*Idolatry*

# IDOLATRY

*Moshe Halbertal*
*Avishai Margalit*

*Translated by*
*Naomi Goldblum*

*Harvard University Press*
*Cambridge, Massachusetts*
*London, England*
*1992*

Copyright © 1992 by the President and Fellows of Harvard College
All rights reserved
Printed in the United States of America
10  9  8  7  6  5  4  3  2  1

This book is printed on acid-free paper, and its binding materials
have been chosen for strength and durability.

*Library of Congress Cataloging-in-Publication Data*

Halbertal, Moshe.
Idolatry / Moshe Halbertal and Avishai Margalit : translated by
Naomi Goldblum.
p.    cm.
Translation from Hebrew.
Includes bibliographical references and index.
ISBN 0–674–44312–8
1. Idolatry.   I. Margalit, Avishai, 1939–   .  II. Title.
BL485.H34   1992
291.2'18—dc20

91–33312
CIP

*To*
*Heniah and Meir Halbertal*
*Edna Ullman-Margalit*

# Acknowledgments

The first formulations of our ideas on idolatry began in a seminar given at the Shalom Hartman Institute for advanced Jewish studies in Jerusalem. We benefited a great deal from the stimulating conversations with its members. In particular we wish to thank David Hartman, the director of the institute, for his encouragement and support.

Several people read the manuscript and offered valuable criticisms and advice: Wendy Doniger, Moshe Idel, Sidney Morgenbesser, Michael Sandel, and Judith Shklar. We are grateful to them for their contributions and friendship. Special thanks are owed to Tova Halbertal and Edna Ullman-Margalit; their constant encouragement and valuable suggestions made this book possible. The manuscript also benefited a great deal from the wisdom and dedication of its translator, Naomi Goldblum, and from the attentive reading of Elizabeth Hurwit of Harvard University Press. We also wish to thank Lindsay Waters, Executive Editor of Harvard University Press, for the support and advice he offered us throughout the writing of this book.

# Contents

*Idolatry*

# Introduction

In addressing the central question—What is idolatry and why is it viewed as an unspeakable sin?—we do not trace the historical vicissitudes of the concept of idolatry; rather, we are interested in various models of this concept in the monotheistic[1] religions, especially in Judaism. Of course, for the purposes of this conceptual analysis we have made use of textual and historical analysis of material from the nonpagan religions, but only as a starting point. The chapters of this book reflect transitions from one model to another, a kind of tour among the various approaches: different concepts of God create, when reversed, different concepts of idolatry. Different religious sensibilities conceive of the alien or the enemy in totally different terms.

According to the anthropomorphic concept of God, which is characteristic of biblical faith, idolatry is a sin within a system of interpersonal relationships, a sin analogous to those people commit with respect to other people, such as betrayal and disloyalty. In Chapter 1 we explore the sin of idolatry in the framework of the anthropomorphic picture of God through an analysis of one central religious metaphor, the metaphor of the biblical marriage relationship. As this is a metaphor of an exclusive relationship, it gives meaning to the sin of idolatry.

But the metaphor of the marital relationship explains only one facet of idolatry, namely, the worship of other gods. The prohibition against idolatry entails not only a ban on the worship of other gods but also a ban on certain ways of representing the right God. It is forbidden to represent God in images and paintings, and the ban on idolatry is, among other things, a determination of the permitted and forbidden ways of representing God, which raises a whole series of questions. What is the reason for this ban on the representation of

God, and why are linguistic representations of God apparently permitted while visual representations are forbidden? If it is permitted
to describe God as possessing a hand, why is it forbidden to draw it?
What is the difference between a statue of God and a verbal description of him? When does a symbol become a fetish, and what is the
difference between a symbol and a fetish? Furthermore, given that
God may also be represented in narratives and dramas, stories and
myths, are there narrative representations that are particular to
idolatry, and is there an internal relation between myth and idolatry?
Chapters 2 and 3 deal with these questions of the relation between
idolatry and representation and attempt to define the boundaries of
legitimate representations of God.

The fight against idolatry, which was a central theme in biblical
religion, disappeared during the period of the Second Temple. "The
temptation for idolatry was slaughtered," records the Talmud, and a
legend tells that the Rabbis of the Great Assembly shut it up in a
barrel.[2] The temples of Baal and Astarte ceased to be real enemies;
they no longer threatened the hegemony of God in the Jewish community, and the problem of the temptation of idolatry was removed
from the spiritual agenda of the period. The fight against idolatry
was renewed in a later period, by Maimonides. This was not because
the old temptation for idolatry had been reawakened, but because a
new religious sensibility had appeared, accompanied by a different
conception of God, which reformulated the problem and defined the
realm of the alien in a completely different way. The renewal of the
fight against idolatry, its central position in religious life, and its
reformulation in terms of philosophical religion are the concerns of
Chapters 4, 5, and 6, which address the connection between idolatry
and error.

The central effort of philosophical religion is the attempt to attain
a proper metaphysical conception of God. This conception not only
is a necessary condition for the worship of God but also constitutes
the high point of religious life. Philosophical religion, which
attempts to purify the divinity from anthropomorphism, considers
the crux of the problem of idolatry to be the problem of error.
Idolatry is perceived first and foremost as an improper conception of
God in the mind of the worshiper, thereby internalizing the sin. The
fight against idolatry is no longer against those who worship at the
Temple of Baal, but instead against those who imagine God as Baal

within the synagogue. The criticism of idolatry is transformed into the criticism of folk religion, and the fight against idolatry into a struggle against imagination, superstition, and the masses' projection of their own world onto that of God. This opens the door to the diversion of the criticisms of idolatry against the monotheistic religions themselves, as was done by the Enlightenment and the nineteenth-century critics of religion. The intra-religious criticism is now projected against religion in general: what the elite religion has done to the folk religion now revenges itself against the elite religion itself. The entire project of religion is now placed under suspicion of being idolatry, or false worship, since if there can be a kind of worship that is false then there can be no guarantee that there is a kind of worship that is not false. In examining the concept of idolatry as error, we look at how false worship became defined as false belief. The difference in the conception of idolatry resulted from the change in religious sensibility, as the question of consciousness replaced that of loyalty, and as the idea took hold that imagination is the crucial obstacle to religious consciousness. The area of the alien is redefined here to include those anthropomorphic conceptions that gave the sin of idolatry a different sense in the Bible.

The most frequently occurring term for idolatry in the Bible is "the worship of other gods," while the rabbinic term *avodah zarah*, which is generally translated as "idolatry," "idol worship," or "false worship," literally means "strange worship." The adjective in "strange worship" has two senses. One is the strangeness of the object toward which the worship is directed, not the "proper" God but other gods. The other refers to the method of worship. These two concepts of strangeness—the strangeness of the ritual and the strangeness of the object of the ritual—constitute two pivots of our discussion. The ambiguity of the concept of strangeness is expressed, for example, in the interpretation of the sin of the golden calf, which is the epitome of idolatry in the Bible. Was the sin of the golden calf a sin because it constituted worship of the wrong object—one of the Egyptian gods—or because, as Yehuda Halevi thought, it constituted a wrong method of worship, a worship of God by means of the calf? The rabbinic expression *avodah zarah* apparently derives from the biblical expression *esh zarah*, "strange fire." This expression occurs in the story of Aaron's two elder sons, who "brought a strange fire" and died, and in this context it is clear that the expression refers to a strange method of worship rather than a strange object of worship.[3] Chapter 7 deals with strangeness of the method of worship. In this sense, the boundary between idol worshipers and monotheists is not the metaphysical picture of the world in itself, but the method of relating to it, the method of worship.

In many "monotheistic" traditions the gap between God and human beings is filled by the intermediary forces of angels, constellations, and demons. The world of divinity becomes a kind of complex bureaucratic system, or an emanated chain of being according to the neo-Platonist conceptions of emanation, from the one to the many. In kabbalistic traditions God is conceived of as a many-faceted existence, full of tensions and oppositions, the balance between which resembles an organism. Hierarchical and organic conceptions of the world of divinity stand in opposition to the picture of simple unity of the philosophers, and as a result the conception of idolatry is conceived differently. The metaphysical gap between those who reject paganism and the pagans becomes smaller, since pagan conceptions also involve a pantheon with one god at the head. What distinguishes them is not the answer to the question of what forces there are in the world, but rather the answer to the question of who one is permitted to worship, of whether worship must be exclusive to the figure at the head of the hierarchy. The exclusivity of God, as the only metaphysical power who constitutes unity within himself, is undermined, and the argument turns upon the exclusivity of the worship of one power. The area of the strange is defined through ritual worship of that power; intermediate forces exist and have influence, but their worship is nevertheless forbidden.

In spite of the distinction between the two concepts of strangeness, the answer to the question of what is strange in "strange worship" and why it is rejected is not simple. Idolatry, like many other religious and cultural concepts, belongs to the area called "sensibility." This term describes a type of connection between intellectual conceptions on the one hand and perceptual and emotional experiences on the other. "Sensibility" refers to the esthetics of ideas and concepts, where "esthetics" is understood in its original meaning of "feeling." Religious sensibility says that the rejection of idolatry is the rejection of a type of contact between faith and other forms of worship, similar to the esthetic rejection of a work embodying an idea or feeling that arouses disgust. The concepts of religious modesty—

what sort of clothing it is permitted to wear and what form of hairstyle is permissible—are drawn to a considerable extent not from the realm of religious morality but from the realm of religious sensibility. Shared values, derived from the association of fixed visual perceptions, create a certain shared sensibility in people. The rejection of idolatry is the rejection of a type of connection between worship and belief. If someone rejects the concept of courtly honor, for instance, this rejection is not just the rejection of some idea or assumption, such as the masculine exclusivity involved in it or the taking of ridiculous risks in order to defend it. The rejection is also in the area of cultural sensibility and may be expressed, for example, in the rejection of the gesture of kissing ladies' hands.

Those cultural concepts that are in the area of sensibility are the most difficult to analyze because of the complex connection between concepts and feelings, representations and impressions. The isolation of each of these aspects gives one the feeling that one is missing something in the character and complexity of the phenomenon. The commandment "You shall not follow their practices," which is meant as a rejection of the lifestyle of the idolatrous culture, reflects a complex weave of lifestyle, ritual, and faith.[4] It is not insignificant that the Tractate *Avodah Zarah* ("Idolatry") in the Talmud is a formulation of the types of contact between Jews and pagans, as the category of idolatry includes a criticism of the culture in which idolatry developed.

The ban on idolatry is an attempt to dictate exclusivity, to map the unique territory of the one God. The primary context is worship: worship must be exclusive to one force, sacrifices may be made only to God, and no one but him may be worshiped. A secondary context is the attribution of forces and adjectives that are supposed to be exclusive to a single force. The extent of this exclusive domain is a crucial question in our discussion of idolatry. When does a particular attitude become worship? What aspect of addressing this attitude to a force other than God makes it into idolatry? Which adjectives must be attributed to some force in order to turn that force into an invader of the exclusive realm in which idolatry is banned? The prophets speak of protective treaties with Egypt and Assyria as the worship of other gods. A protective treaty, in which Israel relies on a great power that provides it with defense in return for taxes and political subjugation, is considered an insult to the exclusive realm of God, who gives protection to Israel. This exclusivity is extended from worship to protection, where God is defined as the exclusive protector to whom the nation is subjugated in a political sense. In Chapter 8 we discuss the limits of this exclusive realm and its ramifications in terms of political authority. This chapter can thus be considered an analysis of the political model in which God is described as king and leader. In the framework of this metaphor, sovereignty, as well as what is called the area of civil religion, is perceived as an exclusive realm. Whereas worship is paradigmatic of exclusivity, sovereignty is more complicated and calls into question the boundary between human beings and the gods, between hero worship and divine worship, between loyalty to a political system and the deification of that system.

Our discussion brings philosophical concepts to bear on the study of idolatry, in contrast to historical, theological, and anthropological concepts, although there is, of course, some overlap between these areas and our own.

We need look no further than the notion of idolatry as error. The critical and liberating role of philosophy is the uncovering of deep illusions. Philosophy, by its nature, or at its best, is iconoclastic, in the sense of removing ideological masks or breaking idols. In this context the idols are the creatures of the human imagination that take control over people and their lives, and the breaking of idols means the uncovering of the fictional and illusive character of these creatures of the imagination. The war against idolatry has the same role of liberation from error and the attempt to break the bonds of the imagination.

Our conceptual analysis of idolatry thus has two aims. One is to understand idolatry as a central concept in the history of religion by analyzing texts from monotheistic religions. The other is to use these analyses to elucidate a number of classical problems in philosophy. Our discussion is not historical; it is not arranged in chronological order and does not follow the transformations of the concept over time. It is an analysis of the various understandings of the concept as we find them and as they confront one another. What organizes the discussion is thus a problem or a viewpoint, not a historical chronology. Nevertheless, the discussion is not an abstract philosophical one;

we interpret specific texts in the context of the particular traditions that lived with them.

Idolatry may be considered from three different perspectives: from the view of those who reject paganism, from the view of the pagans themselves, and from the view of an observer who looks at both groups from the outside. The principal viewpoint, although not the only one, that we use in this essay is the first one, the antipagan view. This view of idolatry is obviously neither sympathetic nor impartial: the very identity of the monotheists depends on the negation of idolatry. From their term for idolatry alone ("strange worship") we can infer the negative character the monotheists ascribe to the phenomenon. In the Jewish tradition a positive description of idolatry is not only nonexistent, it is forbidden. In reference to idol worshipers the scripture says, "Do not show mercy unto them" *(lo tekhanem),* and the rabbinic exegesis of this injunction is, "Do not ascribe charm *(khen)* to them," that is, do not admit that there can be anything attractive in idolatry.[5]

Hatred distorts one's perception, even though it occasionally also sharpens one's insights. In places where the pagans defend themselves, such as in debates during the second century between the church fathers and the pagan elite, we get a totally different picture of paganism. These debates reveal how pagans and Christians can interpret the works of Homer completely differently, with the Christians interpreting them literally and ridiculing them, while pagans like Celsus see the descriptions of the gods as metaphorical personifications of the forces of nature. The debate between the pagans and the Christians is sometimes a debate about the right to give texts a sympathetic metaphorical interpretation.

Like the concept of "false worship," which is a clearly polemical concept, the concept of "paganism," as it is used by Christians, is also a far from flattering one. "Pagan" is a derogatory term for an idol worshiper, and its Latin root means "rustic." But as with other ideologically derogatory terms, there have been people in the modern age who have adopted the label of "pagans" for themselves, whether with the intention of provoking the attackers of paganism or in order to confront them with a system of values that rejects its critics. The concept of "pagan" has changed from a purely derogatory concept to a qualitatively differentiating one, that is, to a concept that divides people into groups with respect to their positive or negative attitude toward its connotations. Among the modern connotations that have accrued to the label is the idea of pluralism. Monotheism, in its war against polytheism, is an attempt to impose unity of opinions and beliefs by force, as a result of an uncompromising attitude toward the unity of God. Polytheism, by contrast, by its very nature includes an abundance of gods and modes of ritual worship, and so it has room for different viewpoints and beliefs and therefore is pluralistic. This pluralism is not just the product of compromise but is in fact an ontological pluralism that constitutes a deeper basis for tolerance. In addition, paganism comes as a challenge to Christian ethics, and this also reflects a change of values. Nietzsche contributed greatly to the evolution of this change. He described paganism as a life-affirming viewpoint, as opposed to the Holy God of Christianity who imposes a life-denying, ascetic spiritualism on His followers.

Our book, however, is principally a conceptual analysis of idolatry as it is seen by its opponents, and especially as it is seen in Jewish sources. It is an attempt to understand a phenomenon through the way it defines the "enemy." The assumption is that we can find the answer to the question of what the monotheists consider the proper worship of the proper God by seeing how they define the alien realm. The choice of Jewish sources is not essential, and certainly there is much to learn about the subject from Islamic sources, and from Islam's interesting interface with Hinduism. Moreover, we will not discuss systematically the iconoclastic debates in Christianity, or the worship of saints and the struggle against this worship at the end of the Middle Ages, although these matters are part of the background of our discussion. Our assumption is that the conceptual elucidation of the question as it arises from Jewish sources will be an important contribution even for those who are more familiar than we are with other traditions.

# 1

## Idolatry and Betrayal

### Understanding Idolatry Metaphorically

The biblical depiction of God's relation to human beings draws on images of human relationships. God is king, father, bridegroom, husband, woman in labor, and judge.[1] These images create a conception of God, and responses from him and to him are understood through them. The multiplicity of images, and their use alongside one another, create complexity in the relations between humans and God. As an analogy, consider a person who, in addition to being a father to his son, is also his teacher or his employer, and relates to him sometimes in one aspect and sometimes in another. Occasionally the boundaries between the aspects become somewhat blurred, and it is not easy to tell if the present relation is a father-son or a master-servant relation. Our understanding of the image of God in the Bible depends on our ability to enter into the heart of these images with all their connotations of prevalent interpersonal relationships.

The use in the Bible of variegated metaphors drawn from the realms of interpersonal relationships and human institutions is also applied to idolatry. The Bible explains idolatry by means of anthropomorphisms describing flawed personal relationships. As in understanding the biblical religious world in general, the analysis of these anthropomorphic metaphors is vital to understanding the status of idolatry in the Bible and the question of why it is such an unspeakable sin. This chapter is mainly an analysis of one metaphor, that of marital relations, which is a "root metaphor" for the understanding of idolatry, and which thus demonstrates the importance of metaphors in general.

The explanatory power of a metaphor derives from the familiarity of the realm it is drawn from (the realm of human relations), and in the metaphorical process we attempt to extend our understanding beyond the image to the realm it represents. This is the transition from the primary, or representing, realm to the secondary, or represented, realm. The way the Bible explains what is bad about idolatry by using images of flaws in human relationships teaches us that the basis of our understanding of the sin of idolatry is our moral standpoint with respect to what is permitted and what is forbidden in interpersonal relationships. Idolatry is thus not an obvious "primary evil"; rather, its prohibition is based on moral intuitions and views about the character of interpersonal relationships and the various expectations people have of one another. The comparison of idolatry to adultery, for example, depends on the assumption that adultery is a serious sin in human society. Moreover, within the framework of this metaphor our understanding of this prohibition depends on our ability to identify the element that makes adultery a sin as being present in worship of other gods as well. Hence there are two factors in its vitality: its reliance on shared moral assumptions, and its ability to convey to the reader or hearer the existence of some similarity between the metaphorical image and what it is meant to explain. This similarity is relevant to the extension of moral revulsion from the primary realm of the metaphor to the realm it represents—that is, from the relations among human beings to the relations between them and God. The comparison process intentionally blurs the primary distinction that ostensibly exists between them and God and transforms God into a fellow human being. Thus the central theological principle of the Bible—the rejection of idolatry—is actually based on an accepted moral intuition in human relationships.

In attempting to understand the sin of idolatry through anthropomorphic imagery in the Bible, we are taking a different approach from those who consider anthropomorphism one of the outstanding signs of idolatry itself, and who therefore minimize anthropomorphic interpretations of the text as much as possible. We take the anthropomorphic metaphors at face value and argue that it is anthropomorphism that gives meaning to the sin of idolatry. We will return to this controversy at the end of the chapter, once we have a real picture of the role of anthropomorphic imagery in the creation of the meaning of the sin of idolatry. For now let us assume that it is not an avoidance of anthropomorphism that distinguishes the Bible from paganism.

The process that anchors the sin of idolatry in another, obvious sin in the framework of human relationships is the reverse of the process that anchors other sins by comparing them to idolatry. For example, in the post-biblical comparison "A proud person is like an idol worshiper," the severity of idolatry is considered obvious, and through the imagery of idolatry an attempt is made to clarify the severity of the sin of pride. Once the sin of idolatry has been elucidated by analogy with other sins, this sin itself becomes a model sin through which the evil in other acts is explained: it is transformed from the represented image to the representing image.[2] The biblical imagery we discuss works in the opposite direction, that is, the severity of idolatry is elucidated through an analogy with an interpersonal act whose undesirability is taken for granted. It thus turns out that the primary force of the moral assumption anchoring the prohibition of idolatry is not conditional on the acceptance of the monotheistic principle; rather, this principle is conditional on the image anchoring it.

## Forbidden Sexual Relations

The principal image in common use by the prophets for the elucidation of idolatry is the relationship between husband and wife, in which Israel is compared to the wife and God to the husband. The power of this image derives from the exclusivity of that relationship, which forbids the wife to have sexual relations with any other man; thus, by analogy, Israel is forbidden to worship other gods. In this respect the image captures the uniqueness of the biblical religion: God unlike the pagan gods is a jealous God who forbids the worship of other gods.[3] According to this metaphor idolatry is a sexual sin; even in the early strata of the Bible idolatry is identified as such: "You must not make a covenant with the inhabitants of the land, for they will lust after their gods and sacrifice to their gods and invite you, and you will eat of their sacrifices. And when you take wives from among their daughters for your sons, their daughters will lust after their gods and will cause your sons to lust after their gods" (Exodus 34:15–16).[4]

In this excerpt the use of sinful sexual relations in reference to idolatry is especially salient, as the verb *zanu,* translated here as "lust after," literally means "to have sinful sexual relations." The text explicitly refrains from calling the act of marrying the daughters of the land a sexual sin—with regard to these women the verb "take" is used, denoting a legal act of marriage, while their enticement of the men to worship idolatry is denoted by the verb for sinful sexual relations. The idea of sexual sin is thus intentionally transferred from its natural context—the lust of the Israelites for the daughters of the land—and attributed to the worship of other gods. The image of idolatry as sinful sexual relations also occurs in other parts of the Pentateuch, but it is in the Prophets that the metaphor is fleshed out extensively.[5]

The prophets were the first to refer to Israel as a wife and to God as her husband. Hosea, Jeremiah, and Ezekiel developed the metaphor by adding various images and additional content. Israel's history is seen as the story of a woman who was married and then betrayed her husband, while God's role in this story is that of a betrayed husband who is torn between the feelings of shame and disgrace brought upon him by his faithless wife, causing a fierce desire for revenge, and the strong love the jealous husband retains for his wife, impelling him to search for any means to bring her back to him. Hosea and Jeremiah prepared the ground for the daring way in which Ezekiel described this analogy. We begin with Hosea:

When the Lord first spoke to Hosea, the Lord said to Hosea, "Go, get yourself a wife of whoredom and children of whoredom; for the land will stray [literally "whore away"] from following the Lord . . . Pursue her lovers as she will, she shall not overtake them; and seek them as she may, she shall never find them. Then she will say, 'I will go and return to my first husband, for then I fared better than now.' And she did not consider this: It was I who bestowed on her the new grain and wine and oil; I who lavished silver on her and gold—which they used for Ba'al. Assuredly, I will take back My new grain in its time and My new wine in its season, and I will snatch away My wool and My linen that serve to cover her nakedness . . . I will lay waste her vines and her fig trees, which she thinks are a fee she received from her lovers; I will turn them into brushwood, and beasts of the field shall devour them. Thus I will punish her for the days of the Ba'alim, on which she brought them offerings; when, decked out with earrings and jewels, she would go after her lovers, forgetting me"—declares the Lord. (Hosea 1:2, 2:9–11, 14–15)

Hosea constructs the metaphor with the image of Israel as a whoring and faithless wife, giving content to the notion of God as the betrayed husband of the wife Israel. The main function of the husband in Hosea's metaphor is the satisfaction of the wife's material needs. Extending the metaphor, it is God who satisfies Israel's needs by giving grain, wine, and oil. When God sees that he has been betrayed, he swears to kill his wife by thirst and to have no mercy on her children. The betrayal is analyzed as an extension of the same motif—that Israel prefers other lovers because she thinks they satisfy her needs more successfully: "Because she thought, 'I will go after my lovers, who supply my bread and my water, my wool and my linen, my oil and my drink'" (Hosea 2:7). The betrayed husband brings it about that the wife will no longer be able to find her lovers: "Assuredly I will hedge up her roads with thorns and raise walls against her, and she shall not find her paths. Pursue her lovers as she will, she shall not overtake them; and seek them as she may, she shall never find them" (Hosea 2:8–9). Then the wife, who is consistent after her own fashion, decides as a result to return to her husband. The pain of the betrayed husband is doubled because he had supplied even the goods that the wife had attributed to her lovers. When his wife returns to him empty-handed, in the hope that he will fulfill the needs that her lovers are no longer fulfilling, the time has come for the enraged husband to revenge himself on his faithless wife: "Now I will uncover her shame in the very sight of her lovers, and none shall save her from Me" (Hosea 2:12). The husband is the cause of his wife's returning to him in her desperate state, and when she returns he punishes her.

The sin of idolatry is whoredom. Israel gives her favors to whoever pays her the highest fee, but idolatry is worse than ordinary prostitution because in this case the fee is always being paid with the husband's money, as he is the sustainer of the world. The sin of idolatry as whoredom is made even worse by the great gap between the husband's faithfulness and love for his wife, and the wife's faithless behavior. For the wife sexual relations are based on pay, and she believes that the lover pays more. In theological terms, the Israelites relate to God as to a supplier of material goods, and when he seems to have disappointed them they turn to other gods. Thus Hosea says, "The Lord said to me further, 'Go, befriend a woman who, while befriended by a companion, consorts with others, just as the Lord befriends the Israelites, but they turn to other gods and love the cups of the grape'" (Hosea 3:1). God loved the Israelites as a man loves a woman, and she betrayed him.

Hosea also alludes to the date of the couple's marriage in his description of the end of the crisis: "Assuredly, I will speak coaxingly to her and lead her through the wilderness and speak to her tenderly. I will give her vineyards from there, and the Valley of Achor as a plowland of hope. There she shall respond as in the days of her youth, when she came up from the land of Egypt" (Hosea 2:16–17). The reconciled couple return to the place where they first met and renew the days of their youth. A clear romantic flavor has been added to the metaphor, as God is not only a supplier of material goods but also a lover. Moreover, this passage shows us that the couple met in the desert at the time that the Israelites left Egypt.

*Nymphomania*

Following Hosea, Ezekiel makes extensive use of the same metaphor, adding a detailed biography to the story of the marriage and reconstructing the entire history of the relations between Israel and God around the metaphor of husband and wife. He also gives a detailed account of the betrayal, but his analysis of the crisis is different from Hosea's. The later prophets had a tendency to add homiletic interpretations to the material they received from the earlier prophets, and this is what Ezekiel does with the image of husband and wife that he received from Hosea and Jeremiah:

> The word of the Lord came to me: O mortal, proclaim Jerusalem's abominations to her, and say: Thus said the Lord God to Jerusalem: By origin and birth you are from the land of the Canaanites—your father was an Amorite and your mother a Hittite. As for your birth, when you were born your navel cord was not cut, and you were not bathed in water to smooth you; you were not rubbed with salt, nor were you swaddled. No one pitied you enough to

do any one of these things for you out of compassion for you; on the day you were born, you were left lying, rejected, in the open field. When I passed by you and saw you wallowing in your blood, I said to you: "Live in spite of your blood." Yea, I said to you: "Live in spite of your blood." I let you grow like the plants of the field; and you continued to grow up until you attained to womanhood, until your breasts became firm and your hair sprouted. (Ezekiel 16:1–7)

Israel is depicted as a baby girl abandoned by her natural parents without receiving the treatment customarily accorded to newborns.[6] God happens to be passing the place where the baby was abandoned and he grants her life by saying, "Live in spite of your blood." After she has attained puberty God passes by the place again:

You were naked and bare when I passed by you [again] and saw that your time for love had arrived. So I spread my robe over you and covered your nakedness, and I entered into a covenant with you by oath—declares the Lord God; thus you became Mine. I bathed you in water, and washed the blood off you, and anointed you with oil. I clothed you with embroidered garments, and gave you sandals of *tahash*-leather to wear, and wound fine linen about your head, and dressed you in silks. I decked you out in finery and put bracelets on your arms and a chain around your neck. I put a ring in your nose, and earrings in your ears, and a splendid crown on your head. You adorned yourself with gold and silver, and your apparel was of fine linen, silk and embroidery. Your food was choice flour, honey, and oil. You grew more and more beautiful, and became fit for royalty. Your beauty won you fame among the nations, for it was perfected through the splendor which I set upon you—declares the Lord God. (Ezekiel 16:7–14)

When God passes by the place again, he sees that the girl has grown up. She is showing signs of sexual maturity and her time for love has arrived. Here the foster father turns into a husband, and he enters into a marriage contract with the girl. Different interpretations have been given to the specific content of the metaphor. Who were the girl's parents? Why was she abandoned? Is this a description of the Israelites in Egypt or at an earlier stage of their history?[7] In any case it is clear that Ezekiel is trying to weave the image extensively into Israel's history. The marriage apparently occurred at the time that the Israelites left Egypt and the various gifts were given in the desert.

Later, the poor abandoned baby turns into a surpassingly beautiful girl, by virtue of her husband.

> But confident in your beauty and fame, you played the harlot: you lavished your favors on every passerby; they were his. You even took some of your cloths and made yourself tapestried platforms and fornicated on them—not in the future; not in time to come. You took your beautiful things, made of the gold and silver that I had given you, and you made yourself phallic images and fornicated with them. You took your embroidered cloths to cover them; and you set My oil and My incense before them. The food that I had given you—the choice flour, the oil, and the honey, which I had provided for you to eat—you set it before them for a pleasing odor. And so it went—declares the Lord God. You even took the sons and daughters that you bore to me and sacrificed them to those [images] as food—as if your harlotries were not enough, you slaughtered My children and presented them as offerings to them! In all your abominations and harlotries, you did not remember the days of your youth, when you were naked and bare, and lay wallowing in your blood. After all your wickedness (woe, woe to you!)—declares the Lord God—you built yourself an eminence and made yourself a mound in every square. You built your mound at every crossroad; and you sullied your beauty and spread your legs to every passerby, and you multiplied your harlotries. You played the whore with your neighbors, the lustful Egyptians—you multiplied your harlotries to anger Me . . . In your insatiable lust you also played the whore with the Assyrians; you played the whore with them, but were still unsated. You multiplied your harlotries with Chaldea, that land of traders; yet even with this you were not satisfied. How sick was your heart—declares the Lord God—when you did all these things, the acts of a self-willed whore, building your eminence at every crossroad and setting your mound in every square! Yet you were not like a prostitute, for you spurned fees; [you were like] the adulterous wife who welcomes strangers instead of her husband. Gifts are made to every prostitute, but you made gifts to all your lovers, and bribed them to come to you from every quarter for your harlotries. You were the opposite of other women: you solicited instead of being solicited; you paid fees instead of being paid fees. Thus you were just the opposite! (Ezekiel 16:15–26, 28–34)

Ezekiel associates Israel's harlotry with specific events in its history: the covenants with Assyria and Egypt and the alliance with the Chaldeans. The insatiable woman denies her entire identity: she sacrifices her children to her lovers and gives them all the property she received from her husband. Sexual passion controls her so thoroughly that she neglects all her other needs for the sake of adultery. For this she pays good money, the opposite of the prostitute, and here Ezekiel stresses, in a tone that seems to be directed at Hosea's wording, "Thus you were just the opposite!" In Hosea's description adultery is a means for obtaining other goods, whereas in Ezekiel's portrayal it is the very good desired. Where Hosea describes idolatry as prostitution, Ezekiel portrays it as nymphomania: "Yet you were not like a prostitute, for you spurned fees." The metaphor of husband and wife is the same for Hosea and for Ezekiel, but the analysis of the crisis and the ensuing corruption is different. Ezekiel portrays the relationship between the Israelite nation and their God in erotic terms: "I spread my robe over you" is a euphemism for sexual relations,[8] and this occurs after the foster father has discovered his adopted daughter's sexuality. Idolatry is also described in erotic terms: "and you made yourself phallic images and fornicated with them," as opposed to Hosea's description, which stresses the economic dependence between the husband and wife. For Ezekiel, the motifs of losing control and forgetting are central to the sin of idolatry. With this sin the woman Israel subjugates her identity to her sexual drive and detaches herself from her entire past. Among other things she forgets that this is what happened to her in her childhood. The worship of other gods thus reflects an insatiable need for love detached from any ties of faithfulness.

To see how Ezekiel developed and reinterpreted Hosea's metaphor, we must look at Jeremiah's words. Jeremiah also compares the relationship between God and Israel to the relationship between husband and wife: "I accounted to your favor the devotion of your youth, your love as a bride—how you followed Me in the wilderness" (Jeremiah 2:2). Unlike the prostitute described by Hosea, however, Israel followed her beloved into a desert, a place of unlikely remuneration, out of love and devotion. Beginning at chapter 2:4 and ending at 3:5 there is a prophetic passage in which Jeremiah uses the metaphor of marital relations for idolatry. In this passage Jeremiah begins by addressing Israel in the second-person masculine form: "Thus said the Lord: What wrong did your fathers find in Me that they abandoned Me and went after delusion and were deluded? They never asked themselves, 'Where is the Lord, who brought us up from the land of Egypt, who led us through the wilderness?'" (Jeremiah 2:5–6). Afterward Jeremiah changes the gender of his address to the feminine, as if speaking to a woman: "What, then is the good of your going to Egypt to drink the waters of the Nile? And what is the good of your going to Assyria to drink the waters of the Euphrates? Let your misfortune reprove you, let your afflictions rebuke you; mark well how bad and bitter it is that you forsake the Lord your God . . . On every high hill and under every verdant tree, you recline as a whore" (Jeremiah 2:18–20).

The transition from Israel as a man to Israel as a woman prepares for the comparison of idolatry to whoredom, and thus Jeremiah begins to speak about idolatry. In this prophetic passage Jeremiah paves the way for Ezekiel by referring to Israel's covenants with Egypt and with Assyria as idolatry. And Ezekiel, as is his way, adds erotic imagery.

*Reconciliation—Metaphors of Marital Relations and Monogamy*

The metaphor of the relationship between husband and wife is extended to the reconciliation stage, but here the metaphor is liable to become inappropriate. If God and Israel are husband and wife, and the wife committed adultery, then reconciliation seems impossible, since a wife who has committed adultery is forbidden both to her husband and to her lover. One possible response is that such a question extends the metaphor beyond its limits, as if one asked whether it was time to shear the fleecy clouds. Although God is the husband in the metaphor, he is not exactly like a husband. Examining the reconciliation stage will help us understand the limits of the metaphor of marital relations. According to Ezekiel, the woman is treated like an adulteress; she is publicly taken out naked and then put to death by fire or stoning: "I will inflict upon you the punishment of women who commit adultery and murder, and I will direct bloody and impassioned fury against you" (Ezekiel 16:38). But this does not end the husband's inner struggle—the woman comes back to life after her death. As Ezekiel puts it, "Nevertheless, I will remember the covenant I made with you in the days of your youth, and I will establish it with you as an everlasting covenant" (Ezekiel 16:60). As opposed to the forgetful woman, God remembers. He remembers the covenant he made with her in her youth, and he establishes an everlasting covenant with her. Here it seems that putting the wife to death is a cathartic element in the story. After she has been put to death, even if only verbally, God discovers that he does not really want to be separated from his beloved, and he brings her back to himself for eternity. His new certainty that the relationship will be eternal stems not from the imprinting of the monotheistic idea in the minds of the Israelites, but from the wife's feelings of guilt and shame over the gap between her own wayward behavior and the generosity of heart with which her husband takes her back and forgives her for the sin that initially seemed to be unforgivable: "I will establish My covenant with you, and you shall know that I am the Lord. Thus you shall remember and feel shame, and you shall be too abashed to open your mouth again, when I have forgiven you for all that you did—declares the Lord God" (Ezekiel 16:62–63). The solution of the problem of the sin of idolatry is depicted as a reunion accompanied by such deep gratitude and guilt feelings as to guarantee that the adultery will not recur. This description demonstrates the extent to which the sin of idolatry is perceived as an event taking place within a framework of human relationships.

Thus the wife returns to her husband. But how is it possible, according to biblical law, for an adulterous wife to return to her husband? Jeremiah asked this question long before we did. The word of the Lord came to him as follows: "If a man divorces his wife, and she leaves him and marries another man, can he ever go back to her? Would not such a land be defiled? Now you have whored with many lovers: can you return to Me?—says the Lord" (Jeremiah 3:1). Jeremiah brings an argument from the lesser to the greater evil: if a woman who was properly divorced and remarried may not return to her first husband, then this prohibition must surely apply to an adulteress with many lovers. The question Jeremiah asks reveals the richness of the metaphor of marital relations, the depth and breadth of this metaphor, in which many different aspects of the relationship between human beings and God are represented. Not only the marriage and the sin are included in the metaphor but the attempt at reconciliation is as well. Jeremiah reveals the extensiveness and seriousness of the metaphor in his quasi-literal references to the legal problem of the wife's return.

A number of different solutions to this problem are offered. Jeremiah's solution is to transmute the metaphor in midstream:

> I had resolved to adopt you as My child, and I gave you a desirable land—the fairest heritage of all the nations; and I thought you would surely call Me "Father," and never cease to be loyal to Me. Instead you have broken faith with Me, as a woman breaks faith with a paramour, O house of Israel—declares the Lord. Hark! On the bare heights is heard the suppliant weeping of the people of Israel, for they have gone a crooked way, ignoring the Lord their God. Turn back, O rebellious children, I will heal your afflictions! "Here we are, we come to You, for You, O Lord, are our God!" (Jeremiah 3:19–22)

In the act of breaking faith Israel is called a woman, but in the act of return the Israelites are called children. An adulterous wife is forbidden to her husband, but an alienated son is a different matter: he is welcomed back with open arms.[9]

The question of the possibility of reconciliation arises as well in a rabbinic midrash. There a different answer is given, one which reveals a great deal about the use of metaphor. In the future the Israelites will say to God, it predicts, "Lord of the Universe, you have already written, 'If a man divorces his wife, and she leaves him and marries another man, can he ever go back to her?'" And God says, "What I wrote was 'a man,' but it has already been written, 'For I am God, not man' (Hosea 11:9)" (*Sifrei on Deuteronomy,* 306). Here the Israelites are expressing to God their fear that it will not be possible for them to be forgiven, since God himself has written that once a woman has been married to another man she may not return to her first husband. The midrash takes the metaphor to the limits of its literal meaning in asking how reconciliation can be possible and finds an answer in the difference between human beings and God. The verse from Hosea, "For I am God, not man," which deals with God's forgiveness of Ephraim for the sin of idolatry, is the verse that defines the limits of the anthropomorphic metaphor. When the metaphor has reached a dead end, with no solution but the severance of the relationship, the verse explicitly attests to the metaphor's limitations as a description of the ways of God. God is not exactly like a person, and the human institution of marriage is not exactly like the marriage between Israel and God.[10]

## Personal Obligation and the Ban on Idolatry

A personal, anthropomorphic God is essential in order for it to be possible to speak of the sin of idolatry. If God were not a person, then it would be difficult to speak of betraying him. And if God had not created an attitude of loyalty toward him within the framework of a specific history of human relations, then there would not be any betrayal. It is this kind of god that gives the story of the Exodus from Egypt its importance as a basis for the prohibition of idolatry. The event of the Exodus is the foundation of the relation of obligation between Israel and God. As we have seen, this event creates an obligation because it is the event in which God consecrated Israel as a wife, or—according to the romantic interpretation—in which God revealed his love for Israel and Israel revealed her willingness to follow her beloved into the desert.

The Exodus from Egypt has been discussed as part of the story of a marriage. But it takes on other meanings in metaphors of other types of human relationships, especially the master-servant relationship. According to this metaphor, the Exodus was the event that established this relationship: "For it is to Me that the Israelites are servants: they are My servants, whom I freed from the land of Egypt, I the Lord your God" (Leviticus 25:55). The assumption behind the verse is that freeing a servant from another master is a basis for establishing ownership over him. The first commandment, "I the Lord am your God who brought you out of the land of Egypt," is the reason for the prohibition immediately following: "You shall have no other gods besides Me" (Exodus 20:2). According to this reading the first commandment is not God's identity card but his bill of ownership.[11] Chapter 8 fully analyzes this metaphor and its ramifications for the question of idolatry; here we want only to present an alternative metaphor used to give meaning to the sin of idolatry on the basis of the history of a human relationship.

The exclusivity of both the husband-wife and master-servant metaphors explains why other nations are exempted from the prohibition against idolatry. Exemplar of monogamy, God has married only Israel and has taken only the Israelites out of Egypt.[12] The biographical conception of the sin thus also defines those to whom the sin does not apply: It does not apply to those who do not share the history that created the exclusive obligation. The ban on idolatry is not universal because it was shaped by the metaphor of an exclusive relationship. Moreover, in the process of creating the image that explains the sin of idolatry, the prohibition becomes morally anchored in customary norms, principally in the area of sexual morality. If, for example, there had been no prohibition of adultery, then the power of the metaphor would have been nullified. There is a "moral monotheism" here, and not only in the sense that the descriptions of God are principally moral adjectives, or that the objective force of morality depends on the belief in one omnipotent and omniscient God. The moral element exists because the very obligation to worship one God stems from the fact that God in Heaven chose Israel on earth as his wife, and so according to the norms of marital life idolatry was forbidden for Israel. The anthropomorphic metaphors are not only representations of that force which cannot be represented, in the sense that God spoke in ordinary human language because that is the only language people could understand. Here the figurative language serves as a basis for more than the description of God, for the understanding of man's obligation to God in terms of a personal obligation. The Israelites' obligation to God is anchored in interpersonal relationships, it is integrated into a history of relations, and it is understood on a human basis.

So far we have described the ban on idolatry as the prohibition of the worship of other gods. But can one infer from this conception any answer to the question of whether there exist other gods besides the God of Israel? It is entirely possible that the Bible admits the existence of other gods and merely forbids their worship—a standpoint called "monolatry" by scholars;[13] it is also possible that the Bible not only forbids the worship of other gods but also denies their very existence.

In either case, even if the existence of other gods is denied, the sin of idolatry is not identified with the cognitive error of believing that other gods exist. The error in such a case is not the sin, but only the cause of the sin, which is the worship of and following after these gods. The error exacerbates the insult to the betrayed husband, as not only has his wife betrayed him, but she has done so with a worthless rival: "For My people have done a twofold wrong: they have forsaken Me, the Fount of living waters, and hewed them out cisterns, broken cisterns, which cannot even hold water" (Jeremiah 2:13).

But this verse itself, being ambiguous, exemplifies the difficulty of elucidating our question in the Bible. Jeremiah does not say that Israel is worshiping nonexistent gods, as in the same chapter he speaks about the covenants with Egypt and Assyria: "What, then, is the good of your going to Egypt to drink the waters of the Nile? And what is the good of your going to Assyria to drink the waters of the Euphrates?" (Jeremiah 2:18).[14] Here it is obvious that existent forces are being spoken of—actual cisterns—even if they cannot hold water. That is, there is nothing in the understanding of the sin of idolatry, as we have presented it so far, to permit a judgment on the metaphysical question of whether there exist other gods besides the God of Israel. We will return to this question later and discuss it extensively, but for now we will say only that in the Bible the negation of idolatry stems from the special relationship between Israel and God. Unlike the pagan gods, the God of Israel has the additional characteristic of jealousy which is unique to him. But one cannot derive from this any metaphysical standpoint concerning the existence of other gods, as this is not the essence of the sin.

## Sexual Morality

The view that the sin of idolatry is not a cognitive error but a sin associated with sexual morality is reflected in a number of places in the Talmud. "Rabbi Judah said in the name of Rav, 'The Israelites knew that the idols were nonentities, and they engaged in idolatry only in order to allow themselves to perform forbidden sexual relations publicly'" (Babylonian Talmud, *Sanhedrin* 63b). According to the Talmud, not only is it the case that idolatry is not identified with a metaphysical error, but there is no cognitive error here at all, because the Israelites worshiped idols for other (sexual) reasons. Yet the Talmud also cites contradictory quotations which demonstrate that the idolaters among the Israelites were willing to die for their gods. How can these descriptions be reconciled? The Talmud's solution is to suggest that the initial motivation for idolatry—evading constraints on sexual relations—in time led to actual belief in and attachment to the idols. The sexual connection arises again here, but in a different way. There is thus an internal relation between the ban on idolatry and sexual morality on two levels: first, idolatry itself is described as a sin akin to adultery; second, the worshipers of idols do so in order to permit adultery. According to the internal logic of the biblical metaphor, if sexual sins in the sphere of the family are permitted, then idolatry in the sphere of the relationship between human beings and God will also be permitted, and vice versa.

The idea that idolatry is not a cognitive error but is performed in order to permit forbidden acts is also mentioned in the Jerusalem Talmud:

> When Jeroboam reigned over Israel he began to seduce the Israelites and say to them, "Come and worship idols, idolatry is permissive . . . The Torah says, 'The fat of My festal offering shall not be left lying until morning' (Exodus 23:18), while idolatry says, 'Bring your offerings in the morning.' The Torah says, 'It shall be eaten on the day you sacrifice it, or on the day following' (Leviticus 19:6), while idolatry says, 'For three days out of ten.' The Torah says, 'You shall not offer the blood of My sacrifice with anything leavened' (Exodus 23:18), while idolatry says, 'Bring your thanks-offering with leaven.'"   (Jerusalem Talmud, *Avodah Zarah* 1:1)

Here once again appears the motif that idolatry's permissiveness is its primary appeal. The problem of idolatry is not the inability of the people to grasp the abstract concept of the transcendental God of Israel. What is operative here is what the Talmud calls the "evil desire" or the temptation for idolatry.[15] The attraction of idolatry is embedded either in the erotic temptation of idolatry itself, or in the lifestyle accompanying idolatry. The decision to worship idols reflects a way of life rather than a particular metaphysical worldview. In the description of the Israelites' sin at Ba'al Pe'or the midrash gives an instructive answer to the question of how the Israelites came to worship idols:

> When the Israelites had their fill of the spoils of war they began wasting them, tearing garments and throwing them away, because they did not want anything but gold and silver vessels, as it is written: "We retained as booty all the cattle and the spoil of the towns." (Deuteronomy 3:7) They went and sat down at Shittim— in the place of *sh'tuth,* of foolishness. At that time the Amonites and the Moabites arose and built themselves markets from Beit Yeshimoth until the mountain of snow, and they put women there to sell all kinds of delicacies, and the Israelites would eat and drink. At that time a man would go out for a walk in the marketplace and would ask for a certain article from the old woman and she would

sell it to him at its market price. Then the young woman would call to him from inside the shop and say, "Come here and get it for less," and he would buy it from her that day and the next day. On the third day she would say to him, "Come inside and see for yourself if you are a member of the family." And he would go in with her and there would be a stone jar full of Amonite wine next to her. At that time the wine of Gentiles had not yet been forbidden to the Israelites, so when she asked him if he wanted to drink some wine, he would drink it, and the wine would burn within him. And he would say to her, "Do my bidding," and she would take out an image of [the idol] Pe'or from her bodice and say to him, "If you want me to do your bidding, bow down to this." Then he would say to her, "I do not bow down to idols," and she would answer him, "What do you care if you only expose yourself to it?" and he would expose himself to it. Therefore it is said, "Exposing oneself to Ba'al Pe'or is the way of worshiping it." (*Sifrei on Numbers,* sec. 131)

Idols are worshiped here because of sexual temptation. The atmosphere preceding the sin itself is one of rebelliousness and light-headedness. First the taking of spoils is described, then the destruction of property, then going to the fair, and out of all these elements the temptation is created: bargaining in the idolaters' marketplace, drawing near to the young woman, drinking the wine, and worshiping the idol. Idolatry is part of a lifestyle, and it is the tempting power of this lifestyle that leads to idolatry.

## The Husband's Jealousy of the Lover

One of the most important questions arising from the discussion of anthropomorphic metaphors is the image of God. The key element characterizing the husband in the metaphor, and by extension God, is jealousy.[16] If not for God's jealousy there would have been no reason for the family quarrel to have become so serious. "For you must not worship any other god, because the Lord, whose name is Jealous, is a jealous god" (Exodus 34:14).[17] God's jealousy is the justification for the prohibition of idolatry here, as well as in many other places in the Bible. From the point of view of the wife, Israel, the analysis of idolatry is an analysis of betrayal, while from the point of view of the irate husband the issue is jealousy, in all its various and complex aspects. This anthropomorphic tone is especially salient in a number of midrashic passages that deal with the problem of jealousy. In the perplexities they raise and in the solutions they offer, these passages explore jealousy through analogies with human institutions:

> A philosopher asked R. Gamaliel, "It is written in your Torah, 'For the Lord your God is a consuming fire, a jealous God.' Why is he jealous of its worshipers and not of the idol itself?" He replied, "I will give you a parable. It can be compared to a human king who had a son, and this son reared a dog which he named after his father, so that whenever he took an oath he would say, 'By the life of the dog, my father.' When the king heard about it, with whom was he angry—his son or the dog? Surely he was angry with his son!" The philosopher said to him, "You call the idol a dog, but there is some reality in it." R. Gamaliel asked, "What is your evidence?" He replied, "Once a fire broke out in our town, and the whole town was burnt except for a certain idolatrous shrine." He said to him, "I will give you a parable. It may be compared to a human king against whom one of his provinces rebelled. If he goes to war against it, does he fight the living or the dead? Surely he wages war against the living!" The philosopher said to him, "You call the idol a dog and you call it a dead thing. If that is the case, then why doesn't your God simply destroy it?" He replied, "If it was something unnecessary to the world that was worshiped, He would destroy it, but people worship the sun and moon, stars and constellations, streams and valleys. Should He destroy His world because of fools? . . ."
>
> The General Agrippa asked R. Gamaliel, "It is written in your Torah, 'For the Lord your God is a consuming fire, a jealous God.' Is a wise man jealous of anyone but a wise man, a warrior of anyone but a warrior, a rich man of anyone but a rich man?" He replied, "I will give you a parable. It may be compared to a man who marries an additional wife. If the second wife is her superior, the first will not be jealous of her, but if she is her inferior, the first wife will be jealous of her." (Babylonian Talmud, *Avodah Zarah* 54b–55a)[18]

The stories deal with the question of God's jealousy from two different points of view. In the first dialogue the question is why God is jealous only of Israel and not of the idol itself. In the terms of the biblical metaphor, the question is why God expresses his rage at the woman and not at her lover. This question hints that perhaps God has chosen an easy target for his rage and has avoided confronting the lover. In the second dialogue the assumption is that God is jealous of the idol, and the question is why the omnipotent God should be jealous of insubstantiality and nothingness. It seems as though God has been placed in an untenable position: if he does not confront the idol this may be seen as a sign of his weakness, while if he is jealous of it this is seen as a sign of the idol's importance. Here the midrash grasps the internal contradiction within the feeling of jealousy itself.

The answers to the questions are given by two different relationship metaphors. In the first dialogue God is the father, Israel is the son, and the idol is the dog that is named after the father. The father is angry with the son for calling the dog by his name, but not at the dog, which does not threaten him. The dog's inferiority is the reason that the father is jealous only of his son. In the second dialogue, unlike the first one, the inferiority of the idol does constitute a reason to be jealous of it. Israel has married an additional wife of lesser importance, and this is a cause for jealousy. If Israel had married a more important second wife, the first wife would not have been jealous. The difference between the answers stems from the change in the metaphor. In the second dialogue Israel is the husband, God is the wife, and the idol is an inferior woman that the husband has married in addition to his first wife. It is important to note that the second parable represents God as the wife, unlike the biblical marriage metaphors in which God was always the husband.[19] In the parable of the romantic triangle, whether Israel is the woman and God and the idol are men who are jealous of each other, or whether Israel is the man and God and the idol are co-wives, a very intimate relationship has been affected, and so there is an obvious reason for jealousy. In the parable of the dog, by contrast, the relationship between the son and the dog does not have any intimate significance, and naming the dog after the father does not give the dog any special status—it only insults the father.

Jealousy has two sides. One is a threat to the jealous person's power, in which case a person is not jealous of another unless his own self-esteem has been undermined by his rival's achievements. Therefore God's jealousy arouses the suspicion that the idol must have some real substance if it can disturb the equanimity of the omnipotent. The other side of jealousy is the humiliation. When a wife leaves her husband for a nonentity, there is no real threat, but there is a very deep sense of humiliation. The two stories described here deal with the two contradictory aspects of jealousy and the psychological tangle in which the jealous person is caught. If he expresses his jealousy he demonstrates the value of his rival, while if he does not express his jealousy and ignores the matter, he will be suspected of not being man enough to fight for the object of his love.

Moses made good use of the dilemma facing the jealous husband in defending Israel after the sin of the golden calf:

> R. Nehemiah said: When Israel committed that act, Moses was trying to appease God. He said: "Lord of the Universe, they have given You an assistant, so why are you angry with them? The calf they made will be Your assistant—You will make the sun rise and it the moon, You the stars and it the constellations, You will make the dew fall and it will make the winds blow, You will make the rain fall and it will make the plants grow." God said: "Even you are making the same mistake as they are, as surely there is no substance in it." Moses replied, "If that is so, then why are You angry with Your children? 'Let not Your anger, O Lord, blaze forth against Your people.'"
>
> Another interpretation of the verse "Let not Your anger, O Lord, blaze forth against Your people" (Exodus 32:11): It can be compared to a royal dignitary who entered his house, found his wife embracing a eunuch, and became angry. His best man said to him: "If he could beget children, it would be proper for you to be angry." The dignitary replied: "He does not have this power, but I must teach her not to act this way." Thus did God say: "I know that there is no substance in it, but they must not be allowed to worship idols," and Moses retorted: "If there is no substance in it, then why are You angry with Your children? 'Let not Your anger, O Lord, blaze forth against Your people.'" (*Shemot Rabbah* 43:6–7)

Moses acts here like a wily defense lawyer. He encourages his witness to say that idols are insubstantial and worthless. Moses says that the Israelites have acted properly in finding an assistant for God, and God retorts that Moses too must be thinking idolatrous thoughts, as he should know that idols have no substance. Once Moses has extorted this declaration from God, he immediately uses it to effect an appeasement: if that is so, he replies, then what is the anger about? The midrash compares the situation to that of an irate husband who is expressing his anger pointlessly because his wife is embracing a eunuch. Idolatry is not a threatening male, it is an unsubstantial eunuch. In this defense of Israel there is an expression of the problematic motif of jealousy over a nonentity. To be jealous of one's inferiors shows a lack of dignity that is all the more inappropriate for the creator of the world.

The motif of the husband's jealousy is tightly connected here with the sin of idolatry. God does not waive his rights—he demands exclusivity in his relationship with Israel because he sees himself as a husband and his nation as his wife. But his demands are not considered a reflection of envy, domination, or insecurity. Joshua, for example, said to the people of Israel: "You will not be able to serve the Lord, for he is a holy God. He is a jealous God; he will not forgive your transgressions and your sins. If you forsake the Lord and serve alien gods, He will turn and deal harshly with you and make an end of you, after having been gracious to you" (Joshua 24:19–20). Unlike the gods of the gentiles, the God of Israel does not tolerate other gods beside him—this is his name, his essence and his uniqueness. The Israelites accept their God willingly with the awareness that they are now forbidden to worship other gods. They answer Joshua's warning with the reply, "No, we will serve the Lord" (Joshua 24:21), thereby demonstrating a positive aspect of this jealous relationship: their great love and the devotion of the lover for the beloved. A lack of jealousy—equanimity in the face of betrayal—can raise the suspicion that love (as well as passion) is lacking, and in such cases equanimity is interpreted more as an insult than as tolerance.

There are other ways that God's jealousy is shown to have two sides. It has a certain benefit to Israel, which is well expressed in the Song of Songs, where the love of the man and woman is interpreted as a parable for the love of God and Israel: "Let me be a seal upon your heart, like the seal upon your hand. For love is fierce as death, passion is mighty as Sheol; its darts are darts of fire, a blazing flame" (8:6). But God's jealousy has a dangerous aspect, for jealousy distorts the judgment of the jealous person. Thus the Hebrew word for jealousy, *kin'ah,* is also used to denote uncontrollable rage, as in the phrase, "My rage for Your house has been My undoing" (Psalm 69:10). Because of the danger inherent in jealousy other biblical verses dealing with idolatry stress God's ability to overcome his

anger: "How can I give you up, O Ephraim? How surrender you, O
Israel? How can I make you like Admah, render you like Zeboiim?[20]
I have had a change of heart, all My tenderness is stirred. I will not
act on My wrath, will not turn to destroy Ephraim. For I am God,
not man, the Holy One in your midst: I will not come in fury"
(Hosea 11:8–9). God declares that as God he can leave behind the
aspect of personification and take up the aspect of divinity, which is
the ability to overcome anger. He controls his anger rather than
allowing his anger to control him. Despite the feelings in his heart
concerning Ephraim's straying after other gods, he overcomes his
anger and takes up the aspect of mercy. Thus jealousy is seen to
have an ambivalent status. It distinguishes the God of Israel from the
other gods, but the ability to overcome it is what distinguishes God
from human beings.

## The Fading of the Metaphor

As we have seen, the ban on idolatry is anchored on all levels in the
analysis of marital relations, betrayal, and jealousy. It thus depends
on acceptance of the prevailing attitudes toward the family and
societal obligations. The changes that have taken place in these basic
attitudes in modern society create an outstanding example of the
possibility threatening all metaphors of this type, namely, the fading
of the metaphor. The weakening of the image of marital relations as
a metaphor for idolatry results in part from the changes in the
punishment for adultery and in the attitude toward jealousy in marital affairs.

In Western societies adultery is no longer punishable by death. If
jealousy leads a husband or another family member to kill the wife,
the killer will be brought to criminal trial, and his jealousy will be
seen by most people as excessive, as an outbreak of archaic drives.
One reason for this about-face is the changed economic relationship
between the members of a couple. Betrayal is now considered the
violation of mutual trust rather than a sort of robbery or improper
usage of another's property. This violation of trust does not justify
legal intervention because it is a matter of the mutual understanding
between the members of a couple rather than of the abrogation of
someone's legal rights. But such changes deprive a metaphor dependent on outdated human relationships of its relevance and power.

There has also been a devaluation of the concept of loyalty as a key organizing concept in a system of obligations. The emphasis on obligation toward an individual has shifted to obligation toward rules or institutions. For example, personal loyalty to a king—a loyalty that was often accompanied by oaths and promises and that was the basis for political obligation during the feudal society—has shifted toward political obligation to a state or ideology.[21] The question that arises from time to time in the contemporary philosophy of ethics about the source of a person's obligation to his parents could not have been raised at all in a system in which all other obligations were derived from those based on personal relationships.

In this context it is important to emphasize that the Israelites' obligation to God is formulated in the Bible not as an obligation to a principle, or to truth for truth's sake, but as a personal obligation based on a history of relations that began with the Exodus from Egypt. The denunciation of idolatry in the Bible is often accompanied by the expression "other gods that you have not known." In other words, what is lacking between those divinities and Israel is "knowledge," *yedi'ah,* a term used to denote a personal and intimate relationship.[22] As opposed to the worship of God, which has a historical or personal basis, the worship of other gods is characterized by the lack of a history or relationship. Idolatry is associated with forgetfulness, whereas God demands remembrance again and again. The obligation of remembrance, and the basing of many commandments on the commemoration of the Exodus from Egypt, show how important personal loyalty, accompanied by an oath or covenant, is to the biblical concept of obligation.[23] Thus any change in attitudes toward the betrayal of that obligation shakes the foundation of the relationship between human beings and God.

Aside from the change in the judgment of adultery, we find a growing discomfort with the representation of God as a jealous husband,[24] and with the jealousy that causes him to react so severely to his wife's betrayal of him that he actually has her killed. The word *kin'ah,* in addition to meaning "jealousy" and "uncontrollable rage," has two other senses in the Bible. One of these is "envy"; the other reflects extreme devotion to a particular matter and is often translated as "zeal," as in the words of the prophet Elijah, "I am moved by zeal for the Lord" (I Kings 19:10). Both this last sense and the jealousy that a husband feels toward his wife are directly attributed to God.[25]

The fact that the attribution of jealousy to God has come to be considered an inappropriate representation of him is a linguistic reflection of the deep change in sensibility that has occurred in the area of insult and the defense of one's honor. In many societies the defense of one's honor when it has been insulted by betrayal was and still is a matter of life and death. The insulted man is obligated to invite the insulter to a duel and endanger his own life or take the other person's life in order to restore his honor. Betrayal is contempt, an active demonstration of the insulted man's lack of power. That is why it is important for the punishment of adultery to take place in public, so that the insulted man's honor can be restored in front of everyone. God's jealousy in the biblical view is perceived as obvious, like the betrayed husband's demand for the restoration of his honor. The insulted man who does not display jealousy is regarded as if he has proclaimed that he has been deprived of the power to defend his most basic interests, or—possibly worse in the eyes of the adulterous wife—as if he has proclaimed that he has no interest in what occurred. If God is not jealous, then he has lost either his honor or his devotion, and so in the Bible jealousy is not considered an inappropriate representation of God. Jealousy is associated here with honor, and honor is the ability to directly defend one's basic interests.

In clarifying the question of honor, the distinction between honor and dignity is of central importance. The concept of honor is associated with status. An honorable person in this sense is a person with a firm status in his society. In modern society there has been a change in the concept of honor, and it has become more closely associated with the consciousness of dignity, or self-worth, which is an internalization of the sense of honor involving status.[26] A person without honor is a person who has lost not his status but his consciousness of dignity. Honor in this context does not depend on belonging to some class but on a person's dignity as a human being. It is possible, for example, to speak of a person in a concentration camp as a person with dignity if he has preserved his sense of self-worth. Nevertheless, in such a condition one cannot speak of him as a person with honor, as the concept of honor is totally dependent on the person's status with respect to his environment.

This distinction is important in understanding attitudes toward God's jealousy. As concepts of honor change, so do attitudes toward the sort of jealousy that depends primarily on the concept of honor. As a result of this conceptual transformation God is seen as possessing dignity rather than honor, and God's honor becomes associated primarily with his ability to restrain himself, rather than with his ability to demand restitution when he has been insulted. God is counted among those who are insulted and do not return the insult. Thus the sages interpreted the verse, "Who is like You, O Lord, among the celestials [*elim*]" (Exodus 15:11), as if the word *elim* were the typographically similar word *ilmim,* meaning dumb ones, so as to praise God for remaining silent when insulted.[27] It is interesting to note that the motif of restraint as a type of honor appears in the words of the sages in the context of the battle against idolatry. A person who sees an idol that has not been destroyed but remains standing is supposed to pronounce the blessing, "Blessed is He who is slow to anger" (*Tosefta, Berakhot* 7, 2). The jealous God, who demands that all idols be destroyed and who destroys them himself, is now being praised for being slow to anger, for being restrained.

We can learn more about the problem of jealousy and the power of restraint from a marvelous midrash in which Rachel teaches God a lesson about jealousy. This midrash deals with attempts to defend the conduct of the Israelites after the destruction of the First Temple. In the biblical story (Genesis 29) Jacob had worked seven years for Laban in order to marry his younger daughter, Rachel, but the crafty Laban secretly replaced her with his older daughter, Leah, under the heavy wedding veil, which entirely covered the girl's face. According to the midrash, Jacob had suspected that Laban might do this, and so he had given Rachel special signs by which he could know whether he had married Rachel or Leah, as he would not be able to see her face. Rachel, however, could not bear to see her sister humiliated, and so she gave her the signs. The midrash continues with the words of Rachel speaking to God:

> "Moreover, I hid under the bed where he was lying with my sister, and he would speak to her and she would be silent, and I would answer everything he said so that he would not recognize my sister's voice, and thus I did this kindness for her. I was not jealous of her and I did not permit her to be humiliated. And if I, who am only flesh and blood, dust and ashes, was not jealous of my co-wife [Jacob subsequently married Rachel as well] and did not permit her

to be shamed and humiliated, then You, O living King, why are You jealous of idols that have no reality, and why have You exiled my children and allowed them to be killed by the sword and permitted their enemies to do as they wished with them?" Immediately God's pity was stirred and he said, "For you, Rachel, I will return the Israelites to their place." (*Petikhta, Eikhah Rabbah* 24)

Rachel restrained her jealousy in the most difficult situation imaginable and then sought to teach God a lesson. The clear demand is that this destructive jealousy, which led to Israel's ruin, should be replaced by restraint and generosity. Such a midrash could be conceived only when the attitude to jealousy had been transformed and the concept of honor had undergone a substantive change. Moreover, in this midrash God is represented as the wife and the idol as the co-wife. It is possible that the feminine representation of God makes the sin of idolatry less severe, as in this framework it is perceived as the addition of a co-wife to the beloved wife, which is not a sin in a society where polygamy is permitted, although it is a difficult thing for the first wife to tolerate—in contrast to the representation of idolatry as the wife's betrayal of her husband, which is a sin punishable by death.

As a result of all this, the metaphor of marital relations received a different meaning in theology. The use of the aspect of this metaphor associated with betrayal and jealousy encountered difficulties stemming from the change in attitude toward absolute obligation on a personal basis, and from the about-face with respect to jealousy and the defense of one's honor. Metaphor ordinarily works by taking a representing image that is generally accepted as being obvious and extending this image to the area being represented, but this process cannot work if the representing image itself is no longer obvious. The understanding of idolatry and the severity of the sin involved, when the explanation is given in the framework of the marital-relations metaphor, depends on the understanding of social relations, on the rejection or approval of moral concepts such as loyalty, honor, and jealousy. The criticism of theological language in such instances is associated with the social assumptions it takes for granted in its metaphorical way of speaking. The metaphor of marital relations for the relationship between human beings and God still works in the context of a love relationship, but not in the context of betrayal and jealousy associated with it, and it is the latter relations that explain the sin of idolatry.

## The Hermeneutic Circle within the Metaphors

To this point we have analyzed the sin of idolatry by taking the anthropomorphic images at face value and assuming that these are the images through which one may understand what idolatry is. But one could make a claim that the very act of interpreting anthropomorphic images literally is itself idolatry. Now we have reached the hermeneutic circle, in which the very representation of God in anthropomorphic terms is perceived as part of the problem of idolatry. On the one hand we can grasp what idolatry is only by understanding the metaphors that express opposition to it, but on the other hand the understanding of these metaphors, particularly the question of how literal or metaphorical they are, depends on how we understand idolatry in the Bible. For example, consider the expression "the jealous God." The understanding of idolatry requires the understanding of this expression in its various manifestations in a sense very close to the sense in which a husband is jealous of his adulterous wife. But this literal understanding of the word "jealous" is itself suspect as a manifestation of an anthropomorphic conception of God, which is an aspect of idolatry as it is understood post-biblically.

Here we are confronted with another circle within the first circle. Those who read the anthropomorphic expressions in the relational metaphors nonliterally will nevertheless give a literal reading to other expressions connected with the question of whether the Bible only prohibits the worship of other gods or denies their existence altogether. Those who forbid the anthropomorphizing of God as idolatry certainly consider any statement that other gods exist to be a form of idolatry. Therefore, when they encounter biblical verses which may be understood as saying that other gods exist, they will read these verses nonliterally, although they will read literally other verses denying the existence of other gods. Thus, when they encounter phrases saying that other gods are "delusion" or "no-gods," they will read these phrases literally. In contrast, the phrase that, literally translated, says, "Who is like You, O Lord, among the gods," is given the nonliteral translation "Who is like You, O Lord, among the celestials," precisely in order to deny the existence of other gods. The question of which texts to read literally and which to read metaphorically depends on the question of what conception of idolatry the reader holds, a conception which those very texts are supposed to anchor.

We chose to enter the circle from the standpoint of a literal, anthropomorphic reading of the metaphors, because we see the nonanthropomorphic abstraction as a later product of a philosophical viewpoint that regards the concept of God as an abstract concept, and the distinction between idolatry and monotheism as a difference in the degree of abstractness of the concept of God. According to this viewpoint the main problem of idolatry is not the worship of other gods but the improper and erroneous representation of God himself, including anthropomorphic representations. In our opinion this approach does not reflect the anthropomorphic biblical viewpoint, and in this chapter we have explained how a viewpoint that takes seriously the idea of the God of Israel as a person relates to idolatry. In subsequent chapters we defend this viewpoint and distinguish between the anthropomorphic viewpoint and myth in general. For now we will only state what Yehezkel Kaufmann pointed out in his paper "Unity and Abstraction": that the God of the Bible is personified and what distinguishes him from other gods is not his being more abstract.[28]

# 2

## Idolatry and Representation

The prohibitions against idolatry are an attempt to dictate the ways in which God may be represented. It is forbidden not only to worship other gods such as Ba'al, but also to represent God himself by means of a statue or picture. This aspect of the ban on idolatry raises many questions: What are the proper methods of representing God, and which methods are forbidden? Why are representations in pictures and statues forbidden, and why are linguistic representations permitted? What are representations of God by idols supposed to mean? Are they an attempt to represent him by means of something that resembles him, and thus forbidden because there is nothing that resembles God? Or can they be regarded as representations in which there is a special presence of the gods, thus narrowing the gap between the world and God to a greater degree than can be tolerated by the monotheistic religions?

According to the view that distinguishes the ban on the worship of other gods from the making of images and likenesses of the God of Israel, the two consecutive verses in the Ten Commandments, "You shall have no other gods besides Me" and "You shall not make for yourself a sculptured image or any likeness" (Exodus 20:3–4), must be understood as two separate prohibitions. The second verse, in other words, must be understood as a second prohibition: it is forbidden to worship other gods, and in addition it is forbidden to make images and likenesses of God himself.[1] Such an understanding of the prohibition seems explicitly called for in Deuteronomy: ". . . be most careful—since you saw no shape when the Lord your God spoke to you at Horeb out of the fire—not to act wickedly and make for yourselves a sculptured image in any likeness whatever: the form of a man or woman" (4:15–16). Since the Israelites did not see any image on Mount Sinai, they are forbidden to make images or pictures—a clear expression of the fear of the representation of God himself in images and pictures. In the same chapter in Deuteronomy the revelation at Sinai is described as hearing the voice of God without seeing any shape: "You heard the sound of words but perceived no shape—nothing but a voice" (4:12). This emphasis, which is repeated several times in the chapter, is intended to eliminate the possibility that the very revelation which forbade the making of images and pictures would be conceived as a revelation in which a shape of God was seen, and so would be a cause of the making of images and pictures.[2] But the chapter does not tell us why a linguistic description of God's hand is permitted while a drawing of his hand is forbidden. A short discussion of representation in general will assist us in clarifying the distinction between the permitted and forbidden representations of God.

C. S. Peirce divided the various kinds of representations into three categories.[3] The first is representation based on similarity, the second is causal-metonymic representation, and the third is convention-based representation. Representation based on similarity means that one thing represents another because it is similar to it. Thus, for example, a photograph of someone may be said to represent him because it is similar to him. In causal representation the relation between the representing and the represented things is not a relation of similarity; other relations are involved, such as metonymy, in which a part represents the whole. We can say that the handkerchief of a beloved represents her not because it resembles her but because it belongs to her. In conventional representation the representing thing is associated with the represented thing by convention, as the word "cup" represents a cup, without any similarity or causal relation between the word and the object. There is a convention that permits the word "cup" to represent the object we drink from. According to this division of the types of representations, conventional representations are controlled by rules, and in order to know that a particular word represents some object the word must be learned and practiced. This is not true of representation based on similarity, where the representation is natural and obvious and is not controlled by special rules.

This schematic division of the types of representation has been subject to criticism, primarily by Nelson Goodman, who refuted the assumption that there is a natural kind of representation independent of conventional rules. He has argued that there is much more convention than is intuitively apparent in representations generally regarded as being based on similarity. In his opinion similarity-based representations are only a special case of convention-based representations.[4] In spite of Goodman's objections, for the purposes of our analysis we will make use of Peirce's division. In the course of the discussion of the relation between linguistic and pictorial representations we will refer to the problems that this scheme engenders and to what the criticism of this scheme can teach us about the issue of the representation of God.

At first glance it would seem that gods can be represented by any one of the three types of representation. There are similarity-based representations such as sculptures and pictures, metonymic representations such as the Ark of the Covenant and the cherubim, and conventional representations such as linguistic descriptions of a god. The different relations between the types of representation and the prohibitions on representations are the subject of this chapter.

## Similarity-Based Representations

### Idols, the Error of Substitution, and Fetishes

The prophets describe idol worship as the worship of wood and stone. When the idolater bows down to the idol, according to Isaiah, he worships the image itself and not what the image represents. In their polemics the prophets taunt the idol worshipers with the idiocy of worshiping wood and stone; the image is not a sign or symbol of god, the prophets flatly state, it is god.[5] This view of the function of the image as a fetish was clearly influenced by the biblical polemics that attempted to portray the idolaters as identifying their god with wood and stone.[6] The other extreme in describing the function of images and their place in worship is the view that images and icons are mere signs, with no unique powers, capable of serving only as reminders and transparent representations of the gods. Icons according to this view inspire and teach; they are mainly didactic artifacts and not active forces. Such attitudes were expressed by those who defended icons in the church during the iconoclastic debate of the seventh century and by Catholics in arguing against the Reformation in the sixteenth century.[7] These two extreme views, of course, must be distinguished from the more complex views of the worshipers themselves.

Between the two extremes is a variety of attitudes regarding the relationship of the gods to their icons. Those attitudes, free from either polemics or apologetics, describe and reflect more faithfully the role of icons as representations. Not mere transparent signs, icons have independent power; they heal and perform miracles and therefore are addressed and worshiped. Their unique power is due not to the identity between God and the material makeup of the icon, but to the special relationship between the two. The relationship is only partly based on the similarity between the symbol and the thing symbolized. The icon also shares some of the features of the thing it represents. This special relationship is described in a variety of forms. The idol is one of the manifestations of the god— sometimes his place of residence (like the soul in the body) and sometimes a direct concentration of his powers. Moreover, in certain ritual contexts there are special causal connections between the god and its icons. By means of these causal connections an act performed on the icon becomes an act upon the god itself.[8] In the Bible itself there is a similar attitude to the holy vessels. The presence of the Ark of the Covenant could bring life and death: it brought disaster upon the Philistines and killed thousands of Israel's people in Beth Shemesh.[9] Thus there is a "substitution" in idol worship of the symbol for the thing symbolized, in which some of the traits of the symbolized thing are transferred to the symbolizing thing. In this substitution the two prohibitions—the one against the making of sculptures and pictures and the one against the worship of other gods—are actually joined. The prohibitions against making sculptures and pictures is explained by the potential for them to be eventually transformed from representations of god or other gods to other gods themselves. Thus the prohibition against the icon in this conception has two components. First, the gap between the god and the world is blurred by the representation that possesses the features of the god itself. Second, this creates a very deep fear of substitution, in which the idol takes the place of the god in the eyes of the worshiper.

An example will help us clarify what sort of representation we are dealing with. The changing seasons of the year can represent transitions between life and death. There is a metaphorical similarity between the two phenomena, the transition between the flowering of spring and the aridity of summer in subtropical countries, and the transition between life and death. In the Mesopotamian ritual worship of the god Dumuzi the metaphorical similarity between these two phenomena signifies a deeper connection of representation. In the myth of Dumuzi the changing seasons represent the life and death of the gods not only because they are metaphorically similar but also because the changing seasons are perceived as the direct manifestations of the death and resurrection of the gods. Summer arrives because of the repeated mythic event of the death of the god, and it passes because the dead god has come back to life. The changing seasons are direct manifestations of processes in the heavenly world, and it is as such that they represent them. Thus there is a direct causal dependence between the symbol and the thing symbolized. In addition to this causal dependence, the aridity of summer is a manifestation of the death of the god—it is the "same" death.[10] Death has acquired a cosmic dimension. In this sort of representation the symbols are regarded both as manifestations of the god (as a man's footprints in sand may be said to represent him) and as causally dependent upon it (as dark clouds represent rain). These representations are a substitute for the god because they bear his traits and because they stand in a unique relationship to the god, a relationship which cannot be attained by any other sort of representation. The fact that there is a similarity between the phenomena of the changing seasons and the phenomena of life and death is not the reason that these phenomena are capable of representing one another; on the contrary, the resemblance between the two is the result of the internal relations between them. Returning to Peirce's division of the types of representation, we see that the type of representation we are discussing here is closer to metonymy than to similarity-based representations. The tendency is thus to transform similarity-based representations into metonymies, and even more radically to explain the similarity between the phenomena on the basis of the metonymies.

The nonpagans' great fear of similarity-based representation is the possibility of a substitutive error, in which the idol ceases to be the representation or symbol of God and comes to be seen as God himself or part of him. In such a case, the idol is regarded as a fetish that slowly and gradually acquires the traits of the thing it is representing. In a certain sense it becomes the body of the god, the residence of its soul, and an independent object of ritual worship. The purpose of the prohibitions dictating proper methods of representation is to prevent errors of substitution of the representations for God. Thus, in the seventh-century controversy within the Christian church the primary motivation of the iconoclasts was the fear that pictures of Jesus were being substituted for Jesus himself. The debate centered on the question of whether or not representations in pictures and sculptures were safe from substitution. Although defenders of the tradition of paintings and icons in the church also believed that these representations had to be protected from the danger of substitution and therefore prohibited their worship, they claimed that there was no danger of substitution in the act of visual representation itself or in an attitude of respect for the representations.[11]

A fetish is an object to which people attribute powers that it does not have. But not every error in the attribution of powers transforms an object into a fetish. Although such errors occur all the time, we can call an object a fetish only if the error gives the object some control over its worshipers. In such a case the fetish is an object to which people have an attitude of ritual worship. There have been many transformations in the concept of the fetish and the mechanism of fetishistic error;[12] we will discuss only those fetishistic errors that are related to the error of substitution. This error occurs when a representation acquires the features of the thing represented. The mechanism of such an error involves forgetting that it is a representation and seeing it as something autonomous.

The understanding of idolatry as an error of substitution was central to Maimonides' thought. The transition from belief in a first cause, which Maimonides considered a chronologically prior belief, to the worship of idols did not occur in one direct leap. Rather, it took place through intermediate stages in which the worshiped heavenly forces and their images first served as intermediaries between the worshiper and God and only subsequently became gods. Maimonides describes this development at the beginning of the section on the laws relating to idolatry in his *Code of Jewish Law*.

Initially, worshipers thought that worshiping the intermediaries was a way of showing respect for God, just as honoring the servants of a king is a way of showing respect for the king. This view led the people to begin worshiping the moon and the stars, but still as intermediaries—"They did not say that there was no god but this star." Afterward false prophets arose who said that God had commanded them to worship a certain star or all the stars, and so they built temples and filled them with idols representing the stars. The gap between God himself and worship of him was increased further by the claim that God had commanded not only that the stars, which were intermediaries, should be worshiped but also that the images of the stars, which were intermediaries upon intermediaries, should be worshiped. The motivation for worshiping these intermediaries was supported by the assertion that they were capable of causing good and evil events to occur, and that success was dependent on worshiping them. In the next stage there were more false prophets who claimed that these stars had commanded that they should be worshiped, that is, these intermediaries were given the additional status of being able to give commands and prophecies. The end of this process, as described by Maimonides, was as follows:

> And as the days progressed the name of the revered and awesome God was forgotten from the entire universe and no one knew of Him. Thus all the ordinary folk, including women and children, did not know of anything but the images of wood and stone and the stone temples, as they had been taught from childhood to bow down to them and to worship them and to swear by them. The wise men among them, such as the priests and others, pretended that there was no God but the stars and the constellations in whose form the images were made. But there was no one who knew the Rock of Ages. (Laws of Idolatry 1:2)

At the end of the process according to Maimonides there was a fetishistic folk religion, and the masses forgot that the idols in the temples were representations of the stars and not independent forces.

One of the most important components in the process of the transformation of the representation into an independent power was the use of representations of the representations. The religious elite was aware that the idols were only representations of heavenly forces, but even the priests and the wise men made the substitutive error of regarding the heavenly forces themselves as gods rather than as intermediaries for the Rock of Ages. The only difference between the masses and the priests was that the latter made the substitutive error in a later stage and attributed less transparency to the intermediaries as representations. The masses erred at the stage of the idols themselves, in relating to them as if they were fetishes, although they were only representations of the heavenly forces. The priests erred in their fetishistic attitude toward the heavenly forces, although these were only representations of God. Since it is the error of substitution that is the cause of idolatry, according to Maimonides the purpose of the prohibitions against idolatry is to ensure that such errors will not be made. This is the reason that the worship of created beings and symbols was forbidden, even if the worshipers were aware that they were only being worshiped as intermediaries.[13]

Whatever historical validity Maimonides' description may have, what interests us in his description is the analysis of the error of substitution. According to Maimonides, the cause of the error of substitution is the act of worship, as beliefs follow actions. The confusion results from the fact that in a situation of representation only the ways of relating are supposed to be transferred, and not the predicates applying to the represented thing. The king's representative is not the king himself, although some of the ways of relating to the king are transferred to the representative because of his role. The error of substitution occurs in the next stage, when the thing represented is described as if it were the thing it represents. This is what occurs with respect to the heavenly forces and the idols. Substitution occurs again when the attitudes that were derived from the fact that the object is a representation continue to exist even after the object is no longer perceived as such. The attitude of respect and worship toward the heavenly powers was derived from their being representations of God, but this attitude persisted even after they were no longer perceived in this way. In Maimonides' view the purpose of the prohibitions against idolatry was to ensure that the worship of God would be free of the possibility of the substitutive error. Here we see an absolute shift to the worship of one God, which is the crucial meaning of the prohibition on idolatry.

In addition there are also cases in which the substitution is not a specifically cognitive error. Consider the example of the soldier who falls in battle while trying to save his nation's flag. There are those who would claim that there is a substitution here of the flag, which is a symbol of the state, for the state itself. But wars are fought to protect the state, not the flag. The substitution here takes place on the level of attitude, that is, the representation is accorded an attitude that rightfully belongs only to the represented thing. In a case like this, where the error is an attitudinal one, the criterion for the transformation of an object into a fetish is less clear, and the question of when there is an attitude of substitution becomes very complex. The same people who consider the soldier's willingness to die for the flag to be a case of substitution may be shocked by an attitude of contempt toward the flag in other contexts. In any event the criterion for judging when substitution has occurred is not as clear in this case as in cases of error-based substitution.[14]

### Erroneous Representation or Inappropriate Representation?

There is another problem with similarity-based representation even where there is no fear of substitution. In the painting on the ceiling of the Sistine Chapel in which Michelangelo painted God creating Adam there is no problem of substitution. No one has ever claimed that God is present in this painting or confused the painting with God. Those who interpret the prohibition against images most strictly will oppose this painting, however, because there is something forbidden in the very act of representing God in a painting. The prohibition against representing God in a sculpture or painting is the prohibition against a representation that seems to be based on similarity. Why is it forbidden to represent God in this way? If it is assumed that God has no image, then any similarity-based representation of God must necessarily be a wrong representation, a diminution of what he really is. The error is in the very act of making an image of something that has no image.[15] Representation is prohibited as a result of the metaphysical claim that since God has no image, any representation of God, and naturally any worship of such a representation, constitutes the worship of a false god. The problem in this case is that any similarity-based representation is mistaken and causes an error in the conception of God for anyone who sees or worships such a representation.

Although the claim that God has no image is considered by Maimonides as a principle of faith, it is not so clear that it is accepted in the Bible or in the rabbinic traditions. In the Bible it seems that

God does indeed have an image, except that it is forbidden to represent this image in any way. Thus, for example, when Moses asks to see God's face, God answers, "You cannot see My face, for man may not see Me and live" (Exodus 33:20). Elsewhere it is said of Moses that "he beholds the likeness of the Lord" (Numbers 12:8), and of the elders of Israel that "they beheld God, and they ate and drank" (Exodus 24:11). Isaiah saw the Lord "seated on a high and lofty throne" (Isaiah 6:1), and Ezekiel describes him as having "the semblance of a human form" (Ezekiel 1:26). It thus seems that the prohibition against representation is associated not with the metaphysical question of whether God has an image but with the methods of representing God in ritual worship.

The Bible itself does not resolve the question of whether God has an image. Moshe Weinfeld claims that biblical literature does ascribe an image to God, for example, when the priestly source speaks of God as dwelling within the sanctuary. At the same time, according to Weinfeld, in Deuteronomy there is a more abstract concept of God as having no image. In Deuteronomy God's dwelling in the sanctuary is replaced by his name's dwelling there.[16] It is not clear in Deuteronomy how one should interpret the verse "since you saw no shape when the Lord your God spoke to you" (4:15): is this a negation of the existence of a shape of God or only a stipulation that the Israelites did not see any such shape? At any rate it seems that there is a view embedded in the Bible which ascribes a shape to God, and the issue is whether there is any tension within the Bible concerning this question.

These trends within the Bible are developed further in the *Shi'ur Komah* literature, a form of mystical literature from the second and third centuries that discusses the size of the parts of God's body. This literature is filled with visual descriptions of God and describes experiences of seeing him directly. It is entirely possible that this tradition is not a mystic tradition on the edge of the mainstream Judaism but is found within the very heart of rabbinic Judaism, as Saul Lieberman claims. He points out that the midrash on the Song of Songs tells us about traditions of God being seen—at the crossing of the Red Sea and at the giving of the Torah; the midrash about the song at the crossing of the Red Sea tells us specifically that the Israelites saw God at the sea when they said, "This is my God and I will enshrine Him" (Exodus 15:2). The claim that God has no image, which was turned into one of the foundations of Judaism by Maimonides, does not reflect either the Bible or the rabbinic tradition. It would therefore be very difficult to say that the prohibition against idols and pictures was based on this claim.[17]

In keeping with this approach, we argue that the difference between the worship of God and the worship of idols is not in the issue of whether the divinity has an image but rather in the issue of whether it is permitted to make a representation of this image. The important question is thus the following one: if God actually does have an image, why is it forbidden to make a similarity-based representation of this image? One answer is that God does indeed have an image, but no person has seen it, and so there is a danger that any representation will be incorrect. From this argument it would follow that if someone should happen by some chance to see God's image he or she would be permitted to make a representation of it. A possible rejoinder to this is that even someone who had seen God's image would be forbidden to make a representation of it, because every representation constitutes a diminution of respect for the represented object. God would lose his uniqueness in the process of representation and in the fact of having many imitations, and his value would decline, just as the value of a work of art declines when there are many reproductions of it. The sense of the gap between God and his worshipers is based on the fact that they can never see his image, even in a representation. This may be compared to the kings of Persia, who would speak to their subjects from behind a screen and were never seen.[18] In general, there are two opposite approaches to the task of creating a feeling of remoteness and authority: one is to distribute pictures of the king everywhere, and the other is to prevent anyone from ever seeing the king. The prohibition against making images and pictures is a facet of the second approach, which is based on mystery and distance. This prohibition is independent of the metaphysical view that God has no image and relates only to the issue of the permitted methods of representation. The problem here is not one of the error in representation but of the degree of exposure of what is being represented on the basis of similarity, where this exposure is independent of the problem of the substitutive error. The representation is not mistaken, it is inappropriate.

The distinction between the idol worshipers and their opponents is not in the image of God in the minds of the worshipers but in the methods of representing him in ritual worship. In the view of Maimonides, however, as we will discuss at length in Chapter 4, the image of God in the mind of the worshiper is the crucial element. He therefore insists that those who ascribe a corporeal image to God are heretics and will have no share in the world-to-come. Rabad, in his commentary on Maimonides' *Code of Jewish Law* (Laws of Repentance, 3:7), disagrees with Maimonides and returns the focus of the discussion from what is in the worshiper's head to what is represented in the act of worship.[19]

## Metonymic Representations

The biblical tradition, which so clearly forbids similarity-based representations of God, permits metonymic representations of him. Even in the Jewish temple, when one passes from the courtyard to the outer part of the temple building, and from the outer part to the inner part, the Holy of Holies behind the curtain, one does not see any image of God, as is the custom in pagan temples. There is an expectation of seeing God, or at least an image of him, behind the curtain, but the only thing to be seen there are the cherubim. The cherubim do not represent God by resembling him; rather, they are a metonymic representation of God: they represent God because they are directly associated with him, being his chariot. (We do not believe that the cherubim are similarity-based representations of metonymic representations, that is, that the cherubim in the temple are representations that resemble the heavenly chariot; in our opinion the cherubim themselves are the chariot.)[20]

Metonymic representations are permitted because they do not lead to error in the conception of God, as they do not represent him by being similar to him. Moreover, God is not revealed in a metonymic representation to the degree that he is in one based on similarity. An image of God is not the same as his chariot, if the intention is to prevent direct exposure of the image of God himself. The fact that metonymic representations of God are permitted supports our contention that the basis for the prohibition against images and pictures is not the fear of substitution but the struggle against mistaken or inappropriate representations. Substitution can occur just as easily in metonymic as in similarity-based representations. Didn't the Israelites treat the Ark of the Covenant as a fetish when they took it to the war with the Philistines on the assumption that it would grant them victory? If the primary fear was a fear of the substitution of the representation for the represented thing, then metonymic representations should have been forbidden as well.

Often the accusation of idolatry is hurled at some person or group because the accuser has failed to distinguish between metonymic and similarity-based representations. Thus, for example, some scholars claim that equating worship of the golden calves in the northern kingdom of Israel with idol worship is a mistake.[21] The worshipers of the golden calves, according to this claim, did not worship them as similarity-based representations of God but as a substitute for the cherubim and the Ark of the Covenant, which were in Jerusalem. (There are those who explain the sin of worshiping the golden calf in the desert in the same way.) To consider worship of the golden calves in the northern kingdom idolatry is to attribute similarity-based representation to what is only metonymic representation.[22]

This very same process may be applied in reverse to permit what seems to be idolatry, or what seems mistaken from a theological viewpoint, and to make it legitimate. That is, similarity-based representations may be transformed into metonymic ones in order to solve serious problems. For example, when the translator-commentator Onkelos encounters biblical verses describing God as appearing in a cloud or in a fire, he transforms them into manifestations of objects that God created for the purpose of revelation, instead of seeing them as manifestations of God himself or of something resembling him.[23] There is indeed a direct causal relation between God and the cloud, but it is not a relation of similarity. The process of transforming the similarity-based representation into a metonymic one thus legitimizes the representation.

## Conventional Representations

While the biblical tradition regards the making of sculptured images and pictures as a grave sin, it permits linguistic representations of God. In many synagogues the hymn *An'im Zemirot* (I will sing songs) is sung at the end of Sabbath morning services. One of the lines of the hymn describes God thus: "His head is covered with curls of light, his hair is like fragments of the night." Imagine if this line were illustrated and God drawn with a head of curly hair! The idea of drawing such a picture would not enter the mind of any observant Jew, in spite of the fact that the linguistic description in the hymn is one of the accepted parts of the Sabbath service. A never-failing source of blatant anthropomorphic images may be found in the Song of Songs. The song, which is interpreted as an allegory for the love between God and Israel, is full of bold linguistic descriptions of God as lover, whose cheeks are like beds of spices, whose hands are rods of gold, whose belly is a tablet of ivory, and whose legs are like marble pillars (see Song of Songs 5:13–15). It is not by chance that this song aroused the imaginations of the authors of the *Shi'ur Komah* literature, who extended and deepened the linguistic descriptions of the attributes and shape of God. The astounding degree of freedom accorded to linguistic descriptions of God, as opposed to the strictness with which pictorial descriptions were judged, confronts us with a crucial question in the understanding of idolatry: what is the distinction between linguistic representations of God, which seem to be not only permitted but even accepted, and pictorial representations of him? Is there a real difference between speaking about the hand of God and drawing it? Three approaches to this question are discussed below.

### Representation as Metaphor

One view holds that just as linguistic expressions can have metaphorical interpretations, so can pictures. A picture has a transparent quality, and just as the expression "the hand of God" is a metaphor for his power, so a drawing of God's hand can be such a metaphor. Michelangelo's famous painting can thus be interpreted as a metaphor for God's primacy, creativity, and power. The fact that the painting has a reference is not grounded in similarity-based representation. We are not required to say that the painting refers to something because it resembles the thing it refers to; it can also represent something based on a convention. There is no real distinction between a linguistic picture and an actual picture. Thus if the linguistic expression is taken at its face value, then the picture too should be permitted; and if the linguistic expression is interpreted metaphorically, why shouldn't the picture also be considered a candidate for metaphorical interpretation?

In this connection there is an interesting distinction that was made during the Reformation. There were those who regarded representations of Jesus as a lamb as preferable to paintings of Jesus as a man. Their claim was that the representations of Jesus as a lamb were obviously metaphors of his being a sacrificial victim, as no one would say that Jesus resembled a lamb, which was not true of his representation in the figure of a man. Luther therefore asserted that the pictures of Jesus as a lamb are the most appropriate representations.[24] The question that arises here is why one should not have the same attitude toward all pictures of God as toward the paintings of Jesus as a lamb—that is, as metaphors rather than as similarity-based pictures. And if it will be argued that we are liable to take the pictures literally because they are not protected against this possibility the way the paintings of Jesus as a lamb are, then why should it not be said that the same danger exists for words? After all, a "literal reading" may be attributed only metaphorically to a picture, as its first and most natural sense applies to words.

The strategy for defending such a view is to abolish the existing distinction between linguistic representations, which are based on convention, and the similarity-based representations occurring in pictures. This is the view of Nelson Goodman, who believes that what is called similarity-based representation is not a natural form of representation that is innocent of all conventions and prior knowledge.[25] A smile in a painting of one of Jesus' apostles might be interpreted as an expression of amiability, but if it turns out to be a painting of Judas Iscariot the smile will be seen as a representation of guile and cynicism. In other words, the identification of what the smile represents is not dependent on similarity alone. In general, according to Goodman, everything is similar to everything else, and the similarity that is attributed may sometimes be based on a certain trait of the representing thing to the exclusion of its other traits. The painting of a dog beside a knight represents the knight's loyalty, in spite of the fact that there is no other relevant similarity between the dog and the knight. Moreover, the very trait of loyalty possessed by the dog is not a trait that can easily be seen in a picture of a dog outside a specific cultural context. The process of singling out the similar traits depends on various conventions. The difference between similarity-based and convention-based representations evaporates, and with it the distinction between linguistic and pictorial representations of God.

### The Essential Distinction

There is another view, however, which distinguishes between linguistic and pictorial representations in that the linguistic representation does not present the worshiper with an object that can be confronted in an attitude of worship, as an intermediary of God or a fetish. In a pictorial representation the believer is actually confronted by an object. Even if the object is as transparent as language, and even if it can be given a metaphorical interpretation and need not be perceived as a similarity-based representation, there is nevertheless a possibility that the believer will transform the object into a focus of his attitude, into a ritual center of gravity. Thus idols not only represent on a basis of similarity but also become the bearers of the power they represent, because of their similarity to it. This blurring of the distinction between the symbol and the thing symbolized, which is so common in idolatry, does not occur in language because in the latter there is no concrete object that can be endowed with some of the powers of the symbolized thing. With pictorial representations there is always the fear that the representing object will at some stage be transformed into the permanent dwelling place of God himself or into a power with independent identity, whereas language does not create an object that can undergo such a transformation. This argument must be qualified by the fact that names are sometimes considered bearers of the power of the thing they denote, and a Torah scroll can become a fetish no less than any picture or image.

To the above argument can be added another reason for the prohibition of pictorial but not linguistic representations, which is independent of the fear of substitution. When one says, for example, that God has a hand, the constituents of this hand, such as size and shape, remain undetermined. Even the addition of more linguistic details will not give the fullness of description that is provided by a picture of the hand. If the problem is the degree of exposure of God in a pictorial representation, then in the case of a linguistic description, since the representation always leaves some gaps, the degree of exposure of the thing described is less than in a picture. In accordance with this criterion, the Persian kings who spoke from behind a screen could be described linguistically but not represented pictorially. The source of this distinction is the notion that God may be heard but not seen. To the extreme opponents of corporeality this distinction is not meaningful, as they do not see a difference between attributing the power of speech to God and attributing a physical shape to him. If, however, the problem is not corporeality but the degree of exposure of God to the hearer or the beholder, then the distinction is useful.

The intuition that distinguishes between similarity-based and convention-based representations gives priority to the "internal image," created from an accumulation of sense data, over linguistic representations. The following schema is often presented to describe the relationship between language and sense data, especially sight: we see the same object many times and this gives us a picture in our mind that abstracts the fixed properties of the object from the many instances of the object that we have seen. This is the "idea" of the object, to which we attach a word as a tag, and this gives us a linguistic representation.

The linguistic representation is thus distanced from the concrete object because it depends upon an idea that is created from the repeated appearance of sense data. The distance between language and object is mediated by the "idea," which is an internal image that a person has of an object, and this mediation produces the feeling that the linguistic description is less intimate and more distanced from direct contact of the senses, with respect to the object being described. Those philosophical standpoints which attacked this empiricist view of language, and described language as the mediator between objects and sense data, did not accept the approach that distances the linguistic representation from the represented object. The tag attached to a painting in a museum creates a different view of the painting. Changing the tag will create a change in perspective, so that people will see entirely different things in the painting. This is what would happen, in the example we gave before, if the tag under the painting of the smiling apostle were changed from Peter to Judas.[26]

As mentioned, the distinction between pictorial and linguistic representations has been attacked from both directions. On one side are those who abolish the distinction so as to permit pictorial as well as linguistic representations; on the other are those who prohibit both forms of representation and liken preserving the distinction to belittling the force of language and the serious consequences of the linguistic representation of God. To the latter group, language is even more dangerous than pictures because it states propositions and makes judgments. To say "God has a hand" is to assert a proposition, while a drawing of this hand is not a proposition. This propositional character of language can make it more dangerous than visual representations. According to this view, just as there is a ban on representations in images and pictures, so there should be a ban on linguistic representations. The war against sculptured images and paintings is thus extended to linguistic images. The outstanding representative of this view is Maimonides, whose writings we discuss in the following section.

### "The Torah Speaks in the Language of People"

To consider the third view—that there is no distinction between the two types of representation and that they are both forbidden—we must understand the expression "the Torah speaks in the language of people," which is central to Maimonides' treatment of linguistic representations of God, although it evolved from the talmudic sages. The primary meaning of the expression refers not to the use of language in describing God but to the application in the Torah of different rhetorical devices accepted in ordinary language.

The second-century discussion, which is the source of the expression, arose in the context of a debate between the schools of R. Akiva and R. Ishmael over how to interpret the doubled expressions that occur frequently in the Torah. When these expressions are translated into English, the doubling is omitted, as there is no such form of expression in English. In order to translate the expression literally, one would have to say, "Walk you walked," instead of simply "You walked," or "Kidnap I was kidnapped," instead of simply, "I was kidnapped." R. Akiva interpreted these expressions as conveying some additional meaning, because he believed that there is no redundancy in the Torah. R. Ishmael, by contrast, asserted that one should not try to find the source of any halakhah in these doubled expressions, because the Torah simply speaks in the language of people. In his view, these expressions were not meant to convey an additional meaning that was not present in the first term, but constitute a rhetorical device, as in ordinary speech, for the sake of emphasis.[27] The controversy here concerns the proper rules of interpretation that must be applied to a sacred text. At the heart of the issue of interpretation, this issue is not whether the rules of interpretation are being used correctly, or which rules should be used, but whether or not a sacred text requires its own special interpretive code because its language is essentially different from ordinary language.

Interpretation of the expression "the Torah speaks in the language of people" underwent an essential change before it reached Maimonides. This change, which began during the post-talmudic period,[28] culminated in the writings of Maimonides, who treated it as his guiding principle in his great philosophical work, *The Guide of the Perplexed*. Whereas the previous controversy was about the redundancy of language, and whether the Torah uses the same language that ordinary people use, Maimonides turned the phrase into an expression of how the Torah speaks about God. In his view, the Torah describes God not according to the correct metaphysical picture but in a way people are able to understand. The Torah describes God in terms of heightened human perfection, because most people are unable to imagine any other sort of perfection than their own. Thus the Torah depicts God in material terms that the masses are able to grasp, and attributes to God those mental characteristics that people regard as perfection because these characteristics represent perfection when applied to people. The masses believe that "God would not exist if He did not have a body with a face . . . except that it is larger and brighter" (*Guide of the Perplexed*, 1:1). Maimonides applies the words "the Torah speaks" in the expression to speech about God, and the words "the language of people" to the language that people are capable of understanding, not necessarily the language that they speak. "People" at this stage is a term whose precise denotation is the masses—people who are unable to imagine the proper image of God. Thus Maimonides interprets each of the three parts of the expression differently from the talmudic sages.

Maimonides' use of this expression brings us to the relation between language and idolatry. The first part of *The Guide of the Perplexed* is devoted almost entirely to liberating the perplexed person from the difficulties of the language used with respect to God. At the beginning of the book Maimonides attempts to liberate the reader from the hold of the language of the Bible concerning the metaphysical image of God. This is the reason that biblical interpretation has such a central position in Maimonides' book. The language used in the Bible (and our taking this language at its face value) constitutes one of the primary causes of an incorrect image of God, whether in the attribution of material existence or in the attribution of emotionality. Maimonides teaches the reader that the language in which the Bible speaks of God is figurative language.

An example is the use of the word "sitting" as attributed to God, which Maimonides discusses in chapter eleven of part 1. He says the word is not attributed to God with the same literal meaning it has in the expression "Reuben is sitting," but is like the metaphorical biblical expression whose literal translation is "Judea will sit forever." In this expression the word "sit" refers to stability, as it does when it is used to refer to God. "Going up" and "going down" with respect to God also have a slightly altered meaning—something like going up or down in status rather than in space. Many expressions of physicality are used figuratively with respect to God just as they are used figuratively in ordinary language to speak of social relations. We say that a person is "the center of attention," clearly a reference not to a point in space but to a position in a social system. Understanding a figurative expression as a literal one with respect to God is, according to Maimonides, the great linguistic fallacy that leads to an erroneous metaphysical picture of God. In Maimonides' own words:

> When they [the rabbinic sages] said, "The Torah speaks in the language of people," they meant whatever all people are able to understand at first thought . . . Therefore they described Him in terms that refer to material being, in order to teach that He exists, since the masses cannot grasp existence at first glance unless it is the existence of a body. (*Guide of the Perplexed,* 1:26)

Thus metaphorical language blurs rather than clarifies distinctions, and it leads people astray because they tend to read the metaphors literally. A metaphor may often be clearly identifiable, as in the case of the sentence whose literal meaning is "Judea will sit forever" but whose obvious intended meaning is "Judea will be established forever." When the subject matter concerns God, however, the identification of the metaphor requires an extensive philosophical background. People know enough about Judea as a state to be able to identify "sitting" as a metaphor, but they do not know anything about God that would enable them to identify expressions referring to him as metaphors. If all people's knowledge of Judea were derived from the quoted sentence, then it would not be so easy to interpret "sit" as a metaphor. Since the masses do not have independent information about God, whose source is in external metaphysics, they do not have the capability of identifying expressions in religious language as metaphorical, even though they can do this easily in other areas of language. In the chapters that deal with figurative language in part I of *The Guide of the Perplexed,* Maimonides often shows that an expression is figurative by citing an example of its figurative use in a place where it is immediately understood as a metaphor, thus demonstrating that the expression is metaphorical when used to refer to God as well. This procedure is necessary because of the difficulty of identifying expressions as metaphorical with respect to God, in contrast to the ease with which metaphors about ordinary objects are identified.

So far it has been assumed that there exists a pure, nonmetaphorical language that is free of this type of fallacy. In such a conceptual language it would be possible to speak correctly about God, without the heavy burden of the use of figurative expressions for the purposes of the masses. Later in part I of his book, however, Maimonides takes an even more radical stance regarding religious language. He disqualifies language in general from being able to describe God by any positive attributes. He devotes this section of the book not to biblical interpretation or to an attempt to liberate the perplexed reader from the hold of biblical language, but to a general attack on the very attempt to describe God in language. This attack is directed even at those who understand quite well that the Torah uses figurative expressions to speak about God.

Hegel distinguished between religious discourse about the absolute, which is metaphorical, and philosophical discourse about the absolute, which is conceptual. Conceptual discourse, he asserted, is free of the distortions and imprecision of metaphorical language. But Maimonides' criticism of linguistic representation includes not only metaphorical religious language but also conceptual philosophical language. In his view even conceptual language is not transparent in issues relating to God. At this stage "the language of people" does not mean the language of the masses who are incapable of abstract speech but refers to language itself. Maimonides' purpose is to liberate the philosopher from what Wittgenstein would have called the mythological layer inherent in language in general. The discussion of the connection between language and the erroneous picture of God, which is the heart of part 1 of *The Guide of the Perplexed,* confronts us with a similarity between various points in the philosophy of language and in Maimonides' discussion of the limitations of religious language. Maimonides expresses his criticism of language in general as follows: ". . . and these subtle matters cannot be distinguished by customary words, which constitute the great cause of misapprehension." Later in the same chapter Maimonides discusses the words "preexistent" and "one" and their attribution to God, commenting: "None of these expressions are anything but the language of people." Here he is obviously referring to language in general.

What is this misapprehension that results from the use of language with respect to God? Maimonides offers two principal answers. One is that the use of attributes impairs the simple unity of God. The structure of the sentence "God exists" or "God is one" creates a picture of an object to which different predicates can apply. But God's unity is his essence, not something added to his essence, and this is true of his existence as well. If, however, we consider these attributes not as predicates or accidents but as part of the definition of God, then we are creating a plurality in the very definition from a number of aspects. This criticism of the attribution of positive predicates to God is based on the negation of nominalist arguments that oppose granting predicates a different ontological status from that of the object being described. Indeed, nominalist arguments were used by various philosophers against the theory of negative attributes. For example, Ibn Rushed criticizes Ibn Sina on this very point, and the argument was used by Gersonides and Crescas against Maimonides himself.[29]

Maimonides' second argument against the ascription of positive attributes to God is that describing God with universal predicates such as existence puts him into the same category as other things to which these predicates apply. For example, we attribute existence both to God and to a table, but actually God's existence is of a different type, to which the familiar usage of existence does not apply. To give another example, if one says that God is preexistent to the world in a positive sense, then one is attributing the concept of time to God and putting him into a chronological relation to the world. But since, according to Maimonides—who uses the Aristotelian definition of time—time is dependent upon motion, the concept of time does not apply to God at all. One cannot say that God is preexistent; one can say only that since he has no motion the concept of time does not apply to him. The attribution of predicates to God in language is nothing but a category mistake, like the attribution of length to taste. This mistake causes people to perceive God as belonging to the same category as other familiar things to which the same attribute applies.

This error, in Maimonides' opinion, is so grave that the ascription of an attribute to God is an error with respect to his identity as a whole. A person who ascribes attributes to God should not be regarded as talking about God and making some mistake about him. Rather, such a person is not talking about God at all but about something else entirely. Extending familiar language to apply to God creates a category mistake rather than an ordinary error (*Guide of the Perplexed,* 1:58). When we speak about God, it is not really God we are speaking about but something else, and this is independent of the question of what we say about him. According to this view, the theory of negative attributes is meant to determine not the simple unity of God (as in the first view) but the absolute otherness of God and the essential categorical difference that exists between him and all familiar objects. The nominalist argument cannot be used against this claim because it relates to the problem of speech about God and the world with the same categories of predication in language, and not to the ontological duality that exists, so to speak, between the subject and the predicate.

Language is thus limited and misleading in its descriptions of God for two reasons. One is that the basic structure of the sentence creates a duality of subject and predicate. The second is that there is a misapprehension in a description of God using the same linguistic categories that are based on the existence of our familiar reality. Language serves as an instrument for projection of the sort of perfection that is familiar to us onto God, who is the absolute other. Language thus crosses its natural boundary into another reality, and in this extension of language a misapprehension is created with respect to God. Maimonides summarizes these two claims in chapter 59: "And know that whenever you attribute some other thing to Him, you will be distant from Him in two different ways, the one because whatever you attribute to Him is perfection for us, and the second because there is nothing that belongs to Him, but rather His perfections are His essence." The degree of criticism of language in the theory of negative attributes depends upon one's understanding of the starting point from which the theory is approached. One way to describe the motive for this theory is the skeptical way. The meaning of the theory of negative attributes is that we do not know anything positive about God: all we are able to know is what God is not (not what he is). This theory is thus essentially skeptical. Maimonides uses this line of argument when he describes the limits of understanding of the greatest of the prophets, Moses. All he was able to grasp were the descriptions of God through his actions, while everything else was negative. That is, to say that God is not nonexistent is not the same as to say that God exists. Even though the negation of nonexistence is logically equivalent to the attribution of existence, in the case of the theory of attributes the negation of nonexistence is not the negation of an attribute but a categorical negation. This may be compared to our saying of the wall that it cannot see, which does not mean that the wall is blind, because we are negating the use of the concepts of sight and blindness as applicable to walls in general. It would be more correct to say that the category of sight and blindness does not apply to walls. What characterizes a category mistake is that the negation of the proposition is wrong in the same sense as the positive proposition. A categorical negation does not imply anything positive. It thus turns out that the proposition that God is not existent is logically equivalent to the proposition that God is not nonexistent. The familiar category of existence which may be predicated of an object does not apply to God. The fact that we say, "God is not nonexistent," and that this expression is considered preferable to saying, "God is not existent," is a matter of determining which way of speaking is appropriate to God and no more than that (*Guide of the Perplexed,* 1:58).

Another view of the theory of negative attributes is that the problem is not in the impossibility of knowing God's essence but in its linguistic expression, as any attempt to formulate this knowledge in words creates an error. Behind the negative attributes, according to this view, a great deal of positive knowledge about God's essence is hidden, and it is only the attempt to formulate this knowledge in words that fails and is thus misleading. We know that all of God's attributes are his essence and not something added to it, but how could this be expressed positively without creating a duality between his essence and the attributes? This interpretation of the theory of negative attributes, which is not fundamentally skeptical, is taken by Harry Wolfson, and also, in a different version, by Julius Gutman. It constitutes a direct criticism of language. As Maimonides says: "Silence and limiting oneself to the apprehensions of the intellect are more appropriate." Beyond negation there is an intellectual understanding of God. It is possible "to understand appropriately," but the attempt to express this understanding in words is immediately misleading and creates error.[30]

The two trends found in Maimonides' discussion of this issue reflect two different attitudes toward the critique of language. One claims that there is a congruence between the possibilities of linguistic expression and of cognition, as according to this view the theory of negative attributes is based on the fact that nothing can be known about God's essence and thus there is obviously no possibility of expressing such knowledge. The second trend delimits not the boundaries of cognition but the boundaries of speech, and in this view there is no congruence between linguistic expressions and intellectually conceived knowledge about God. The attempt to give this knowledge linguistic expression is what causes error, since language is fundamentally limited in its attempts to describe this type of reality. In Chapter 4 we discuss the content of this knowledge that cannot be expressed, and in Chapter 6 we discuss the relation between Maimonides' theory of negative attributes and the names of God. At this point we note only that the issue confronting us resembles the question discussed by the positivists concerning the meaninglessness of metaphysical expressions in language: does this meaninglessness express a skeptical attitude with respect to all possible metaphysics, or does it only negate the possibility of expressing metaphysical ideas in words?

In our discussion we distinguished among three senses of the expression "the Torah speaks in the language of people." The first sense is that the Torah speaks the way people speak, and so redundancies in biblical language do not require a special type of interpretation that differs from the way we interpret people's speech. The second sense is that the Torah speaks about God in a way that the masses are capable of understanding, that is, metaphorically. The third sense is that the language of people is language in general in its attempt to describe God, and the Torah had to speak about God in language. The last two senses are directly related to the issue of language and idolatry. Biblical language creates a mistaken picture of God if its metaphors are taken literally, and so the reader must be liberated from this language in its literal sense. Moreover, the hold of descriptive language creates a duality in the description of God and impairs his simple unity. It also applies the same descriptive categories to the world and to God and thus impairs the absolute separation between God and the world. Maimonides devotes most of part 1 of *The Guide of the Perplexed* to liberating the reader from the hold of language, and the climax of this process is the silence recommended by the theory of negative attributes. Just as pictorial representations of God are forbidden, so are linguistic representations.

## The Appropriate Linguistic Representation

Even those who did not share Maimonides' view—that all linguistic representations of God are improper metaphysical descriptions and are thus forbidden—saw the need for constraints on representation. They perceived the limits of linguistic representation not in the representation itself but in the question of whether a particular representation is an appropriate one. This view categorized linguistic representations differently, as can be seen in various passages from the midrash. Consider, for example, the following midrash dealing with the revelation in the burning bush:

> R. Eliezer said, "Why did God reveal Himself from the high heavens and speak to Moses from the bush? Just as this bush is the lowest of all the trees in the world, so did the Israelites go down to the lowest level, and God went down with them and redeemed them, as is written, 'I have come down to rescue them from the Egyptians' (Exodus 3:8)." R. Joshua said, "Why did God reveal Himself from the high heavens and speak to Moses from the bush? When Israel went down to Egypt the *shekhinah* went down with them, as is written, 'I myself will go down with you to Egypt' (Genesis 46:4), and when they went out the *shekhinah* went out with them . . ." R. Jose the Galilean said, "Why did God reveal Himself from the high heavens and speak to Moses from the bush? Because it was holy, as the nations of the world did not use it for idolatry." (*Mekhilta of R. Simeon bar Johai,* on Exodus 8:3)

The question asked by the three rabbis is a question that could be considered a metaphysical one: how could the Infinite confine himself to a small bush in the desert? How could the One who has no motion, as all motion is a deficiency, go down from his place and speak from a bush? A metaphysical answer to this question would deny that there was a revelation from the bush and would say that what happened there was only a prophetic vision, like a dream, or that the voice that spoke from the bush was created by God for this purpose and there never was any presence of the speaker himself within the bush. But from the various answers that are given in the midrash we see that the problem that was disturbing the rabbis was not a metaphysical type of problem at all. The question of why God revealed himself in the bush is not a question of how such a revelation is metaphysically possible, that is, how a nonmaterial being can embody himself in the material. Rather, the question is why the king of kings chose to reveal himself precisely from such a lowly object as a bush. If a state hosts a president and gives him a room in a cheap hotel, it is not performing a metaphysically impossible act but is showing disrespect for his status and putting him in an inappropriate place.

Another example of this approach may be found in the *Mekhilta* interpreting the verse, "The Lord went before them in a pillar of cloud by day" (Exodus 13:21):

> "The Lord went before them in a pillar of cloud by day"—How is it possible to say this? Is it not written, "For I fill both heaven and earth—declares the Lord" (Jeremiah 23:24) and "One would call to the other, 'Holy, holy, holy! The Lord of Hosts! His presence fills the earth!'" (Isaiah 6:3) and "And there, coming from the east with a roar like the roar of mighty waters, was the Presence of the God of Israel, and the earth was lit up by His Presence" (Ezekiel 43:2). So how can the Torah say, "The Lord went before them in a pillar of cloud by day"? R. Judah said, "The emperor Antoninus would sometimes be speaking on the dais, and it would grow dark and it would be dark for his sons. When he left the dais he would take a lantern and light the way for his sons, and his ministers would come to him and say, 'Let us take the lantern and light the way for your sons.' And he would say to them, 'I am not doing this because there is no one who will take the lantern and light the way for my sons, but because I want to let you see my affection for my sons so that you will treat them respectfully.' Thus did God display his affection for Israel to the nations of the world, so that they should treat them respectfully. Yet not only do they not treat them respectfully, they even put them to death in harsh ways." (*Mekhilta of R. Ishmael va-Yehi*, 6)

As in the previous midrash, it only appears that the problem is a metaphysical one: how is it possible for one who is said to fill the world, and who is infinite and immaterial, to confine himself into a pillar and go before the camp in a pillar of cloud or of fire? The question seems to call for a response that would try to show that God did not really go before the camp, but rather that an angel who was his messenger or a miraculous cloud appeared. But in this midrash as well one discovers the true nature of the question by studying the responses. The question here is understood as how it can be appropriate for one whose presence fills the earth to go before the camp: is it proper for him to go to this trouble, is it an appropriate appearance for one who fills heaven and earth? The midrash in its answer does not deny that God indeed went before the camp in a pillar of cloud but justifies this action by his wish to demonstrate his affection for Israel, just as Antoninus did for his sons with the lantern. The transition to the metaphor of father and sons explains the degree of closeness with which God behaves toward Israel and his deviation from the behavior expected of a king. The issue, again, is not whether the representation in question is metaphysically possible but whether it is appropriate, or, more precisely, what can be learned from the fact that God's attitude toward Israel is not that of an authoritarian ruler but that of a father toward his sons. What needs explanation is not the metaphysics of the Infinite which reveals itself in a finite pillar, but the type of attitude that is revealed in this appearance, which is neither sublime nor awesome. This is the reason that the transition to the father-son metaphor provides the proper background for the answer.

There are thus two aspects to the problem of anthropomorphism. One is whether it provides an erroneous picture of God. The other aspect of the problem is whether anthropomorphism provides a disrespectful and inappropriate picture of God. The midrash often discusses the problem in its second aspect, and the answers it provides concern the understanding of the relationship between God and Israel. God's confinement within the small bush in the desert is an expression of his sharing in Israel's pain, and his going before the people in a pillar of cloud is an expression of his affection for them.

A different attitude toward the problem of linguistic description is demonstrated in Maimonides' interpretation of the following story, which is related in the Babylonian Talmud:

The leader of the prayers in R. Hanina's presence prayed as follows, "The God who is great and heroic and awesome and mighty
and bold and fearsome and strong and courageous and respected."
R. Hanina waited until he had finished the prayer and then said,
"Have you finished all the praises of your Master? What are all
these for? The three praises that we say—'the God who is great
and heroic and awesome'—if Moses had not said them in the
Torah, and if the Rabbis of the Great Assembly had not determined
that they should be a fixed part of our daily prayer, we would not
be permitted to say them. How then could you add all the others?"
This may be compared to a king of flesh and blood who has a
million gold coins and someone praises him for having silver coins.
This would be a sign of disrespect for the king. (*Berakhot,* 33b)

The extensive sequence of praises of God, which seems to constitute an attempt to exhaust his greatness, is disapproved of as being
inappropriate. Moreover, it constitutes an attitude of disrespect for
the king whose coins are of gold to praise him for having coins of
silver, as any praises one is able to offer to God cannot equal his
actual attributes. The multiplicity of praises beyond the ones that are
determined by the tradition constitute disrespect rather than praise,
and instead of increasing God's honor they decrease it. The problem
of God's attributes here is the problem of appropriate representation:
it is preferable to express fewer rather than more praises because it is
precisely the multiplicity of praises that is inappropriate to the king.

Maimonides, who quotes this passage, says about it, "Look first
and see how the midrash flinches and distances itself from the multiplicity of positive attributes." Later, in his explanation of the parable, Maimonides stresses that the parable describes God's perfections
as gold coins and the praises of him as silver coins, "to teach us that
what are perfections for us are not of this type for Him at all, but
they are all deficiencies with respect to Him. Whatever you may
imagine in these attributes to be perfection would be a deficiency for
God if it was of the same type as what is perfection for us" (*Guide of
the Perplexed,* 1:59). In Maimonides' view, as we might expect, the
story in the Talmud teaches the negation of all linguistic representations, as every perfection is only a perfection for us but is a deficiency
with respect to God. Positive attributes are forbidden in general,
and every ascription of an attribute is erroneous because there is a
categorical distinction between God's perfections and the perfections

that man ascribes to God through the use of language. It is thus in terms of quality rather than quantity that Maimonides explains the difference between gold and silver in the parable. Maimonides sees this passage as a continuation of his system of negating positive attributes in general and recommending silence.

The problem of representation can be viewed from two different perspectives. One understands the danger of representation as a medium that creates mistaken conceptions of God. Therefore, God is not allowed to be represented in images and pictures because he has no image. If this is the logic of the constraints on representations, linguistic representations should also be prohibited, and Maimonides followed that logic and abolished the distinction between language and image. The other view on representation is more political than metaphysical. Representations are prohibited either because of the fear of substitution or because of the approach that minimizes exposure. One may talk about God's image, since the Bible suggests that he might actually have an image, but one may not look at his image.

# 3

## Idolatry and Myth

### The Concept of Myth

Myth is the characteristic expression of idolatrous thought. There are thinkers who consider myth a form of expression unique to paganism, among them Ernst Renan, Henri Frankfort, and Yehezkel Kaufmann. By contrast, Martin Buber and Franz Rosenzweig are of the opinion that there is no living religion, pagan or otherwise, that does not contain myth.[1]

The term "myth" is laden with meanings and interpretations. Suggesting yet another definition of myth would be confusing as well as useless. Our use of "myth" follows common usage of derivatives and collocations of the concept such as "mythic story." We are less concerned with the term "mythology."[2] We are interested in the classification of stories as myth from the viewpoint of the philosophy of religion rather than the philosophy of culture, and these interests are not necessarily the same. We obligate ourselves to one thing only in our use of the term "myth": what we call "myth" is what others also call "myth," but not vice versa. That is, we intend to cover the paradigm cases of myth. This may perhaps suggest that our concept is the core concept of myth, while other concepts are derivative.

In our characterization there is an intimate relation between myth and ritual but not the sort of relation discussed by the people of the "myth and ritual" school. They address the question of which came first, whether temporally or conceptually: is myth an explanation for ritual activities that preceded it, or is ritual a mimetic embodiment of mythic motifs? In our opinion ritual is the extralinguistic context that turns a story or rhapsody about a divinity into a myth.[3]

There are two principal ways of characterizing myth: by content and by form. Characterization by content means classifying myths according to the main themes they deal with. We characterize a love story, for example, as a story whose main theme is love. The attempt to characterize myth by content therefore requires the identification of the main topic of myths. Thus, one might say that myths are stories dealing with the genealogy of the gods. However, one might also try to characterize myth by form, as allegory is characterized in terms of its form rather than its content.

There is another sense of characterization by form which might be appropriate, namely, the sense in which Kant speaks of time as a form. The concatenation of events one after another is the form of time, as opposed to the form of space, which consists of events placed one beside another. In this sense, a myth is a story with a special form of time—mythic time, which is cyclical rather than linear (like historical time). Events repeat themselves in the same way that the seasons of the year repeat themselves.[4]

We are thus confronted with three principal methods for classifying myths: by content, by linguistic form, and by a form of time that is unique to this sort of narrative. Although this division is not exclusive, and may not be exhaustive, we use it as a starting point for studying the relationship between myth and idolatry.

## Paganism and Myth

We begin with Kaufmann's conception, which defines myth by content and considers it the outstanding type of pagan representation. Pagan mythology is an expression of the limits of the gods, of their being part of primordial nature. The pagan drama includes many figures of gods who limit one another, where no force has an absolute will of its own. In pagan myth, the gods are bound to fate and nature—to the processes of birth and death—and they are also bound to the primordial existence out of which they were created. The Israelite story of creation, by contrast, is free of pagan themes such as battles between the gods before creation. God is not limited by fate or nature, just as he is not limited by other divine forces that engage him in a mythic struggle. He creates the world by his word and not by war.

Thus the innovation of monotheistic belief—and the fundamental notion of biblical belief, which distinguishes it from paganism—is the idea of God's absolute will.[5] This fundamental notion liberates the Bible totally from myth. There are, it is true, places in the Bible where there are myths, but in Kaufmann's view these are remnants of myths, broken myths that have been reworked. For example, in the descriptions of creation in the Psalms and Job, which include descriptions of God's struggle against primordial creatures like the *taninim* (often translated as "sea monsters"), these are creatures of God and not primordial divine existences. These reworked remnants left no impression on biblical religion, and they do not reflect its fundamental idea.

This idea of absolute divinity distinguishes all of Israel's institutions—including ritual, prophecy, and morality—from those of the pagans. Since the gods are bound to primordial nature, the pagan ritual is an attempt to compel the gods—by means of this primordial nature—to act on man's behalf. Pagan ritual is a form of magic, and in it man claims to be able to control the gods. In contrast, biblical ritual is the fulfillment of God's will, keeping his commandments, and not a technique for compelling God to act on man's behalf. God consents to do what man asks of him because his will has been fulfilled, and not because he has been compelled, by a magical or ritual technique, to act on man's behalf. Pagan prophecy is a skill: the pagan seer knows what the gods know because he shares their skills. He knows fate and the processes to which the gods themselves are subject; therefore he also knows the future. Biblical prophecy is the prophecy of a messenger. God tells the prophet what he intends to do; he reveals to the prophet a future of which he himself is the author. The prophet is therefore regarded not as a person with special skills but as a messenger to whom God's will is revealed. Pagan morality is, according to Kaufmann, embedded in nature. The gods do not legislate it; rather, they are bound to it. In pagan myths the gods commit sins—they lie, they fornicate, they steal, and they murder. In contrast, the source of biblical morality is God's will, and so it is not a natural morality like that found in pagan literature.

Not only does this fundamental notion of God's absolute will

unify the whole of biblical religion, it also plays an important role in
the history of biblical belief. As noted earlier, Kaufmann does not
attribute the uniqueness of biblical religion to the degree of abstractness it affords God. On the contrary, in Kaufmann's view the
abstractness that involves the denial of God's personality, and thus
the denial of his will as well, is derived from paganism. Spinoza's
pantheism, in which God becomes a substance identical with the
world, is in Kaufmann's opinion the peak of religious abstractness.
The source of this abstractness is pagan because it denies God's personality, and so the difference between God and the world vanishes.
Biblical religion did not constitute an extra degree of abstractness
over and above that which had already been attained in Israel's pagan
environment. Thus, biblical religion did not develop gradually out
of paganism, and Kaufmann rejects any attempt at a historical view
that describes the Israelite belief as developing out of intermediate
steps in its environment. Israelite belief is not a higher degree of
abstractness but an essential turning point whose source is the genius
of the Israelite nation. Israelite belief was cut off from its surroundings by the emergence of the notion of God's absolute will, and it
must not be described as developing out of paganism by adding
abstractions or by an inner development through the gradual refine-
ment of the concept of the one, abstract God.

The Israelite belief, since it is not a product of abstract thought, is
a folk belief. It is not tied to an enlightened elite, as abstract ideas
are. It is not the product of a high culture that reigned in developed
centers like Egypt or Mesopotamia. The argument that monotheism
gained supremacy in Israel only in the later stages of biblical history
depends in part on the covert assumption that monotheism is a
product of abstraction, and that such a notion could only be accepted
after a struggle and in later stages. Kaufmann rejects this picture
partly because the idea of God's unity is not an abstract idea; he sees
the Israelite belief as monotheistic from the outset. The struggle in
the Bible against the Israelites' idolatry is only a struggle against
insignificant remnants of idolatry, such as idols, which were
regarded more as good-luck charms than as revelations of mythic
powers. The basic idea of God's absolute will had become so deeply
rooted in Israel that the Bible does not even recognize paganism,
according to Kaufmann.

We are not concerned here with the twofold historical question of whether Israelite belief developed out of paganism and whether biblical belief was the Israelite belief in its early and popular stages. In his monumental book *The Religion of Israel*, Kaufmann identified Israelite belief with biblical belief. Whether there actually was real idolatry in Israel, to a greater extent than Kaufmann thought, is an important question, but our own concern is with biblical belief rather than with the Israelite belief of that period. Even if the extent of idol worship among the Israelites of that period was greater than Kaufmann estimated, his assertion that there is an essential difference between paganism and the Bible, in all its layers, is still valid. Kaufmann assumed that the Bible was a popular work, and this assumption turns the religion of the Bible into a religion that was salient in dictating the lives of the Israelites during that period. Whether this was actually the case, and whether it is supported by the evidence of the Bible itself—which often distinguishes itself from the Israelites of that period—is an open question. The issue discussed here, however, is Kaufmann's definition of myth as it relates to the idea of God's absolute will.

It is certainly possible to offer other definitions that would include the Bible as mythological literature. It is also possible to contend that Kaufmann defines myth according to the difference between biblical stories and pagan narratives, rather than vice versa. If myth were defined, for example, as thinking of the godhead in images as opposed to abstractions, then even according to Kaufmann's description the Bible would be a mythological text. We do not discuss the question of what is the best definition of myth because this concept may be given many different definitions. In our opinion, Kaufmann has indeed put his finger on an essential difference between the two worlds, and this difference exists even if it is not analogous to the difference between mythological and nonmythological literature. The questions we actually discuss, then, are the following: Did Kaufmann succeed in identifying in the Bible an essentially different concept of divinity? Did he describe the concept of the biblical God correctly? Is the Bible a myth according to Kaufmann's own definition? If there actually are no myths in the Bible, does this mean that the Bible knows nothing about idolatry?

It is possible to discern Kant's and Schopenhauer's influence on Kaufmann's formulation of the idea of the absolute will of God. His conception of the will as a force divorced from the natural tendencies of a personality, and as a hidden free force, reflects the Kantian conception. Moreover, the definition of personality as individuated by the existence of will, which permits free decisions, rather than by the causal world of nature, is also a deep Kantian conception. According to Kaufmann—in Kant's terms—God is the holy will.[6] The biblical conception, in Kaufmann's description, is anthropomorphic in the sense that it always preserves the factor of will in God, but it is distinguished from the pagan conception in that this will is an absolute and unlimited will.

In contrast to Kaufmann's emphasis on the will, it seems to us that as a personality the God of the Bible has a rich emotional life that transforms him into a person rather than a force. God hopes and is disappointed, he loves and becomes alienated, he is jealous and he is appeased. The tangle of this emotional life is so complex that it is not clear if there really is an absolute will here that is free of emotional tendencies. After God has tried to destroy the world in the flood, and Noah, who has survived, offers him a sacrifice, the Bible says: "The Lord smelled the pleasing odor, and the Lord said to Himself: 'Never again will I doom the earth because of man, since the devisings of man's mind are evil from his youth; nor will I ever again destroy every living being, as I have done'" (Genesis 8:21). God's disappointment with human beings leads him to destroy the world, but after he has destroyed the whole of creation he expresses remorse. His knowledge of man's limitations is the key to the prevention of such absolute anger against man. When high expectations are disappointed, they lead to the desire for annihilation; lowering these expectations also guarantees the moderation of the disappointment. Do we find absolute will in the God who tests Job out of suspicion that the latter loves him only because he is good to him? This is analogous to a rich husband who is gnawed by the suspicion that his wife loves him only because of his wealth, which makes him decide to put her love to the test. The God of the Bible is free from nature and fate, but he is not free from emotional tendencies. In modern terms we would say that he is free of physics and biology, but not of psychology.

In this context it is interesting to note that the Bible and Kaufmann do not use the word "will" in the same way. The Hebrew word for "will" is *ratzon,* and in the Bible this noun is associated with the verb *lehitratzot,*[7] which means "to be reconciled" and does not denote an occult power that moves a man or God to act one way or another.

*Lehitratzot,* to be reconciled, means to love, to desire; to be *ratzui,* desirable, means to be lovable, to be dear; and *nirtza,* reconciled, means to be received willingly. *Ratzon* here is not used in the modern sense of "will"—of a power that lies beyond the heart's tendencies and rules them; rather, it is the emotional tendency of desire. To do an act willingly, out of *ratzon,* means to do it out of desire, gladly, and not necessarily to do it freely, unrestrained by any previous emotional tendencies. Kaufmann has forced upon the Bible a Kantian anthropology that was never there. One might say that the biblical narrative transfers myth from nature to human drama, a drama in which man and God are involved in a deeply interdependent relationship. Even if God afflicts man and alienates himself from man, he cannot prevent himself from feeling the pain that accompanies such alienation. What stands opposed to God in the Bible is not nature or other cosmic forces in the image of gods but man. Man stands before God not as a personality that limits him by its power but as a personality that engages God in a conversation interwoven with all the characteristics of the human heart. The concept of God's personhood is broader than the existence of will, and the question is whether such a person can also include an absolute will that lies beyond the tendencies of the heart.

This alternative definition of God as a person does not nullify Kaufmann's important distinction. In recognizing that God is independent from the world in terms of nature and fate Kaufmann discovered a deep and important distinction between paganism and the monotheistic religions, even if it does not provide a successful definition for all the uses of myth. There is, however, an emotional interdependency that involves God in a complex relationship with the world and gives the biblical story a mythic dimension even in Kaufmann's own terms. It is important to note that this dependency is not a causal subjection like the subjection of the gods to nature and fate in myth, and so Kaufmann's significant distinction remains intact.[8] The dependency we have identified is like a person's dependency on his beloved, or upon prior obligations.

## The Bible and Myth

There are thinkers who regard myth as a form of expression exclusive to pagan thought. How then do they explain the fact that there is no ban on myth in the Bible, even though idols are prohibited? Why did the Bible identify idolatry with the making of engraved images but not with myth, even though there are those who claim that the association between paganism and myth is even closer than that between paganism and the making of images?

Kaufmann's answer to this question is simple and decisive. Biblical Israelite faith did not recognize paganism except in popular fetishistic manifestations that were observable as engraved images. It did not recognize the pagan myth as a means of expression of higher forms of paganism. Remnants of pagan myths did indeed seep into the Bible, but only as decorations and not as living stories. We would not suspect a contemporary of ours, when he says that someone is full of bile in order to describe a state of chronic anger and resentment, of believing in Galen's theory of the humors. The term "bile" in contemporary usage has lost the meaning it had in the ancient theory of humors. According to Kaufmann, mythical expressions appearing in the Bible have a similar status. Consider, for example, the verse: "It was You [God] who drove back the sea with Your might, who smashed the heads of the monsters in the waters; it was You who crushed the heads of Leviathan" (Psalm 74:13), or God "drew a boundary on the surface of the waters . . . By his power He stilled the sea, by His skill He struck down Rahab" (Job 26:10, 12). Such expressions, and many similar ones, were not forbidden for the simple reason that they were perceived as sublime poetic expressions of the greatness of God, without recognition of the mythic beliefs underlying them.[9] Beliefs in a struggle between God and the sea monsters were not recognized any more than people today who use the term "bile" recognize the theory of humors.

Is there a convincing alternative explanation for the lack of any prohibition against myth in the Bible, besides the explanation that it was not recognized? One alternative explanation is censorship. Although we do not know what considerations influenced the editors of the Bible, we may conjecture that they employed censorship against alien myths. But is concealment really a preferable alternative to lack of knowledge as an explanation for this phenomenon? In regimes with totalitarian ideologies, which demand uniformity of opinions from their subjects, a heretical ideology often becomes widely known as soon as the regime condemns it. The regime's ideologists are faced with two alternatives: condemnation, which will lead to familiarity with the heresy; or concealment, which may prevent the heresy from becoming widespread. The price of concealment is the lack of a confrontation in which the heresy is openly condemned. A clever though evil regime will take the tack of condemnation only when the heretical theory is widely known independently of the act of condemnation. (Thus, for example, was Hans Jonas able to reconstruct the Christian Gnostic heresy from the attack on it by the Church Fathers.)[10] If the dangerous ideas are not widely known, then the most logical procedure from the regime's standpoint is concealment. In this sense, even if the absence of pagan myth in the Bible was not due to the editors' ignorance, and there was intentional concealment on their part, the very act of concealment is prima facie evidence that the people from whom they were concealing the ideas were ignorant of the pagan myths.[11] This is the important point for Kaufmann's theory. In other words, concealment in the case of a clever regime does not contradict the claim of ignorance. What differs is only who has the knowledge: in cases of concealment the editors have the knowledge but not the readers; in cases of ignorance no one has the knowledge. In either case the situation of the editors of the Bible was totally different from that confronting the Christian apologists. The latter had to use the technique of condemnation because the pagan ideas they were confronting were very widely known. The upshot of all this is that censorship is not really an alternative explanation to ignorance.

Another criticism of Kaufmann's thesis is that the state of closeness and friction between the biblical society and its idolatrous environment makes the hypothesis of ignorance implausible. Is this so? Remaining within the framework of relevant historical parallels, we can find a similar type of interpretive controversy among archaeologists studying a post-biblical period. On a Jewish grave from the Mishnaic period (first to second century A.D.) in the village of Beit Shearim a sharp and clear relief sculpture of Helios, the sun god, was found. The archaeologist Nahman Avigad considers this relief a decoration whose significance the builders were unaware of,[12] whereas Erwin Goodenough regards the relief of Helios as an expression of a living symbol rather than a meaningless decoration. The answer to the question of whether this is a decoration—a kind of dead metaphor—or a living symbol depends here as well on the degree of cultural and geographical closeness between the communities of believers. During the Hellenistic period this closeness was extreme, and so the hypothesis that the relief was a decoration seems prima facie less likely. When it is the biblical period that is under consideration, specifically the mythology of that period, the issue becomes more complex because of the distance in time and the dearth of evidence. In addition, we are left with the question of who is supposed to have known about the beliefs of the pagans: the later editors or the Israelites who came into close contact with them?

We propose changing the nature of the question. Instead of asking whether what was included in the Bible was recognized as myth or only as "decoration," let us ask if the pagan myth—whether it was recognized as such by the editors and readers of the Bible or not—created a "mythic gap" that had to be filled in with mythic content sooner or later.

Paul Tillich asserted that when a religious worldview passes through a period of crisis it is replaced by a new worldview that adopts fragments of the myths which nourished the old view.[13] This idea of Tillich's seems quite appropriate to the description of the embedding of pagan myths in the Bible as "broken myths." We will adapt his idea and say that the myths are not broken, but only bent. If mythic motifs seeped into the Bible, whether they passed through a censorship that considered them to be mere decorations or whether there never was any censorship, a "mythic gap" was opened up. A gap is any point in a story that invites detailed filling in by an interpreter, while a mythic gap is a gap for which, due to the mention of mythic creatures or events, the required completion is a mythic story. Whenever a mythic gap is opened up one may presume that over the course of the generations it will be revived as a myth, although the new myth may differ from the original one.

Thus, for example, the fragmented description of the mythic event that occurred to Enoch, who walked with God and was taken into heaven, is an invitation for filling in the gap.[14] The story of the mythic creatures who in the form of divine beings took wives from among the daughters of men also opens up a mythic gap, and there are many other such examples. We suggest there is in effect a kind of "law of conservation of myth." The "law" states that if remnants of myths seep into a sacred literature of the sort that is subject to continual reflection, then sooner or later they will be revived as myths.

What makes the filling in of such a gap a mythical completion is an issue we will return to later, when we discuss the types of interpretation that make a story or narrative poem mythic. In any case, the filling in of a story with a narrative about events occurring to a divinity is a sign of myth. When the Book of Enoch fills in the unwritten part of the story of Enoch's going up to heaven by describing a "peek behind the scenes," then at a first approximation this is a mythic revival of the story.

There is another sense in which one can speak of the revival of a myth. This sense is expressed in the reading of metaphorical expressions as if they were literal. For example, if the verse "He mounted a cherub and flew, gliding on the wings of the wind" (Psalm 18:11) is given a literal reading, such a reading will be a revival of a myth— even if the original myth underlying the verse was forgotten or was not identified as a myth before.

We may note parenthetically that there is an interesting analogy between what we have called here, almost ironically, "the law of conservation of myth" and a similar view in contemporary philosophy. Philosophers such as Wittgenstein, Ryle, and Austin, among others, suspected that linguistic metaphors might become dead in ordinary language without becoming dead in philosophy. Dead linguistic metaphors may be revived in philosophy when they are taken literally. This may be good for the metaphors, but it is bad for philosophy. The revival of metaphors is a source of serious cognitive errors because there is something magical in the hold such expressions have over us. A linguistic myth, according to this view, is a dead metaphor based on a category mistake and erroneously understood as literal.[15] Both Ryle and Wittgenstein used the term "myth" in this context, and they considered the role of philosophy to be the demythicization of these linguistic myths—that is, the exposure of their true nature as dead metaphors.

Let us return to Kaufmann. An alternative to his hypothesis of ignorance is the theory that what was operative in the Bible was not ignorance but censorship. The fact that the Bible regards idolatry as mere fetishism and not as a comprehensive mythic worldview may be a polemical strategy whose purpose was to ridicule idolatry. Moreover, in the Bible itself there are mythic elements, and even if they are only unfamiliar remnants of an entirely alien language, they still open up mythic gaps that are destined to be filled in. In sum, even if the Bible is free of myth in Kaufmann's sense, it is not free of mythic gaps.

The question of mythic gaps brings us to the issue of interpretation. Not every reading of a sacred story makes it a myth, that is, a story with pagan characteristics. Sacred stories may be read in different ways; there are not merely alternative interpretations of the stories but alternative uses of them—uses that determine one's attitudes toward them. A sacred story may be pagan in content, in the sense that it speaks about many gods, yet not be a living myth, if the reading or use of the story does not turn it into one. The relation we are interested in clarifying is not so much the one between myth and paganism as the one between living myth and paganism.

## From Myth to Living Myth

Myths raise the problem of linguistic representations conveyed by the story as a whole, and not only by the isolated expression or sentence. The question is whether there are limits on the sort of story that one may tell about the divinity—whether there is a sort of story that is essential or typical of paganism and must be avoided in representing the monotheistic divinity—or whether there is no real difference between paganism and monotheism in this respect.

Our interest in the relation between myth and idolatry is confined to myth as a linguistic entity composed of sentences and does not include "mythic thought" or "mytho-poetic thought" as a stage in the development of preconceptual thought, which some critics consider specific to paganism.[16] We are narrowing the extension of the term "myth" so greatly that one might argue we are stipulating rather than discovering what myth is. This narrowing may be seen as serving the idea that myth is related internally to paganism but only externally—that is, not essentially—to the monotheistic conception of God. The suspicion regarding our view is that the characteristics of myth we have focused on are made to order for the characterization of pagan myths rather than myths in general.

Our response to this criticism is simple and direct. If the set of characteristics arising from our discussion actually delineates pagan myth as a type of myth that is distinct from any other type of story, and if these characteristics are also the most typical characteristics of myth (those that characterize prototypical examples of myth), then we have accomplished what we set out to do. We must only see whether other, nonpagan sacred stories are also worthy of being called myths. Obviously the characteristics of myth that distinguish idolatrous myths must not be tautological ("a myth is a story about many gods and their struggles"), but there are no tautological characteristics of pagan myths in our account.

Thus, for example, one outstanding characteristic of myth is that it is a narrative of the supernatural, and not just an ordinary narrative but a dramatic one, a story of struggle between its heroes. Paganism, with its multiple gods, is well-suited to such a supernatural narrative. Of course, a multiplicity of supernatural figures with which the divinity comes into narrative contact is not limited to paganism: angels of various types provide a heavenly troupe that can supply the cast for many dramas, and the midrash does actually make use of this heavenly troupe for sacred stories. Pagan casting in and of itself is not any richer than the "heavenly troupe" at the command of monotheistic ontology. The latter has at its command an entire angelology that can be used to populate stories of heaven with as many figures as there are stars in the sky. But the requirement that the story be a drama in which the cast consists of independent figures, even if they are not equipotent with the divinity, is what differentiates pagan from monotheistic narratives. In the monotheistic narrative there is no multiplicity of beings (whether divine or demonic) with a will capable of limiting the divine will. This is where Kaufmann's condition, of the unrestricted divine will, plays a crucial role in the characterization of the prototypical myth.

Every myth is a mythology but not vice versa. The kind of beings involved in the story determine what kind of story it is. The chain of being underlying the distinction between myth and mythology begins with nonhuman living creatures that are nonrational and mortal (animals, the first race), goes on to human beings, who are mortal but rational (the second race), and then continues on to the third race of beings, who are immortal and rational.[17] The chain ends with the "fourth race," gods who are not only immortal but also govern the universe, with the help of the third race or other forces. Between these groups are "in-between creatures," such as mortal heroes whose activities resemble those of the third race and who sometimes earn the right to become immortal and join the third race as a reward for their activities. There are also in-between creatures that span the gap between the first and third races, in the form of monsters with supernatural powers. According to this classification we may say that a mythology that is not a myth is one in which the heroes of the narrative are figures of the third race. In a myth, although it may contain figures from all the levels, the principal heroes are gods.

In a sacred story there are narratives similar to idolatrous narratives. These narratives may be considered myths according to their degree of similarity to the characteristics of those idolatrous myths that supply the prototypical examples of myth. The Manichaean myths are certainly very similar to the prototypical pagan myths, as are the Gnostic myths.[18] The difficult case is, of course, the story of the Christian Trinity, in which one of the divine figures has a complete theogenic biography. On the one hand, to outsiders the myth of the Trinity seems similar to pagan myths, since the three personae of the deity are salient to them. On the other hand, to insiders the story is fundamentally different from idolatrous myths because there is no struggle of wills among the personae. The outsider regards the three dramatic personae in the deity as sufficiently independent to make the story into an idolatrous narrative, while the insider, even if he sees them as three personae, nevertheless regards them as three dramatic roles being played by one actor.

A pagan myth, according to the characteristics we have ascribed to it, may be prevalent in a society or part of a society without being interpreted by the society in a way that would allow us to consider it a pagan society in the belief sense of the term. Christian society at the time of the Renaissance, for example, made widespread use of stories of pagan myth, but the stories served as allegories rather than living myths. A representation is thus not only a relation between linguistic expressions and what they are supposed to be representing but also a manifestation of the ways in which the community telling the myth uses these expressions. Hence our interest in what makes a myth a living myth.

What exactly is a "living myth"? We distinguish four senses of the term: in one sense a myth is a living myth for a community if the members of the community believe literally what is told in the myth, if it is perceived as a true description of reality.

In another sense a myth is alive for all those who are deeply impressed by it, whether or not it is perceived as literally true.[19] The lives of the people who live this myth are significantly different from what they would be if the myth did not shape their world. The interpretation that is appropriate in this case for the vitality of the myth is the literal meaning, in the sense of the simple linguistic meaning, but not in the sense that the sentences composing the myth are regarded as statements about reality. The myth is impressive partly because it reveals existential views of the human situation, such as people's attitude toward birth, death, and other basic aspects of life. On a personal level the myth may be impressive to the extent that it expresses man's deepest wishes, such as those expressed in the biblical story of the Garden of Eden, wishes for total freedom without want or rivalry. The supernatural component of the myth in this case is of secondary interest. The story of Oedipus also fulfills the conditions for living myth in this sense because it is a story that impresses us deeply. Such a myth does not necessarily have to be impressive within the context of a particular society, and so it is not defined as alive with respect to a particular society. Other types of stories that compete with myths, such as epics, sagas, and folktales, are not living myths in this sense precisely because they do not impress us: they are more entertaining than impressive. It is possible to speak of the deep social impression of a myth when the myth plays an important role in shaping a moral community. In this sense the role of Oedipus's story in the Athenian community is different from its diffuse influence today among people belonging to very different types of communities. "Impressive" in this sense is thus a social characteristic.

A third sense of living myth is the sense in which "living" is understood as "fresh," as opposed to wilted or institutionalized. This is the sense in which the Garden of Eden in Paul Gauguin's painting is fresh, and Henri Rousseau's tropic forests create living pictures— living not because they contain "lots of green" but because they create a feeling of a primeval situation, before civilization existed. The concrete and pictorial language of myth in its descriptions of primeval situations is what creates the feeling of greater closeness to the forces of nature than to civilized states. The figures populating myths also appear to us as "greater than life," as all their actions, even the most trivial ones, have the status of constituting the order of things. In this sense of "living" as primeval freshness, mythic time is the time before there were patterns and order, as opposed to civilized time, which is not "fresh" because it contains fixed patterns.

To the third sense of living myth we must add the idea that it is a myth whose characters are vital and brimming with energy. An "absolutely good" divinity may not appear this way; it is precisely the capricious divinity that expresses energetic vitality. Often a sacred story seems mythic to us when the divinity within it radiates vital energy, and this in turn demands a description of the divinity as capricious. The monotheistic religions thus face a dilemma between the presentation of a living and vital God, which may open the door to myth, and a concept of God which is pure but not vital. The pure concepts uproot the myths, but the price is the dissipation of the vitality of the "living" God.

A fourth sense of living myth is the sense we will concentrate on, as it is the most important sense for religious life. A myth is "living" in this last sense if it is associated with a sacrament—if it plays a role, in the consciousness of a community of believers, in a ritual that is intended to influence divine events. When we speak of the sacramental reading, we are proposing not a semantic interpretation of linguistic expressions but an understanding of the seriousness of the expressions in the mythic story in the light of its association with a sacrament. We do not tie this reading to any specific semantic interpretation of the mythic expressions. In general, a sacramental reading requires some ontological commitment to the beings in the myth, even if it is not necessary for everything described in the myth to be accepted as true. The myth of Dummuzi can acquire a sacramental character in a community that participates in ceremonies of the death and rebirth of the god, but this does not mean that everything in the mythic story must be taken literally, let alone believed literally.

In subsequent sections we focus on two readings of myth that guarantee its vitality within a given community: the literal and the sacramental. In addition, we discuss a reading that is traditionally considered to constitute an extinction of the myth: the allegorical reading, which interprets anything that appears philosophically or theologically confusing in a proper but lifeless way. We also mention the typological reading of a mythic story, as this is an important intermediate case between allegory and living myth. But we have a particular interest in the contrast between allegory, which emasculates myth, and symbol, which revives and perhaps even constitutes myth. This is true mainly because the symbolic reading suggests itself as an especially appropriate reading for those stories in the monotheistic religions that seem closest to myth. The vitality of a myth when given a symbolic reading is a result of the vitality of the symbolic worldview. This matter requires preliminary clarification.

Opposite to the symbolic worldview stands the scientific worldview. Roughly, the scientific worldview regards reality as a collection of objects and events in space and time that exist within a system of causal relations. This picture, in whose grip we have been held since the seventeenth century, makes it difficult for us to understand what it means to be gripped by a symbolic worldview as a living thing. Perhaps our attitude to dreams, which we expect to be meaningful, is a remnant in our lives of the symbolic mentality, a picture of events and objects as connected with one another by symbolic as well as causal relations, even when the objects are not man-made. The symbolic worldview is anchored in a Platonic idea, according to which concepts and ideas have substance.[20] This is accompanied by another step: not only are the symbols substantive, but their existence is similar to that of living creatures. This is the crucial step in making symbols constitutive of myth. The substantiality of the concepts and ideas is that of a living substance. These are not concepts fitted into defined molds; rather, their existence must be described in terms appropriate to the description of organisms—that is, in anthropomorphic and dramatic terms.

## Four Readings of Myth

### The Literal Reading

Reading a myth literally means taking it at its face value, both from the standpoint of the linguistic expressions and from the standpoint of the linguistic acts that are performed by means of the utterances of the mythic story. A literal reading in terms of linguistic acts means that the expressions of the myth are understood as declarative sentences that state propositions, whether true or false, describing reality, even if it is a very unusual reality. The status of the sentences in a myth that is given a literal reading is thus like the status we accord to linguistic acts in a history book. This is the strong sense of the word "literal." There are also weaker senses of the word—for example, reading the myth literally in a semantic sense but not as a description of reality. In the weaker sense the linguistic acts are considered not propositions but at most simulations of propositions— the sort of literal reading we give to a historical novel like *War and Peace*. Literalness does not exclude the possibility that there are metaphorical expressions in the story that must be read as such. Literalness means accepting the story at its face value.

Philosophical criticism of myth, as it appeared within pagan societies, attributed to the masses a literal understanding of the myth. Critics regarded the vulgar believers as a bunch of fools who believed in imaginary tales as if they were descriptions of reality. The criticism of literal readings in pagan societies was a criticism of folk religion. The monotheists, for their polemical purposes, attributed the literal reading to all the pagans without distinction. But the pagan elite did not believe the myths literally any more than the monotheists did.

There is a problem with this account. When we say that a person takes some sacred story at its face value, say the biblical story of creation, this seems at first glance to be a simple matter. But actually it is not clear at all what such a person is supposed to believe, since if we take the descriptions at their face value there is more than one story of creation in the Bible.[21] Interpretation is required to determine that these are only two versions of the same story, yet biblical criticism originated in pointing to the existence of these two versions. So what does the believer believe—that the first man and the first woman were created together or that the woman was created from the man's rib? The principled answer to this quasi-difficulty is that there can be more than one version, just as there can be multiple versions of some historical event. This is not a problem for the cognitive status of the historical statement.

To give another example, when we attribute to a person the belief that human beings descended from the apes, there arises the question of which particular species of ape they descended from. Some people may believe in man's descent from one species of primate, and others in his descent from a different species. But when the contrast is between someone who believes in man's descent from the apes and someone who believes in the direct creation of all species, then the difference between one species of primate and another is irrelevant. The same is true of belief in the biblical story of creation. The degree of detail necessary in the attribution of a belief depends on the question of what other beliefs it is being contrasted with, and this in its turn depends on the context. There is nothing deep here, no special difficulty beyond the ordinary difficulty of deciding what someone believes when more than one version exists. This is no more a difficulty for myth than for science or the courtroom.

This last argument seems correct to us. Nevertheless, when one attributes to another person a belief in the literal reading of a myth with several versions, then one is attributing a belief in what all the versions have in common, which is liable to be something abstract that resembles a theological statement more than a simple story. Thus the believer in the story of creation turns into a believer in creation as opposed to preexistence. This is especially likely to happen when the versions are very different and a high degree of abstraction is required to see them all as versions of the same story.

Myth in its literal reading is not only theology. It can also be considered science, the collective science of a traditional society. This is what W. R. G. Horton, for example, believes.[22] In other words, myth is likely to be regarded as a science of the world and of society, in addition to being a science of divinity. It is a science that, according to the positivist schema, has both observational and theoretical sentences, where the theoretical terms are those that are supposed to refer to gods and divinities. As in a proper scientific theory, in myth as well there is an attempt to explain what can be observed by means of what cannot be observed. What distinguishes myth from modern theories is not the obvious falseness of myth and the principled correctness of theories, nor even that myth is primitive and theories are developed. The difference between them is social. Myth serves a closed society, and modern scientific theories serve an open society. In a closed society the traditional theory is not confronted by rival theories—this is the sense in which it is closed—but is handed down from parent to child by force of tradition. Its power is derived from the authority of tradition rather than the test of experiment. These differences between the two types of society are obviously of great importance, though not in terms of the status of the statements appearing in myth. The status of these statements, as we have already seen, is the same as in any scientific theory. The transition from myth to logos is thus not the transition from an obvious falsehood to a theory that is correct at first approximation. It is the transition from a closed society to an open society. The difference lies not in what the theory says but in the social context of what is said.

Myth as science thus maintains the strong literal reading: it both interprets the myth according to its literal meaning and considers the sentences of the myth to be declarative sentences stating propositions. But we have already pointed out that there is another reading, the weak literal reading, which maintains the literal meaning of the sentences but not their role as descriptions of reality. Such a reading of myth changes its role from quasi-science to quasi-literature, the literature of a traditional society. However, myth differs from other types of literature, such as the epic, the saga, or the folktale, in that it is taken seriously. This is not the seriousness of a true description of reality; rather, it is the seriousness of an expression of the fundamental values of the society that maintains the myth, as well as the basic human situations this society considers sublime and impressive. At times the sublime and the impressive are such because of the involvement of the divinity in the story, but this is not always the case: the story of Oedipus is impressive and moving in spite of the negligible role of the supernatural in it.[23] It is the power of myth to express and shape fundamental attitudes toward life. For example, life and the world are perceived as gifts according to the biblical myth of creation, and this is a fundamental attitude toward life that is totally different from that of believers in the preexistence of the world.

The reading of myth as serious literature taken at its face value is not unique to or even typical of paganism. If the monotheistic religions object to myth in its serious though nondescriptive reading, this is mainly because of the values embodied in it, but perhaps also because of the danger that it will nevertheless be read by many people as a description of reality. When this last suspicion has disappeared, then pagan myth can be domesticated by the monotheistic religions, as occurred, for example, with the Greco-Roman myths in Christianity.[24]

A story about gods, when it is taken at face value, stands in clear contrast to the sacred stories of the monotheistic religions. The opposition to pagan myth is not an opposition to the mere fact that it represents the divinity, but to the content of the stories and especially to the fact that it is given a literal reading and that it is believed. It is sometimes difficult to attribute belief in the face value of a mythic story when there is more than one version of the story. The difficulty relates to the question of which of the versions the believers in the myth actually believe. This difficulty may be resolved not by choosing a particular version of the story, but by asserting that they believe what all the versions have in common. The reason for this is that it is highly probable that the believers would be willing to endorse all the prevalent versions of the story, or at least to endorse most of them, sometimes even without noticing that there are contradictions between the various versions. Therefore a belief in what is common to all the versions of the myth should be attributed to the believer. But what is common to all the versions may have the abstract character of a theological statement, and so belief in the myth is no longer simply belief in a story that is concrete and alive.

## The Allegorical Reading

A reading of myth may be said to be allegorical either because the reading is not the literal reading or because the myth is identified with a particular type of literary form known as "allegory." We use the term "allegory," like the terms "myth" and "symbol," to denote first and foremost linguistic works. These terms also have a wider reference according to which "allegory," for example, may also apply to sculptures and pictures, but we are limiting it here to its linguistic component. Allegory and myth are forms of expression for which the typical linguistic unit is greater than the sentence—in contrast to metaphor or metonymy, for example. An allegory is sometimes an extended metaphor, like the state as a beehive (in Bernard de Mandeville's allegory) or the state as a ship (in Horace's ode). The typical allegory, unlike the typical metaphor, requires extralinguistic knowledge for its understanding. We know enough about Albert Camus and the circumstances under which he wrote *The Plague* to see his denoting the year of the plague as "194 . . ." as a key to understanding the novel as an allegory about the war against Nazism. It is true that this reading is not essential, but it is a reading that is suggested by the historical and literary background of the work.

Interpretation is a policy with respect to what is being interpreted. The interpreter has the power to represent what he is interpreting in a good light or a bad light. The possibility of interpreting a person who says "yes and no" as believing an explicit contradiction, rather than as saying that the situation is ambiguous, shows how much power one has to make a person seem irrational if one takes all his or her expressions literally. W. V. Quine formulated a "charity principle" that says, roughly, that one should not make one's fellow human being seem more irrational than necessary. That is, one should not attribute a literal meaning to an interlocutor's expressions if it will make him seem crazy or stupid, when it is more plausible to assume that he is neither of these and that a deviation from the literal interpretation will clarify his meaning.[25] But religious interpretation—the interpretation a community gives to its sacred writings—requires true charity. The principle here is to present what is written in the best possible light. What this light is obviously depends upon the values and beliefs of the society in question.

Pagan philosophers, especially those of the Stoa but not only those, thought that the myths of their society's culture should benefit from the maximal extent of the charity principle. This is what they tried to offer their myths by giving them an allegorical interpretation. The monotheists did the same thing for the myths of their own society. There were even isolated attempts to formulate criteria for cases in which it was proper to deviate from the literal meaning. Saadia Gaon, for example, recommended that one should tend toward an allegorical interpretation whenever the text contained contradictions or anything else that seemed unreasonable, or when the text could not be reconciled with another sacred text, or when it was in direct opposition to an explicit rabbinical tradition. But Saadia Gaon was the exception. In general no explicit criteria are given for resolving the question of when to deviate from the literal meaning and seek an allegorical interpretation.[26] What we generally find among interpreters is that such deviation occurs not when the myth taken literally is false or contradictory to reason, but primarily when it is grasped as an improper representation of the divinity.

The aspect of allegory that has always seemed most suspect is its arbitrary character, its lack of a fixed interpretive code. This is an intrareligious suspicion and not merely the taunting polemical accusation of a rival religion. Origen, for example, referring to the

Judeo-Christian myths, was impressed by the possibility of transforming stories of war and conquest into sublime spiritual truths.[27] His students, however, accused him of "uncharitable subjectivity" because his interpretations were unsystematic—that is, they lacked a fixed interpretive code. But even a fixed method for allegorical interpretation is not a guarantee against arbitrariness. There is a method in the madness of Philo of Alexandria, says one of his commentators, but his interpretation is nevertheless a mad one that does not make the biblical text more rational. Moreover, the requirement of a fixed code is not a clear requirement. If the four rivers flowing out of the Garden of Eden are interpreted allegorically as the four elements (by Ibn Gabirol, for example), does this mean that only four rivers can represent the four elements, while the four kings headed by Chedorlaomer (Genesis 14) are not even to be considered as representing them? Or, on the contrary, should every mention of the number four in the Bible, as in the four sins of Aram, be considered as having no other purpose than the representation of the four elements?

Interpretation, as mentioned, is policy, and in politics the use of double standards is routine. Indeed, in the controversy between the pagans and the Christians the most prominent characteristic of both camps was the blatant use of the double standard: the charity principle for their own stories and the "meanness principle" for the rival interpretations: my stories are allegorical, but yours are literal; my stories are deep spiritual truths dressed up as simple tales that anyone can understand, but your stories are old wives' tales and a bunch of superstitions. Arnobius, one of the most sophisticated of the Christian apologists and competitors in the famous Christian-pagan debate, complains that the allegorical interpretation offered by the pagans is selective. Within the very same text they interpret some of the expressions allegorically and others literally, without any criterion. This assertion is correct, but it should be directed at everyone—Jews and Christians as well as pagans.

Arnobius demands that the pagan interpreters decide whether the text is completely allegorical or completely literal: any other policy is deception.[28] But the ones who are especially vulnerable to Arnobius's demand are the Jewish allegorists. They must be selective, if only because they are neither willing nor able to interpret the commandments allegorically. An allegorical interpretation of the commandments would necessarily be antinomian. This is the interpretive policy that the Christians used against Jews in their allegorical interpretation of the verses containing commandments. They interpret circumcision as the removal of the rigid covering of the heart that prevents understanding, and so the commandment of removing the actual physical foreskin loses its basis. Even radical allegorists on the style of Philo were careful not to allegorize the commandments. They went far in their allegorical interpretations of the reasons for the commandments, but they never gave an allegorical meaning to the commandments themselves. The kabbalists were the ones who came closest to toying with interpretive procedures that bordered on antinomian, while taking advantage of the ambiguity between interpreting the reason for a commandment allegorically and interpreting the very existence of the commandment allegorically. At any rate, Judaism, being a religion based on commandments, is more limited in its allegorical interpretations than Christianity, and certainly more than paganism.

We have seen that myths can tolerate allegorical interpretations—pagan myths more easily than monotheistic myths because they do not contain commandments. Does this mean that the difference between paganism and monotheism cannot simply consist in the very existence of myths? Philosophical allegories, for example, show that if someone is a neo-Platonist it does not matter if he is a Muslim, a Jew, a Christian, or a Hellenist: all of these are primarily neo-Platonists in their viewpoints. Which writings they interpret this way is a secondary issue dependent on the biography of each person. Interpreting myths allegorically is an activity that might be captioned "Philosophers of the world, unite." Which religion you happen to have been born into is not so important, since the allegorical interpretation will show that you all believe the same things, and this interpretation depends in turn on your philosophical beliefs.[29]

But not all allegorical interpretations of myths are philosophical rationalizations. Nonphilosophical allegorical interpretations fill the temples of all the religions. The Bible itself perhaps suggests an allegorical reading of a myth. For example, the typically mythic story of Jacob's struggle against the angel is apparently given an allegorical interpretation by Hosea (12:4–5), where the struggle is understood as a battle of prayer rather than a battle of physical might: "He strove with an angel and prevailed—the other had to weep and implore him." Not every allegorical transformation of the physical into the spiritual is philosophical in character.

Israel's loss of political sovereignty as a result of the exile also served as a reason for a spiritual allegorical reading of power-based political conditions. Following this event the military battles in the Bible were allegorically transformed into halakhic controversies in the rabbinic academy. The battlefield became the rabbinic academy, and the battle array was the halakhic debate. The process of spiritualizing the interpretation thus has an intrareligious justification, and it does not serve only to satisfy philosophical needs.

Once we have reminded ourselves that there are also nonphilosophical allegorical interpretations of myth, let us return to the original question: what after all is the difference, if there is one, between an allegorical-philosophical interpretation of a pagan myth and a monotheist's allegorical-philosophical reading of a sacred text in his own religion?

An interesting answer, even though only partially correct, is that of Athenagoras: the worldview reflected by the pagan philosophers' allegories for myths is actually a view in which everything is material, and it is therefore an atheistic view; by contrast, philosophical allegories from monotheistic sources are spiritual and religious. There may be a difference between the types of philosophies that are likely to be given allegorical interpretations in various religions, but the difficulty we presented concerned philosophers from different religions who held the same philosophical view (neo-Platonist, for example). The difference between them, in the final analysis, is not in ideas but in ritual. However, there is another important difference relating to the symbolic representation of the world. This difference stems from the fact that each philosopher makes use of images and symbols taken from his or her own religion. Thus even though there may be complete identity between their fundamental views, their allegories, cultural references, and philosophical interpretations will relate to different texts and to a different world of images. This may entail profound differences, even if they are not cognitive ones.

Does interpreting a myth allegorically emasculate the myth? The idea that philosophical allegory emasculates myths is based partly on social observations claiming that these allegories are understood only by the intellectual elite and that allegorical interpretations are incapable of nourishing a living folk religion. After all, who can get excited about a myth if it is understood as a parable about the active and passive intellect? In other words, since allegory is abstract and schematic it removes the drama from the story and with it the vitality in the concrete details of the story.

There is some truth in this view, but it is not completely true. An allegorical interpretation is not necessarily a means for emasculating a myth: sometimes it is the condition that creates the myth. For example, the face value of the Song of Songs as a collection of love poems is not mythic. There is, however, a far-reaching claim that the Song of Songs was originally a myth borrowed from the Egyptian ritual about the love of Osiris (Solomon) for Isis (Shulamit), even if this is not the literal biblical meaning. Moreover, the rabbinic interpretation of this collection of love poems is that it describes the love between God and Israel. Whether this allegorical interpretation was created to fill a mythic gap in the Song of Songs, or whether it was originally just a series of love poems, it is the allegorical interpretation that turns the Song of Songs into a myth.[30]

Seeing an allegorical interpretation as mythic is not only, or even primarily, dependent on the allegory being abstract. Whether the allegory is about God and Israel, or the church and Christ, or even man's soul and the passive intellect, there are mythic possibilities in these readings if the concepts are grasped as independent reifications, that is, as active forces in this or higher worlds. But even if a reifying allegorical interpretation provides the possibility of understanding a sacred story as a myth—even a live myth—such a myth lacks vitality, because the concrete details of the story are liable to be uprooted in the allegorical interpretation. The Garden of Eden in the biblical story is no longer perceived as a garden in which trees are planted but is seen as a place in which the idea of planting good character traits appeared (Philo). Even if the planting of good character traits is a reified act with mythic potential, the story is apt to be robbed of its vitality in the allegorical interpretation.

We do not claim that the direction of every allegorical interpretation is necessarily from the concrete to the abstract. There are some allegorical interpretations that work at least partly in the other direction. In Maimonides' interpretation of the ladder in Jacob's dream (Genesis 28), for example, the angels climbing up and down the ladder in the biblical description are interpreted as prophets. Even if prophets are not more concrete than angels, they are certainly more earthly. Yet the ladder too disappears in Maimonides' interpretation, and thus the myth is uprooted from the allegorical interpretation.

In the previous paragraphs we emphasized the view that religious allegory is a method of censoring perplexing parts of a mythological story and turning it into a system of abstract ideas that are grasped as being religiously or philosophically kosher. Moreover, we emphasized the view that religious allegory is a tool for reining in the power of the imagination and a means for rationalizing religious stories and transforming them into dogmatic theology. The allegory defeats the imagination and ties it down with conceptual bonds. Primarily, it is a form of representation that is incapable of nourishing religious life, except among pietistic seminarians and clergymen.

In opposition to the allegory the romantics place the symbol. The symbol is supposed to be intuitive, preserving simultaneously its ties to the concrete and to the supernatural, untranslatable and unparaphrasable, expressing such deep and impressive feeling that it can direct one's life; it is a creature of the imagination rather than the intellect and as such expresses the individual and the general inseparably. The symbol is an authentic experiential and cognitive category, a category from the area of religious sensibility and not a figure of speech in the narrow sense.

These and similar contrasts are the central pillars of Schelling's philosophy, and they have a strong hold on the literature of religious studies.[31] The religious interest in the contrast between symbol and allegory is based on the expectation that it will serve as a means for resolving the tension between the philosophical deity, who is conceptually pure but lacks vitality among believers, and the living godhead, who is anthropomorphic or corporeal. In Kant's terminology, this is the tension between deism and personification, where deism is the representation of God in abstract terms that do not retain the sense of a living and active God, and personification is the representation of God in terms that are anthropomorphic and alive but misleading.

Allegory and symbol share the fundamental assumption that the deity cannot be known and understood except through the world of the senses. From the linguistic viewpoint this means that it is necessary to use sensory and observational language to speak about the deity. But the symbol, in contrast to the allegory, is perceived as an unconventional and purposeful means of connecting the visible and the invisible. We will return to this characterization later. Now we turn to the role of the symbol in the constitution of myth, as revealed in the context of the Jewish Kabbalah—or, more precisely, Gershom Scholem's account of the Kabbalah.

Scholem believes that while rabbinic Judaism made an intentional effort to distance and suppress myth from commentaries on the Bible, the interpretations of the Kabbalah revived the myths. The revival of myth in the Kabbalah, according to Scholem, raises the question, "Is the Kabbalah pagan?"—a question which served as the title of a book by a critical scholar at the end of the nineteenth century.[32] The underlying assumption is that if the Kabbalah really restored or introduced myth into Judaism, then this act brought pagan forms of representation and thought into Jewish religious life.

Scholem accepts Schelling's view that symbols are constitutive of myth. In the spirit of both Schelling and Goethe, he characterizes the mystic symbol as the expressible representation of the inexpressible. This characterization of the symbol is an apparent contradiction. One way to resolve the contradiction is to adopt a Wittgensteinian distinction between saying and showing: "There is indeed the inexpressible. This *shows* itself; it is the mystical."[33] According to this distinction, the symbol shows—but does not say—what cannot be said. We escape the contradiction here in that the concept of "expressing" is understood as being ambiguous: it may mean either "showing" or "saying." The symbol therefore cannot state propositions about the deity, since this is the meaning of its being unable to say things, but it is capable of showing things.

We believe that much of what disturbed Scholem in the distinction between symbol and allegory can be presented, even if not fully explicated, in terms of this Wittgensteinian distinction between saying (asserting) and showing. Allegory is perceived as something whose content can in principle be stated, whereas symbol is held to be something that can only be seen or seen through. Allegory has a mapping system which guarantees a representation that says something; the mystic symbol is not constructed according to such a mapping system, as it is a symbol of something that cannot be mapped. All these are hints of a possible direction for the explication of the concept of the mystic symbol, and they may also explain why the use of terms from the area of vision are so prevalent in Scholem's writings when he tries to explain what a symbol is and what it does.

The presentation of the difference between allegory and symbol in terms of saying and showing still does not get us very far in understanding the relation between symbol and myth, the relation that Scholem considered all-inclusive for kabbalistic myth. But perhaps this is as it should be; perhaps there is no direct relation between the two. As evidence we will bring symbolist poetry, which is a version of esthetic mysticism from the school of Charles-Pierre Baudelaire, Stéphane Mallarmé, Paul Verlaine, Rainer Maria Rilke, Stefan George, and others, who made the symbol the focus of their poetry but did not thereby create myth. Symbolism in poetry is mystic in the sense that it possesses great intensity, that it is nonrational and logically inconsistent, and especially that it hints at a supersensory world of ideal beauty. Poetic symbolism arouses without referring, and it creates an aura through vagueness and obscurity with a spiritual effect.[34] Poetic symbols are perceived as symbols in a world of ideal beauty that the experienced reader is supposed to discover behind the sensual description, a beauty that can be seen but not spoken as one walks in the "forest of symbols." All this converges into a "mystical atmosphere" but not into a mythic story. The upshot is that the use of symbols is not a sufficient condition for myth.

Goethe takes the symbol in a different direction. He calls a symbol "a living revelation," meaning a revelation from the point of view of the perceiver: one who in the blink of an eye and without any inference sees in a symbol a totality that cannot be analyzed. But there is, of course, the other aspect, the aspect of that which is being revealed. The symbol is the appearance of what cannot be studied in the realm of the revealed. The revelation is the symbol of that which is being revealed. Between the symbol and that which it symbolizes there is a quasi-causal relation rather than a commonality of shared characteristics.

In the Kabbalah the forms of divine revelation are called *sefirot*. What makes these forms of revelation living symbols is the organization unifying them and the dynamics created among them. One form of organization, for example, is the divine tree. Another is the primeval man. These symbols capture the mystical observer in the grip of the picture of God as an organism. The godhead, more precisely, the divine revelations have a complex structure. This structure is represented by a symbol that stands in a causal relation to the divinity that cannot be analyzed, the "infinite." The divine revelation, whether in the form of the divine tree or the divine man, is not pantheistic: it is not a revelation in the world. But from this structure causal relations, called "roots," go out to objects and events in the world, so that these in turn serve as lower-level symbols for the divine symbols. A nonkabbalistic example may make this clearer. The lamb for the divine sacrifice is a symbol for God's trait of mercy, which is in turn a higher symbolic revelation of the hidden godhead. The lower symbols are causal and metaphorical expressions of the higher symbols, but the higher symbols are not metaphorical expressions of the hidden godhead.

But what does all this symbolic structure have to do with myth? A necessary condition for myth is that it should contain a narrative about divinity. In pagan myth this narrative is a story of events taking place among gods, as well as between gods and other supernatural forces. It can, of course, also include "natural" figures, that is, mortal beings, but not only these. Scholem contributed to the study of myth in drawing attention to the fact that the events in mythic narratives can also take place within an entity that is considered a single deity—on the condition that this deity is perceived as possessing a structure of various forces not wholly dominated by the divine personality and thus to a considerable degree "independent." This is similar to the way a person's struggle against his or her instinctual drives may be described mythically as a struggle against a quasi-external force that limits the person's good intentions.

When the symbolic aspects of the divinity are reified, and the dynamics among them are described in terms of male-female relations, including sexual intercourse, the divine plot thickens and the sacred story attains mythic potential. This is only potential, however, since the fact that a story is a narrative about the divinity is not a sufficient condition for myth. There are narrative legends in which the divinity is involved but which nevertheless do not constitute myth. Myth requires more than a divine narrative: it requires seriousness. This is the same sacramental seriousness we discussed before, a seriousness lacking in legends. But there is another limitation here on the type of narrative to be found in myth or, more precisely, on the nature of the participants in the narrative, as opposed to the legends in the midrash, for example. Legends about God and his angels are not myths because the participants in the narrative are not the sort of figures that are capable of limiting God's will. Thus another necessary condition for myth is that additional figures, whether external or "internal" to the divinity, possess a will that is alien to the divine will, or that they are forces which constrain the divine will even if they do not have a will of their own, like fate.

From all that has been said so far a conclusion may be drawn concerning kabbalistic myth. This is myth not because it uses symbols but because it reifies the symbols as quasi-independent forces, and especially because it produces narrative and dramatic relations among the symbols. What opposes myth is the theological view of God as possessing simple unity. The complexity of the divine, whether it is an organic complexity or a bureaucratic one (as in the image of a royal court), steals mythic possibilities into the representation of the divinity.

## The Typological Reading

The typological reading of sacred stories is built on analogies relating to foundational situations and prototypes. In general the analogy is between figures, situations, and events from the distant historic or quasi-historic past and later figures, situations, and events, some of which may not yet have occurred. Typology is not just a general historical analogy but a symbolic or quasi-causal analogy. That is, the prototype or foundational situation is connected by a supernatural and noncontinuous causal relation with the analogous figure, situation, or event. The combination of symbolic connection and supernatural causation is what makes typology similar to myth. This is our claim, and it will be elaborated in the following section dealing with the sacramental reading of myth.

Christianity made extensive and conscious use of the typological reading, partly because it considered the New Testament a document containing proofs and evidence of the fulfillment of prophecies in the Old Testament. But even the New Testament has an interest in demonstrating a repeated pattern of foundational situations and prototypes beyond pointing out that a certain prophecy was fulfilled once. Christian typology is accompanied by the idea that is called "mystery" in Christianity. "Mystery" means that concrete signs provide the attentive and sensitive believer with enlightenment about the great divine plan. Foundational situations and prototypes provide the believer with anticipatory hints concerning the divine plan. If someone thinks about the incident in which Joseph was thrown into the pit, for example, or about Jonah's stay in the belly of the great fish, he or she may be able to understand the divine plan involved in the burial of Jesus and his rising from the tomb as analogous to those involved in the removal of Joseph from the pit and the rescue of Jonah from the belly of the fish. The understanding of signs is not a semantic understanding of linguistic expressions. It may perhaps be seen as the understanding of the semantics of objects.

Thomas Aquinas discussed the distinction between what we call the semantics of words and the semantics of objects. He even suggested that a special, spiritual type of understanding is required for the comprehension of the semantics of objects. At first, the whole idea seems strange: how can one explain the attribution of semantic characteristics to objects instead of to linguistic expressions? What is the meaning of the claim that a special type of understanding is required for the semantics of objects?

The matter is much more prosaic than one might expect. It is indeed the case that semantic characteristics are sometimes attributed to physical objects. Printed squiggles, ink scribbles, and chalk marks on a blackboard are physical entities that under appropriate conditions are perceived as linguistic writing. What determines whether an object is perceived as having physical or semantic characteristics is the way the object is being used. A swatch of cloth shown by a tailor to a customer serves as a sample of the cloth from which the suit will be made. The swatch thus has the semantic role of exemplification. The customer is expected to understand that the swatch is denoting something but that it does not exemplify all the characteristics of the cloth from which the suit will be made (it does not exemplify the cut or the size of the cloth but only shows its color and texture). Our way of thinking about the semantic role of the swatch is to see it as a sample of other objects—of other pieces of cloth of the same color or texture, or of other pieces of cloth from the same roll. A sample, as opposed to an example, does not require linguistic mediation. In exemplification the swatch serves as an example of a linguistic expression, such as the term "black." This is a case of literal exemplification. In addition, the swatch of cloth may also serve the purpose of metaphorical exemplification; it may, for example, metaphorically exemplify mourning. The cloth does not mourn, of course, but it is capable of exemplifying mourning metaphorically.[35]

Armed with the distinction between an example and a sample, we can now suggest an explication of the traditional distinction between typology as a figurative mode of speech and typology as a relation between objects. In the first case the typology is built on the fact that the prototype (the figure or the event) literally or metaphorically exemplifies the linguistic expressions that describe the analogous type. For example, Melchizedek exemplifies the expressions "Melchizedek," "king of Salem," and "priest of God Most High" (Genesis 14:18), which are expressions applied to Jesus, the analogous typological figure. In the second case, by contrast, the typology is built on the fact that the prototype serves as a sample for the analogous type coming later in time, as in the case of Adam and Jesus. In both cases we require the semantics of objects: once as a linguistic mediator and once between the objects directly.

In addition to a symbolic relation between the prototype and the analogous type, there is a quasi-causal relation between them. Here an example is needed. The typological reading of the story of Israel against Amalek (I Samuel 15) is not only found in the rabbinic commentaries, but even begins within the Bible itself. Thus, for example, Mordecai is the figure analogous to Saul, where the connection is through Mordecai's genealogy (as given in Esther 2:5) as a descendant of Kish the Benjaminite, who is identified with the father of Saul. The type analogous to Agag, king of the Amalekites, who fought with Saul, is, of course, Haman, who is described in his genealogy as "the son of Hammedatha the Agagite" (Esther 3:1). The analogy between the Saul-Agag connection and the Mordecai-Haman connection is a reverse analogy: Saul had pity on Agag and took him captive instead of killing him; Mordecai fulfilled the commandment of a war of extermination against Amalek. The very story of the original war with Amalek (Exodus 17) already contains typological stage directions: "The Lord will be at war with Amalek throughout the ages" (Exodus 17:16). This indeed is how the rabbinic commentators understood the war with Amalek—that is, as requiring a typological reading. Moreover, the foundational story about the original war with Amalek was itself based on a typological source, on the ancient hatred between Esau and Jacob, as Amalek was Esau's grandson (Genesis 36:12). What characterizes biblical typology is thus the "hereditary hatred" between Israel and Amalek, and the causal connection through which the prototype influences the analogous types is a hereditary connection. This connection may also apply to Gog, which may be a distortion of "Agag," so that the uncompromising struggle between Gog and Magog, a struggle which opens up a great mythic gap, continues the struggle with Amalek into the eschatological future.

The rabbinic sages greatly extended this typological reading of Amalek. They began with the biblical verse "Esau—that is, Edom" (Genesis 36:1) and extended it to an identification of Amalek with Edom, and then to an identification of Rome with Edom. In the chain of typological identifications, Rome is equated with Amalek. The linguistic-metaphorical connection between Rome and Edom becomes, in the typological reading, a quasi-hereditary connection. This is the typological understanding of the rabbinic phrase, "The acts of the fathers are a sign for the sons": both sign and inheritance, or, in our terms, both a symbolic relation and a quasi-causal relation. These are the two components of the typological reading, and the expression "the seed of Amalek" exemplifies this neatly.

Typological readings clearly exist in the Bible itself; such readings of the Old Testament are especially prevalent in the New Testament. But we must make an important distinction between a prophetic and a typological reading of the Bible, although the two types of readings are easily conflated. Prophetic readings (not to be confused with readings of the prophets) come to reveal hints and signs in the Old Testament in order to support the fulfillment of prophecies and promises at the time of the New Testament. Typological readings, however, are not solely or mainly intended to describe the fulfillment of prophecies and promises but indicate basic types that are repeated in the New Testament with greater intensity. The copper snake of the Old Testament is repeated in a more intensive form in the cross.

A typological reading is neither myth nor allegory, although it resembles both. It resembles myth in its ontology, and allegory in the analogies it suggests between states of affairs. In typology myth is not emasculated as in allegory, yet it is not complete myth as in the sacramental reading. Perhaps the religious intensity that the

Judean Desert sect gave its typological readings (which are also prophetic readings) gives what they call "interpretations" the force and vitality of myth, which cannot be found in allegory.[36]

## The Sacramental Reading

The sacramental reading of a story or narrative poem is not meant to be another linguistic figure. The sacramental reading considers what is done with language rather than how language is interpreted. If the sacramental reading is a matter of semantics at all, then it is magical semantics. In magical semantics linguistic expressions serve not merely as symbols but also as forces influencing supernatural—divine or demonic—forces. The prototypical sacramental usages of linguistic expressions generally take place during ritual worship. Not every ritual is perceived by its participants as having a sacramental character, but it is nevertheless true that the typical conditions for sacramental usage occur in the context of ritual. Sacramental ritual is what transforms a narrative story about the deity, under the appropriate conditions, into myth, specifically living myth.

The assertion that words can perform acts is no longer a novel statement. Austin described, for example, how a ship is christened in an appropriate ceremony. A person with the appropriate role who names the ship that is being launched is actually doing the christening, and he thus creates a social fact in the world. His act does not differ from that of his wife, who launches the ship by breaking a bottle of champagne on its side. It is the ceremony which makes the naming "serious" by making it something that creates a social fact. This seriousness has nothing to do with the mood of the person doing the naming. During the rehearsal for the ceremony the role of christener may be played by a child who does it with great seriousness, while during the actual ceremony the man in the role of the christener may be wholly playful.

This Austinian story does not contain any magical elements. The naming is a conventional rather than a sacramental act, whereas in a ritual ceremony linguistic expressions are likely to be perceived as expressions woven of a quasi-causal fabric of other-worldly forces. The ritual provides the conditions for the appropriateness and effectiveness of the expressions. In sacramental semantics there is a nonconventional relation between words and objects. The semantic ideas in Plato's *Cratylus,* concerning language that names the things in the world naturally rather than conventionally, fits the spirit of the conception underlying sacramental semantics. In sacramental semantics, however, there is an additional element, namely, a "natural," non-conventional relation between language and the supernatural. It is sacred worship that fulfills the conditions for the effectiveness of linguistic expressions, while outside the ritual act they are not serious in the sense that they do not have the power to create facts of a sort that we will describe later.

A story or narrative poem can serve for entertainment, where its power to entertain derives from its fancifulness. But the very same utterances may play a sacramental role in the context of ritual worship. The sacramental ritual that turns a story into a myth does not require all or even part of the story to be told or read during the ritual. The connection between the story and the ritual may be less direct. On one hand, it is true that the entire story does sometimes appear at the ritual ceremony. For example, the Babylonian story of the creation (Enuma Elish) was apparently told in its entirety during the new-year ritual. On the other hand, at the Passover Seder, although the participants are commanded to tell the story of the Exodus from Egypt, the story is not actually told as such. In the Seder, which is addressed to the children in the family, the wisest of the children is concerned about the laws and customs of Passover rather than the story. But there is no doubt that the entire ritual of the Seder assumes the story of the Exodus, embodies it in its symbolic acts, and refers to it constantly. The only requirement for a story to be a myth is a connection between the story and some sacramental utterances: the story becomes a sacred story because of this sacramental character, and outside the sacramental context it may not have any sacred status.

We have not yet said anything about what the sacramental usage of a linguistic expression or object is supposed to achieve. Why does it have the power to transform a story into a myth? The answer to this question is, in our opinion, the key to the elucidation of the association between the content of myths and mythic time, which we have mentioned only in passing. The sacramental act is intended to revive a foundational situation or a basic figure that is described in the narrative of a myth. The sense of revivification we are using here is the one exemplified during the sacrament of the bread and

wine in the Catholic mass: by means of the sacramental act the presence of Christ is supposed to be created. The bread and the wine are
not mere representations of Jesus' body and blood; rather, they are
supposed to become, through the sacrament, the actual substance of
the body and blood of Jesus, although obviously without his appearance. The doctrine of transubstantiation is intended to give a nonmetaphorical meaning to the presence of Jesus in the bread and the
wine. For our purposes in illustrating the use of the concept of
revivification the exact details of transubstantiation are unimpor-
tant.[37] All we require is the idea that the sacrament of the bread and
the wine in the appropriate ritual framework is supposed to create
not only a symbolic presence but an actual revivification. It must
nevertheless be stressed that revivification is not resurrection. Jesus'
arising from the tomb was a resurrection in which Jesus was supposed to have appeared in his physical being and not only in his
substance.

What has been said so far may create the misleading impression
that a sacramental utterance which revives the existence of a divinity
can occur only in stories describing a suffering and dying god, such
as Tammuz, Adonis, Osiris, Dionysus, or Jesus—those gods whose
worship is perceived by their believers not only as an enactment of
revivification or as a memorial ceremony but as an objective act of
revivification. Sacramental revivification is not limited to suffering
and dying gods, however. The Passover Seder, which is generally
understood as a memorial ceremony, is interpreted in the Kabbalah
as an act of revivification through sacramental action on the *sefirot*.

According to the sacramental interpretation, myth is a characteristic not of the sacred story itself but of its usage for revivification.
From the story itself it is impossible to determine whether it is a
myth: the context of ritual worship is required to determine this.
The same story may play a role in a memorial ceremony, in which
case it is not a myth, while giving it a sacramental role can turn it
into a myth.

If sacramental revivification is, as we have asserted, the revivification of foundational situations described by myths, we must ask
what foundational situations are, and whether such situations in
pagan stories differ essentially from foundational situations in
monotheistic stories. A common species of mythic narrative are
stories about the origin and creation of the elements of nature and

social institutions. Thus, for example, the story of the banishment from the Garden of Eden describes the source of the snake's poisonousness, the pains of childbirth, and the toils of work, while the story of eating the forbidden fruit in the garden describes the source of shame and clothing. But the most prototypical foundational stories are those describing the creation of the world, and the question we will focus on is whether there is an essential difference between monotheistic and pagan stories of the creation—that is, between the biblical creation story and the creation stories that were prevalent in its environment.

Kaufmann has provided one important answer to this question. The principal difference, in his view, is that either the pagan creation is the product of the gods' procreation, and so the created world is made of the same stuff as the deities, or else the world was created as a result of struggles and wars between the gods, and so it is not the product of the absolute divine will. In contrast, the biblical creation story describes the constitution of the world out of the absolute will of God, who is himself absolutely separated from the world. The biblical creator, according to this claim, is a transcendental God with absolute will, whereas the pagan gods who created the world exist on a continuum with it and do not possess absolute will.

The difficulty in accepting this claim is related to what seems to be the "unbearable lightness" with which one may read theology into mythic stories. It seems as though you can take your choice: you can see the biblical creation story as speaking about God's absolute separation from the world and about a God who created man in his image; or you can see the story of Ptah, who was worshiped in Memphis as the creator of the universe out of nothingness, as being about Ptah's absolute separation and absolute will. Transcendence and immanence are thus in the eye of the interpreter.

There is some truth to this argument against Kaufmann, but it is not completely true. There are definite constraints on the interpretation of creation stories, and within the framework of these constraints it seems that the distinction between the creation story in the Bible and its pagan parallels, along the dimensions of will and separation from the world, is not unfounded. But it is a distinction on a continuum, and not a strict dichotomy, as it was regarded by Kaufmann and by Herman Cohen before him.

Another question that concerns us is whether the creation stories were associated with rituals of revivification. For example, should the ceremony of consecrating the Jewish Sabbath be understood as a ceremony of thanksgiving to the creator or as a ceremony of revivification of the original Sabbath on which God rested from the work of the creation? The same may be asked about the daily reading in the temple of the creation story (Mishnah, Tractate *Ta'anit* 4:2–3)— was it a daily thanksgiving or a daily revivification of the act of the creation? Our answer to the question of whether the story of the creation is a myth in our sense of the word is dependent upon the answers to the questions just asked.

Returning to the sacramental reading of myth, we wish to explore the connection between the sacramental reading and the magical use of utterances of the sacred story and the relation between magic and idolatry in general. According to an old but not outdated account by Emile Durkheim, magic is essentially private and religion is collective. Durkheim did not mean that magic is done only in private or only by individuals. What he meant was that magic is not a product of social commonality even if a number of people participate in it. This relates to the primary distinction between magic and sacrament: performing magic does not create a moral community as observing a sacrament does. A flaw in the order of magical actions may be considered extreme recklessness, but not a sin, whereas a flaw in a sacrament is a sin. The sacrament, as we have already argued, has the role of "improving the world" in the cosmic and not only the social sense; magic is concerned with "exploiting the world." The connection between magic and sacrament is the common assumption that symbolic actions have a supernatural causal effect on divine entities. This common assumption is known as "theurgy."[38]

Given that magic has a utilitarian purpose and sacrament has the moral purpose of creating a fitting social and cosmic order, we must now determine which of the two is associated with myth. To the extent that myth expresses the fundamental values of the society in which it is operative and plays a role in the creation of a moral community, it is associated with sacrament and not with magic. Is magic thus associated with idolatry?

The Bible, which is the foundational document against idolatry, prohibits all forms of magic without exception: "Let no one be found among you who consigns his son or daughter to the fire, or who is an augur, a soothsayer, a diviner, a sorcerer, one who casts spells, or one who consults ghosts or familiar spirits, or one who inquires of the dead" (Deuteronomy 18:10–11). All these acts are the "abhorrent things" that are done by the nations whose land Israel is to inherit. From the language as well as the reason given it is clear that no real distinction is being made between these magical acts and idolatry. Thus, for example, consigning one's children to the fire may be considered an act of ritual worship in the narrow sense or a magical act; the distinction between magic and ritual worship as far as idolatry is concerned does not exist in the Bible.

One reason offered for the prohibition of magic in the Bible is that it is a form of rebellion: "For rebellion is like the sin of divination" (I Samuel 15:23). In turning to alien forces, both the idol worshiper and the person who performs magical acts rebel against God. Magic is an expression not only of rebellion but also of the pretensions of the magician, who feels a divine power in himself because of his ability to do wondrous deeds, as is described by Isaiah: ". . . your many enchantments and all your countless spells. You were secure in your wickedness . . . And you thought to yourself, 'I am, and there is none but me'" (Isaiah 47:9–10). The reasons for the opposition to magic in the Bible—rebellion and conceit—are the same as the reasons for the opposition to idolatry in general.

The Bible's attitude toward the effectiveness of magic is ambivalent, like its attitude toward the question of whether there is any reality in idolatry. The feeling one gets is that there is some reality in magic. Thus, for example, when Moses and Aaron turned their rods into serpents at God's behest, Pharaoh's magicians were able to copy them: "Then Pharaoh, for his part, summoned the wise men and the sorcerers; and the Egyptian magicians, in turn, did the same with their spells" (Exodus 7:11). The purpose of the story is to show that Moses and Aaron's power is greater than the power of the Egyptian magicians, as their serpent swallows the magicians' serpent, and not to show that their magic has no reality. (This is the case in the New Testament as well: Simon Magus, the greatest of the magicians from Shechem, saw for himself that the power of Jesus' miracles was greater than his own power, but there too the purpose of the story is not to show that magic has no reality but only to say that it cannot compete with one who operates with God's power—neither in effectiveness nor in moral content.) Nevertheless, there are some expressions which do imply that magic has no reality:

"You are helpless, despite all your art. Let them stand up and help you now, the scanners of heaven, the star-gazers" (Isaiah 47:13).

In addition to the two concepts of idolatry we have already discussed—idolatry as the ritual worship of other gods and idolatry as false belief—there is also another important concept, which we address at length in Chapter 8, of idolatry as a complete form of life. Not limited to ritual and belief, idolatry encompasses other lifestyle issues such as dress, hairstyle, tattoos, entertainment at theaters and stadia, turning to sorcerers, and many other aspects. Idolatry is thus "following the paths of the gentiles" in a wider sense than ritual worship—including magic and idolatrous lifestyles in general. All these are examples of idolatry in a wide sense. A distinction can be made between two different views of the relation between magic and idolatry in the narrow sense. One view regards magic as a kind of "soft drug" whose excessive use may lead to addiction to the "hard drug" of idolatry in the ritual sense. The other view is an organic approach, which fits the biblical viewpoint better. According to this view, there is no serious distinction between magic and ritual idolatry since both of them constitute one ideological and practical unit.

In conclusion, let us return to the question we began with: what is the relation between myth and paganism? Of our four types of reading of sacred stories, the sacramental reading is the one that is explicitly or implicitly related to theurgic activity, that is, acts that are supposed to have "ontological" effects on the divinity and the world. It is the sacramental reading that transforms our understanding of a sacred story into a myth—in addition, of course, to those cases in which the sacred story can be perceived in the literal reading of the narrative. To the extent that the sacramental reading infiltrates the sacred stories of the monotheistic religions—and this infiltration sometimes occurs through the intermediary of a typological reading—"idolatrous" myths find their way into these religions.

# 4

## Idolatry as Error

The story of the war against idolatry in the Bible is the story of a struggle against the idol-worshiping nations who seduced the Israelites into joining their acts of ritual worship. The worship of idols is described as a foreign import, especially as something brought in by gentile women: "The Israelites settled among the Canaanites, Hittites, Amorites, Perizzites, Hivites, and Jebusites; they took their daughters to wife and gave their own daughters to their sons, and they worshiped their gods" (Judges 3:5–6). This was the case when the judges ruled over Israel, and it continued when the judges were replaced by kings, whose wives—King Solomon's and especially King Ahab's wife, Jezebel— served as the great importers of alien worship. At any rate, the three large classes of idols in the Bible—the gods of the other side of the river, the gods of Egypt, and the gods of the Amorites—all represent alien gods from a foreign source. One exception was perhaps the worship of the golden calves introduced by King Jeroboam (I Kings 13), whose source, according to Hosea, was in Israel. But in general the war against idolatry in the Bible is a war against forms of ritual worship imported from foreign nations.

We have already stressed that idolatry was perceived in the Bible as a demonstration of disloyalty and that the sin of idolatry was regarded as a sin of betrayal. To the sexual sin of the worship of other gods the Bible adds the commission of error. The error was in the longing for gods that are "no-gods" (Jeremiah 2:11), which may be compared to "broken cisterns" (Jeremiah 2:13). Nevertheless, the focus of the sin remained the sexual aspect rather than the aspect of error. A woman who commits adultery with a worthless lover is obviously committing an error; however, her sin is not in the error but in the adultery. The error in the worship of idols adds to the sin, but it is not the sin itself.

When Maimonides presented the war against idolatry as the main principle of the Torah he confronted a reality very different from the biblical reality. The meaning he gives to idolatry is therefore significantly different from the meaning given in the Bible. Idolatrous rituals no longer constituted a temptation in Maimonides' community. The saying in the Talmud that "the temptation for idolatry was slaughtered" describes this new reality. In Maimonides' thought there was thus a change in the concept of idolatry, and this change was in the direction of internalization.[1]

Internalization occurs in two ways: socially and mentally. When socially internalized, idolatry is no longer a form of worship that takes place within other nations, with the Israelites following after them, but becomes something occurring within the monotheistic society itself. This social internalization within the community is made possible by the mental internalization whose essence is the shift from external worship to internal belief. Certainly it was possible for a man to pray alongside Maimonides in the synagogue and behave in a manner externally indistinguishable from that of the great monotheist, while actually being an idolater. The man's concepts of the divinity could be so distorted by errors and corporealizing that his intention in his prayer would be described not as the worship of the right God but as the worship of an alien god.

The focus of the concept of idolatry was thus transferred from the performance of alien rituals to the harboring of alien beliefs. The worship of idols is a symptom of alien belief, and is therefore a sin, but it is a sin derived from the belief it expresses and not primarily from the act itself. The transition from alien worship to alien beliefs constitutes a crucial shift in the conception of the sin of idolatry as well: from the sexual sin of idolatry to the sin of the great error.

According to Maimonides the great error is anthropomorphism, which is manifested in two ways: perceiving God as a body and attributing to God emotions and psychic life. One who makes such errors concerning God is worse than an idol worshiper who worships idols as intermediaries. The prohibition against images is due to the fear that at the end the multitude will believe exclusively in the image, but one who believes in the corporeality of God has already internalized the image of God that the prohibition is trying to eradicate: "Know accordingly, you who are that man, that when you believe in the doctrine of the corporeality of God or believe that one of the states of the body belongs to Him, you provoke His jealousy and anger, kindle the fire of His wrath, and are a hater, an enemy, and an adversary of God much more so than an idolater" (*Guide of the Perplexed,* 1:36). Embodiment in matter refers to a description of the deity that uses material expressions in a literal sense, such as the following verse: "Then the Lord will come forth and make war on those nations as He is wont to make war on a day of battle. On that day, He will set His feet on the Mount of Olives, near Jerusalem on the east" (Zechariah 14:3–4). Mental realization refers to a description of the deity that uses mental expressions in a literal sense: "But the Israelites implored the Lord: 'We stand guilty. Do to us as You see fit; only save us this day!'" (Judges 10:15).

This internalization is reflected in another aspect of idolatrous error, according to Maimonides: the false belief in multiplicity. For Maimonides the belief in the oneness of God meant not merely denial of polytheism, which is obvious, but, more important, denial of the perception of God himself as a complex being. The description of God as one according to Maimonides refers mainly to his own "simple unity." "Multiplicity" is therefore not only the belief in many gods, it is also an error that concerns God himself, which may be called "internal polytheism." The strict demand on unity implies a rejection of corporeality, which assumes that God is divisible like any body and which excludes more subtle violations of unity such as linguistic predication in general. To predicate a positive attribute to God is a violation of God's simple unity, because it assumes a complexity of a subject and his predicate, a complexity of substance and attribute or substance and accident. As analyzed at length in Chapters 2 and 6 of this book, strict compliance with the demands of unity leads Maimonides to the exclusion of the possibility of any linguistic description of God. The concept of unity is understood differently by different monotheists and many of them perceive God as a complex entity. Maimonides' peculiar understanding of the error of multiplicity, and his rejection of anthropomorphism is therefore an internal critique of believers in his own community.

The two big mistakes, corporeality and multiplicity, vitiate God's perfection. Corporeality is a gross error in being the vulgar notion of the common people. The idea of matter is associated with decay, and it is also conceptually connected with finitude. Both decay and finitude are most unfitting notions to combine with the idea of a perfect God. Moreover, corporeality entails divisibility, and hence the notion of a corporeal God undermines God's unity. This leads us to the second error, that of multiplicity. In its basic form multiplicity is the idea of many gods. It is clear why the idea of many gods is incompatible with the idea of a perfect God, since many gods limit one another. In its slightly modified yet still vulgar form multiplicity takes the form of participation *(shituf)* which also violates the perfection of God, insofar as he is not self-sufficient.

In Maimonides' thought the error of multiplicity takes a sophisticated twist in the idea of God's complexity. Here the relation between complexity and God's lack of perfection should be exposed. Complexity undermines God's perfection in two ways. A complex God is a being in whose definition the components (properties) take logical priority over the "whole." Thus the "whole" cannot be perfect since it is not self-explanatory. A parallel move can be formulated in causal terms. A complex being is causally constituted by its parts, hence it is not its own cause of being. Perfection entails the notion of being self-caused. Perfection is a causal and conceptual autarky.

Another way in which complexity undermines perfection is through predication. Ascribing attributes to a complex God means that there are properties which he shares at least in principle with other beings. An attribute is what by definition can be shared with others. Hence there is an implied comparison in all attribution which leaves room only for a relative notion of perfection, not for the absolute one. God's absolute perfection means that he is like nothing else. Therefore, logically, he cannot be a bundle of properties. Our main claim, then, is that the two big errors with regard to God, multiplicity and corporeality, stem from the more basic misconception about God's perfection.

Maimonides was exceedingly skeptical about the possibility that finite and limited creatures like us humans could form the right notion of God's perfection. But he did believe that limited as we are we can avoid projection of our misguided ideas of human perfection onto God. God is not perfect in the image of a perfect human being.

## The Chain of Criticism of Religion

Our discussion of the causes of error in this chapter and of other aspects of error in the next two chapters is based on an important conceptual chain composed of the following links: the criticism of idolatry by the monotheistic religions, the criticism of folk religion by the religious Enlightenment, the criticism of religion in general by the secular Enlightenment, and finally the criticism of ideology. The claim is that at every link of this chain the same intellectual moves were made.

The first link of the chain, the criticism of idolatry by the monotheistic religions, includes arguments and claims that critics adopted from the criticism of pagan folk religion by the intellectual pagan elite. As we have seen, the monotheistic critics used these arguments against the idolatrous religions in general, without distinguishing between the elite and the folk religion.

The criticism of folk idolatry was often expressed in the form of criticism of the poets who narrated the stories and were thus held responsible for the distorted concepts about the gods that populated the views of the ignorant masses.[2] (This criticism of the poets as the creators of misleading mythologies about the gods reminds us of the current criticism of the media as "responsible" for distorting the views of the "people.") Criticism of poetry and poets as distorters of the truth about the divinity was the way the pagan philosophers expressed their criticism of folk religion as a religion molded by imaginative, manipulative, entertainer-poets who lacked any concern for the truth. The use of this intrapagan criticism for the purpose of external polemical attack on paganism was characteristic of Christian criticism of idolatry at a time when Christianity was still intimately connected with it. This move is also characteristic of other links in the chain of criticism: on the one hand the earlier criticism is adopted, and on the other hand it is turned upon the critic himself, as one whose criticism applies to himself as well and not only to the objects of his criticism.

We have given the Leo-Straussian name "religious Enlightenment" to the second link in the chain, which refers to the religious trend whose criticism of idolatry was influenced by philosophical conceptions about religion.[3] The community of enlightened monotheists who criticized folk religion argued that it contained idolatrous assumptions and errors with respect to the divinity, especially on issues such as God's corporeality and the plurality of deities. We use the term "religious Enlightenment" because a considerable number of the identifying traits of the secular Enlightenment were preceded by trends in the religious Enlightenment among the monotheistic religions.

In general, the criticism of folk religion by the religious Enlightenment had two components. One was the claim that folk religion, the religion of the masses, is crucially affected by the power of the imagination, which directs the masses in their cognitive and emotional impressions. The second was the claim that tradition played a major role in the strengthening and preservation of great errors with respect to the divinity.

The third link in the chain is the criticism of religion in general by the secular Enlightenment. This criticism shares many points with the criticism of folk religion by the religious Enlightenment, but it directs its arrows against the traditional monotheistic religions themselves.[4] The criticism by the secular Enlightenment of tradition, all tradition, as a source of epistemic authority was much more radical than the criticism offered by the religious Enlightenment. The latter was characterized by ambivalence with respect to tradition, as it considered tradition to be a source of authoritative knowledge on the one hand and a source of the preservation and strengthening of illusions on the other. The criticism of social illusions as anchored in the imagination is also an important motif in the secular Enlightenment. But in addition to the dimensions of imagination and tradition as important categories for the classification of errors, two new points of classification appear in the secular Enlightenment: illusions whose source is motivational and illusions whose source is the very structure of cognition. Thus, for instance, in the context of idolatrous errors sexual license as a cause of idol worship is a motivational source, while the idea that idolatry relies on what is visible is based on an illusion whose source is in the structure of cognition.

If asked to point out the outstanding thinkers who stressed one of these two points, we would mention Descartes as one who emphasized the importance of the will in the creation of error, and

Kant as one who regarded the very structure of cognition as the principal source of systematic error. Error, according to Kant, is a side effect of human cognition and the price we pay for its efficiency. For example, we see the surface of the sea in the center of our visual field as higher than its surface at the sides of the visual field. This is an error, but it is the price we pay for our ability to encompass such a large area in one glance. By contrast, those who stress the role of motivation in the creation of error will give the example of the perceptual illusion in which hungry people see steaks as larger than well-fed people do.[5]

We should add that the deep analogy between cognitive and motivational illusions on the one hand and perceptual illusions on the other did not go unnoticed by the religious traditions, especially with respect to idolatrous error. Thus in the chapter "The Ant" in the Koran, as well as in the midrash on Proverbs, there is a story about the idol-worshiping queen of Sheba who saw the glass floor in King Solomon's palace as a pool of water and "bared her legs." When she was informed of her error she proclaimed, "Lord, I have sinned against my own soul," made peace with Solomon, and became devoted to Allah. Let us leave the queen of Sheba and return to our own concerns, the Enlightenment classifications of the causes of systematic errors. If the first division into imagination and tradition divides the sources of error into psychological errors and social errors, the second division into errors whose source is motivational and errors whose source is in the structure of cognition shifts the contrast to one between two types of psychological errors. Above all the secular Enlightenment is characterized by a shift from the criticism of folk religion to the criticism of religion in general. Religion is seen as an alien belief in which man subordinates himself to the creatures of his illusional imagination and is thus alienated from himself and from his most vital interests.

The last link in our survey, which we consider a product of the secular Enlightenment, is associated with the shift from the criticism of religion to the criticism of ideology as a type of collective illusion. In this view there is no need for idols or for God to induce man to subordinate himself to the creatures of his imagination: he can and does do this with respect to imaginary reifications such as "race," "nation," "class," "blood and earth," and the many other reifications that populate ideologies. Ideologies as interest-dependent social beliefs manipulate the masses by making use of the power of the imagination, as well as illusion-preserving institutions like the educational system and the church. These ideological illusions are so blatant, according to the critics, that there is no reason to investigate their truth value. Only the causes of the errors, and not their content, is worth examining.

The term "idols" has acquired the sense of "great illusions," primarily as a result of Francis Bacon's writings. Bacon used the word "idols" to name his categories of fallacies, which are types of systematic illusions.[6] He classified the various fallacies as types of "idols," such as "the idols of the tribe" and "the idols of the cave." Bacon's classification cuts across both sorts of classification we have mentioned: both the division into imagination and tradition, and the division into motivation and cognition. In his "idols of the marketplace," which encompass tradition-based errors, he also included errors resulting from the use of language or, more precisely, from the uncritical use of language. There is nothing exceptional in Bacon's mention of language as a source of systematic error. The religious Enlightenment, like analytical trends in contemporary philosophy, placed upon language the primary responsibility for systematic error.

Bacon included the causes of the errors that are particular to idolatry in the narrow sense in his category of "the idols of the tribe." In his opinion these are errors that are created as a result of our tendency to project onto the environment characteristics that are unique to man, in the sense that man created the world in his image. The explanation of idolatrous error as a product of illusion-creating projection is an ancient argument. Xenophanes, the "enlightened pagan," long ago voiced his famous criticism that the gods are given the form of men as a result of projection: the gods of black people are black, and if horses had gods, they would look like horses.[7] All these are direct projections of human characteristics onto the creatures of human imagination. The innovation of the criticism of religion in general as a projective enterprise is in the idea that a superior device for illusion exists in the form of reverse projection: if the earthly family is poor and miserable, then the heavenly family is resplendent with riches and honor. Feuerbach and Freud attributed much of the explanation for the error-creating device to reverse projection.

The chain we mentioned, from the criticism of idolatry to the criticism of folk religion, from there to the criticism of religion in general and then to the criticism of ideology, overlaps the historical development of these matters to a great extent. But our argument is not historical. If we wanted to present a historical thesis we would have had to qualify what we said with all sorts of reservations. For example, we would have had to show that internal religious criticism in terms of "idolatry" sometimes appeared as a criticism of folk religion by the religious elite. This would also be the case for the criticism of the Catholics by the Protestants, and for the criticism of the "high" Protestant church by the "low" church. But, as mentioned, the chain of ideas we are discussing is conceptual rather than historical.

## Tradition as a Source of Error

Behind false worship and false belief stands tradition. Tradition strengthens and preserves idolatrous beliefs, just as it strengthens and preserves idolatrous practices. The Talmud recognizes the fact that tradition, even if it is idolatrous, has the power to arouse true awe and great readiness for sacrifice. Idolatry is not only nourished by orgastic yearnings and license. Its great hold on its followers also derives from its being anchored in ancient tradition. This idea is expressed very forcefully in the talmudic story of the starving child who was found by the prophet Elijah and who was ready to die for the religion in which his parents had brought him up rather than adopt the Israelite religion. As mentioned in Chapter 1, the Talmud distinguishes between the motivation for the adoption of idolatry, which is orgastic license ("permitting forbidden sexual relations in public"), and the reasons for preserving faith in and worship of idols, which are education and ancient custom (*Sanhedrin* 63b–64a).

Ancient tradition as an anchoring of error in customary usage— whether error in general or idolatrous error, including the error of the embodiment of God, in particular—is not unique to idolatrous societies. Monotheistic societies, which are organized around sacred writings, are especially vulnerable to the influence of tradition, even more so than idolatrous societies, whose religion is not defined by written texts. This at any rate is the interesting thesis of Maimonides (*Guide of the Perplexed*, 1:31), which appears as the "fourth cause" of error that he adds to the three causes listed by Alexander of Aphro-

disias. Alexander's three causes are: the love of power, which distances a person from the truth because he is preoccupied with power
struggles and has no time for quiet and truly disinterested contem-
plation; the difficulty of the achievement, that is, the complexity of
the object to be known; and the lack of ability, or, the limitations of
the knower. In positing a fourth cause, Maimonides considers the
fact that people are educated according to the tradition prevailing in
their social environment to be an important cause of error.
According to Maimonides, people have a tendency to adopt whatever is customary: this is the reason that nomads prefer their difficult
life of wandering to living in magnificent palaces. People become
blind to the truth and slaves to habit. Thus Maimonides thought
that conditioning is the deep explanation for the strength of people's
belief in God's corporeality.[8] The habit of corporealizing belief
comes from repeated readings of the sacred writings in their "external" meaning, in a corporealizing sense, which is the meaning that
everyone can understand. It therefore turns out, according to
Maimonides, that it is precisely the Jewish faith, which is centered
on sacred texts, that is more liable to the error of corporealizing the
creator than the idolatrous religions. Tradition as mediated by sacred
texts is a source not only of traditional truths but also of grave
errors.

Considering tradition a cause of error poses a serious problem for
religions that anchor the source of their authority in tradition. The
attitude of the monotheistic religions toward tradition is thus an
ambivalent one. On the one hand, tradition is a cause of idolatry:
the Abraham of the midrash is literally an iconoclast—he breaks the
idols in his father's (Terah's) house and thus symbolizes the destruction of the tradition of his ancestors. On the other hand, the adoption of "gods they had never known, new ones who came but lately,
who stirred not your fathers' fears" (Deuteronomy 32:17) is considered a reason for reproach, partly for the very reason that they are
new gods and not the God that the heritage of one's ancestors enjoins
one to believe in. The issue is particularly complex for religions
based on revelation: the revelation is a turning point and perhaps
even a break with the past, but at the same time the revelation itself
must be transmitted and preserved by tradition.

The attitude toward tradition is crucially different in the religious
and the secular Enlightenments. In general, exponents of the secular

Enlightenment disparaged tradition, because they perceived a connection between ancient belief and superstition, whereas religious Enlightenment thinkers associated tradition with both truth and error. To the views of the two Enlightenments we add another view, the conservative view. According to the conservative view there is a strong presumption in favor of beliefs that are anchored in tradition. A belief backed by tradition is held as true unless there is a counterclaim supported by weighty reasons. These reasons must include the fact that the counterclaim is itself based on a tradition, even if it is not as strong a tradition as the one supporting the original claim.

The justifications for the conservative view are both political and epistemic. From a political standpoint tradition is regarded as a stabilizing social force. Advocates of this view assume that the masses generally honor authority supported by tradition. From a cognitive standpoint the justifications for the conservative presumption in favor of traditional beliefs include skeptical ones as well. In the realm of religion this is expressed as the idea that the individual human mind is limited, and only the wisdom of the religious community permits a proper understanding of divine matters. This "traditionalism," which was formulated in reaction to the French Revolution, maintained that reason is our guide in divine matters; "reason," however, refers here to that of the religious community, as it was formed by the tradition embodied in the Catholic church, and not to the individual's reason. A more radical skeptical view undermines the power of reason in general, both individual and collective, as a guide in divine matters. The act of revelation alone can serve as a foundation for faith, where the revelation is regarded as being transmitted by a chain of authorized tradition from generation to generation. Only tradition is the authorized channel for transmitting the truth in divine matters. Closeness to the source of revelation provides a cognitive advantage for knowledge of the truth, and what is older is closer to the revelation.

According to the view of the religious Enlightenment there is also a presumption in favor of tradition, but it is weaker than the one held by the conservatives.[9] The religious Enlightenment's presumption is that a claim supported by tradition should continue to be held as true as long as there is no proof that it is false. What is important to find out is whether any counterclaim derives logically from principles that cannot be shaken. Even if the counterclaim is more reason-able than the claim of tradition, if it is not based on a demonstrative proof, the traditional claim should be preferred. It is in the light of this presumption that one must understand Maimonides' acceptance of the claim that the world was created over the claim that it always existed. Because the claim of creation was anchored in the tradition to which Maimonides belonged, whereas the claim of the preexis-tence of the world, even if it seemed more reasonable to Maimonides, was not anchored in a proof, he accepted the former.

The religious Enlightenment's view of the relation between ancient beliefs and superstitions is a complex one that incorporates the idea of "double truth." The meaning we give to the concept of double truth is different from the meaning traditionally associated with it. The doctrine of double truth traditionally refers to the idea that there are two sorts of truth, one philosophical and one religious. The religious intellectual compartmentalizes the two types of truth so that there is no relation between them and they cannot engender a contradiction: each truth is correct within its own framework. It is not clear if anyone actually held this version of the doctrine of double truth. The version of the doctrine that seems most reasonable to us is the one claiming that philosophical and theological reasoning methods develop in parallel. The considerations that justify proposi-tions in the two methods are totally different, and they may tem-porarily justify opposite propositions. But these are only apparent contradictions, which can be reconciled over time. The question is which claim has priority in both practical matters and issues of belief until the apparent contradictions are reconciled. In such a case the doctrine holds that there is a presumption in favor of tradition-based religion, unless the philosophical claim is supported by a demonstra-tive proof. If the philosophical proposition is actually supported by such a proof, then the religious proposition is illogical, which shows that we were mistaken in the first place in the interpretation of this claim and we must search for the source of the contradiction and find a new interpretation for the claim.

The concept of double truth thus refers to two sorts of truth, but it also refers to two sorts of believers: the intellectuals and the masses. Holding a double truth (as a temporary standpoint) is the privilege of the intellectuals. The masses may only be presented with the truth of the religious tradition, in order to preserve order and social stability. Only the intellectual elite is capable of dealing with the specious contradiction between the two sorts of truth.[10] Its privilege to deal with these matters, which is in essence the privilege to do philosophy, must be guaranteed, but only after the ignorant masses and naive students are prevented from engaging in this dangerous area of apparent contradictions.

The secular Enlightenment differs from the religious Enlightenment in its attitude toward the truth. In the secular Enlightenment the concept of truth is the same for everyone. The natural light of wisdom is given equally to all, and only alien desires cause people to stray from this light. In the religious Enlightenment, however, wisdom as the power of recognizing the truth is not distributed equally: there are people of understanding who are capable of high knowledge and there are also fools who require traditional religious discipline. The power of habit and conditioning as factors that strengthen error also result in useful errors, such as those that assist in preserving the social order without which the religious intellectual would not be able to exist.

The secular Enlightenment and the conservative approach hold opposite views with respect to the relationship between time and truth. The orientation of the secular Enlightenment is toward the future, while that of the conservative approach—as well as that of the religious Enlightenment—is toward the past. Orientation toward the future depends on a vision of progress toward the recognition of the truth. This concept of progress includes conceptual progress, the acquisition of more abstract concepts that fit reality better as well as the acquisition of increasingly comprehensive truths about reality. The concept of truth which fits the secular Enlightenment's concept of progress is that of truth as coherence: both the coherence of propositions within one comprehensive consistent body of knowledge, and coherence as increasing agreement among rational people. The conservative view, by contrast, sees a connection between truth and the source of truth in the past, a connection mentioned in our earlier discussion of revelation and truth. The mottoes that express this difference are the rabbinic statement, "If the earlier ones were like human beings then we are like donkeys," and the Enlightenment motto, "A dwarf that stands on the shoulders of a giant can see farther than the giant." As is true of mottoes in general, these say too little but suggest too much.

The issue of idolatrous error and its causes is closely associated with the issue of the relationship between time and truth. This close association is connected with the question of whether there was a primeval monotheistic belief that preceded idolatry or whether monotheistic belief was a later stage in religious development that required long prior preparation. The relationship between time and truth is also associated with ethical aspects of idolatrous error. There is an ethical difference between the two orientations in time, the future one and the traditional one, with respect to the perception of idolatrous error as sin. If realizing the truth of monotheism requires long-term development and is not available to people whose thought processes are primitive, then they are not deserving of moral reproach for their error, just as people who are not capable of abstract mathematical thought are not deserving of moral reproach. But if monotheistic belief and the concept of the monotheistic God were available to everyone from earliest times, then those who commit the error of idolatry are deserving of reproach because they are capable of knowing better and believing otherwise.

The developmental theories of the nineteenth century are proto-typical theories of progress. According to these theories, religious development has undergone conceptual transformations from belief in inanimate objects as housing divine powers (fetishism), through animals as divine objects (animism), and thence through the concept of the deity who is supreme over the other gods (hierotheism), until it reached the concept of one sole God who rules over the world (monotheism). In contrast to these theories, Maimonides, as the representative of the religious Enlightenment, shared the conservative approach concerning primeval monotheism, according to which idolatry constitutes a fall from the primeval state of knowledge of the true God.[11]

The religious Enlightenment perceives sacred history as a U-shaped curve. On one cusp of the curve is the ancient past, which is regarded as a golden age of knowledge. The present is at the bottom of the curve. As far as the future is concerned, according to this curve we are marching confidently toward a redemption of renewed consciousness of the truth. In the secular Enlightenment schema, which revolves around the idea of cognitive progress, sacred time ("sacred" because it deals with the development of the concept of holiness) has the form of a rising line / with its low point in the

primitive past and its peak in the enlightened future. It is difficult to
characterize the conservative conception of sacred time, even in our
rough schematic way, but the most typical characterization would
have the form of a falling line \ with its peak in the past. The falling
conservative line may, however, have a discontinuity in the form of
a leap of consciousness in the future. This would be a leap that is not
on the continuum of ordinary time but represents the future of the
messianic age.

This section has dealt with the first cause of error, which is habit
coming from ancient usage. It should be remembered that the explanation of the causes of error is not an objective scientific answer to
the question of why people maintain idolatrous errors. Rather, it is
part of the debate on idolatry, and one of its purposes is the undermining of idolatrous beliefs. One way to demolish a set of beliefs is
to argue that since the causes of its adoption are despicable, the
beliefs themselves are invalid. If people believe in idols because it
gives them license for sexual immorality, for example, then this
belief may be presumed to be immoral and valueless. However, the
case of ancient usage as a source of idolatry is a complicated one,
since ancient usage is not generally considered a despicable source of
belief, but rather is seen as a respectable and even noble source. This
perception creates a serious dilemma for the historical monotheists,
as their loyalties are divided between honoring ancient custom as
part of honoring one's parents, and embracing the revolutionary and
iconoclastic character of their religions, and thereby cutting themselves off from their ancient traditions. Thus, chapter 4 of the Koran,
"The Poets," says: "Recount to them the story of Abraham. He said
to his father and to his people: 'What is that which you worship?'
They replied: 'We worship idols and pray to them with all fervor.'
'Do they hear you when you call them?' he asked. 'Can they help
you or do you harm?' They replied: 'This is what our fathers did
before us.'" On the one hand the monotheistic religions support the
authority of religion, while on the other hand they demand the rejection of the answer that was given to Abraham, for it was Abraham
himself who was commanded to leave his "father's house." Similarly, Jesus' demand (Matthew 4:22) of the brothers John and James
was that they cut themselves off from their father Zebedee and attach
themselves to him and his mission: "And they immediately left the
ship and their father, and followed him." A worthy belief is one that

confronts the believers with the test of cutting themselves off even from their ancient beliefs and cleaving to the great truth. This is the lesson of the cases we cited. Nevertheless, ancient custom and habit is the most understandable—even if unjustified—cause of clinging to idolatrous belief. Since the acceptance of one's ancestors' beliefs is part of honoring one's parents, which is an important commandment, this source cannot be considered a despicable cause of idolatrous belief.

## Imagination as a Source of Error

Imagination is both the power of creating mental images, and as such a precondition of knowledge and thought, and a power unconstrained by logic and reality, and as such an obstacle to true knowledge and a source of illusions. Attempts to reconcile these two senses have resulted in an ambivalence toward imagination dating as far back as Aristotle. The traditional assumptions behind this ambivalent attitude are taken from the psychology of mental faculties, which claims that the mind is divided into separate faculties such as memory, learning, perception, intelligence, and imagination. As the faculty of creating mental images, the imagination is divided into two parts: the faculty of creating copies of what has already been perceived by the senses, which is required primarily for memory, and the faculty of creating images that are new combinations of copies of familiar elements. The constituent elements are always taken from reality, but the combinations may not be. In Aristotelian psychology the first type of imagination is the imitative imagination, while the second type is the creative imagination. It is the second type of imagination that is a cause of illusions.

Today we do not see an essential connection between the imagination and images. We judge acts and people as imaginative without any connection with images. A football player may be considered an "imaginative and inspired passer" not because any image appeared in his or our mind's eye but because he passed the ball in an unexpected way, while his teammate who received the ball may be judged unimaginative not because there was no image that appeared in his or our mind's eye but because he caught the ball as might have been expected. However, this dissociation between the imagination and images is relatively new. Philosophers have traditionally perceived an internal relation between the imagination and images, and the assumption that such a relation exists was common to the rationalists and the empiricists. In addition, both of these schools considered the imagination to be a source of errors and biases. For example, Hume believed that there is nothing more dangerous to reason than flights of the imagination, and that nothing has given rise to more opportunities for error on the part of philosophers (*A Treatise on Human Nature,* book 1, part 4). On the other side, the rationalist Spinoza said something very similar in a famous theorem in the *Ethics* (theorem 41). Spinoza claimed that cognition based upon images and imagination is a source of falsehood. The images, however, no matter how strange they may be, cannot be errors by themselves: they may become errors only when they are accompanied by a judgment (which is a matter of the will). But images seduce us into judging one way rather than another, and thus they contribute to error.

Not every thought, according to the rationalists, is based on images. We have no trouble imagining a triangle, but we are unable to imagine a thousand-sided figure in such a way that it would be distinct in our imagination from a figure with ten thousand sides. It is precisely because we are able to stop thinking in images and think conceptually instead that we are capable of creating an abstract concept of the divinity that is nevertheless not an empty concept. But those people whose thoughts are dependent upon images fall victim to severe corporealizing illusions and errors with respect to the nature of the divinity.

Both rationalists and empiricists believe that the faculty of imagination is a misleading and deceptive cognitive faculty. They differ in their views as to whether people need to use this faculty in their thinking to create visual images.[12] On the issue of the contribution of the imagination to the falsehood of our beliefs about God, however, the contrast is not between the empiricists and the rationalists but between Enlightenment thinkers and Romantics. The Romantics accorded the creative imagination the supreme place in their hierarchy of cognitive faculties, definitely above knowledge acquired through the use of reason. Imagination grants us religious insight, while reason gives us an abstract God rather than a living God. We mention this contrast between Romanticism and the Enlightenment in order to dissociate ourselves from the identification of the Enlightenment

with rationalism, while nevertheless attributing to the Enlightenment the criticism of the faculty of the imagination.

We have inherited from the Eleatics an enigma about the possibility of error, which is essentially the following: in order for a sentence to be meaningful it has to be about reality, that is, some fact
has to fit the sentence. If this is so, then what is a false sentence
about? If, on the one hand, the sentence is about a fact, then this fact
exists and the sentence is not false. If, on the other hand, there is no
fact that fits the false sentence, then it is not false but meaningless.
Therefore it is impossible for a sentence to be false, and so there is
no possibility of error.

Plato's thoughts on error are relevant to our discussion. In his
view error and falsehood are based on wrong combinations.[13] A
wrong combination can occur in a sentence, as in the combination
of words "Theatetus flies": both Theatetus and flying are elements
of reality, but their combination is not an element of reality. An
erroneous combination can also occur within a word, as in the case
of "Pegasus," which is a combination of two ideas that do not go
together—a horse and wings. The paradigm, according to Plato, is
that of a misspelling. Such an error is based on the fact that the
elements of the word (the letters) exist but the combination does not
go together. Similarly, the components of Pegasus—a horse and
wings—are elements of reality, but the combination of the winged
horse is fictional. The creative imagination is responsible for these
fictional combinations and is thus the source of illusion. It is true
that a fictional combination in and of itself does not compel anyone
to believe in it, but it provides the fictional objects for belief.[14]

This argument is a fairly trivial one. It states that the imagination
has the power to represent what does not exist, and if error is the
belief in what does not exist, then the imagination is what provides
us with objects for error. It is still necessary to explain what factor
causes us to believe in the creatures of our imagination: is there
something in the imagination itself that leads us to believe in its
creations? Hume has an answer, which is certainly not trivial but is
doubtfully true, that the degree of our belief is determined by the
degree of vivacity of the images in our mind's eye. It is the vividness
of the image that determines the strength of the belief. Someone
whose mechanism for registering vividness is distorted, such as an
insane person, sees with great vividness images that no one else will

see in this way, and so he is subject to hallucinatory illusions. But this is not only true of insane people and hallucinators. All of us know from our own experience that during a dream we "believe" in the sights of the dream, and the only explanation for this according to Hume is the sights' great vividness. It is the power of the imagination that creates beliefs in us. The explanation for error must be found in the power of the imagination, as it is both the faculty that provides the images and the one that determines their vividness. The vividness of images in ordinary cases is determined not by the creative imagination but by the imitative imagination. The farther we are from the source in reality that creates the image, the more blurred the image will be. But there are people whose creative imagination succeeds in creating within them images that are like the vivid images that a normal person has from a primary impression of something in reality. When this occurs the person is susceptible to illusion, and in the worst case to deceptive hallucinations of the insane.

Hume's discussion, like Aristotle's, is based on the idea that the imagination is dependent upon the formation of images. Although we reject this idea, it remains crucial for understanding the Enlightenment enterprise of criticizing the faculty of the imagination as a separate faculty. It is especially important for our discussion of the imagination as a source of one specific illusion—the idolatrous illusion. The imagination as the ability to form images, and as a continuation of perception, is dependent upon the material. In other words, the source of the imagination, like the source of perception, is in the way material objects act upon us. This "material" character of the imagination has two "idolatrous" effects. One is the tendency to corporealize—to imagine in corporeal terms even those things that are not naturally such. Another is the tendency to multiplicity, since matter is the basis of particularity, and so thought mediated by the imagination is particularized thought. The imagination thus by its very nature leads to the two main elements of idolatrous thought about God: corporeality and multiplicity.

The critique of the imagination as a source of religious illusion does not stop here. It is not dependent upon the problematic assumption of a connection between the imagination and its source in the material world. The question we are asking within the context of the Enlightenment critique of the faculty of the imagination is:

what is actually wrong with living according to the imaginative faculty?

*Living according to the Imaginative Faculty*

Maimonides (*Guide of the Perplexed*, 3:29, 36, 37, 44) and Spinoza (*Introduction to Tractatus Theologico-Politicus*) are useful guides to constructing a worldview on the faculty of imagination. The imagination, according to both of them, is the mental faculty that motivates the masses. Idolatry is the manipulation of the imagination for controlling the masses by means of an image of the world built upon meaningless promises and threats. These promises and threats, in the name of gods and demons that are products of the imagination, constitute a dangerous substitute for a causal understanding of the world.

The faculty of the imagination is activated in an existential situation in which human beings, as finite and limited creatures, live in conditions of uncertainty accompanied by anxieties and fears for the future. An outstanding example of this is the climatic uncertainty confronting farmers—an uncertainty that undermines their basic existential security. Maimonides had good reason to believe that farmers are especially vulnerable to manipulation by means of the imagination, as this faculty is meant to provide solutions for their anxieties. This is the source of the association between agriculture and idolatry perceived by Maimonides, as by Augustine before him.

The order of things, according to this view, is as follows: the uncertainty in our world as human beings is a constant source of fear and anxiety. Increasing or decreasing this fear constitutes an outstanding means of control in the hands of an idolatrous leader. The fear itself increases both the tendency to imagine and the strength of the imagination. The masses are dependent upon their imagination because they lack the critical intellectual faculty required to harness the imagination and attain appropriate causal knowledge.

An immediate counterargument to Maimonides' view is that promises and threats as means of political direction relying on the imagination are not limited to idolatry. Promises of heaven and threats of hell are among the instruments of religious instruction used by the monotheistic religions as well. What differentiates them, in this respect, from idolatry? According to this argument the critique of the imagination should not be confined to the idolatrous religions, but should apply to religion in general.

Maimonides was not unaware of this possibility. His general conception of the Torah commandments provides a possible retort. Maimonides argues again and again (see, for example, 3:29) that "the first intention of the Law as a whole is to put an end to idolatry," where "idolatry" refers to a whole way of life including beliefs, rituals, and magic. If a central idolatrous custom was the placation of the gods by means of sacrifices, consisting mainly of private rituals, then the Torah adopts this means but limits its use (it permits sacrifices only in one temple) and also narrows the categories of the rituals and the reasons for bringing sacrifices. The Torah thus uses the "germs" of idolatry to fight against the "disease" of idolatry.

This immunization model is also appropriate for the description given by Maimonides of the way monotheistic religion uses the faculty of the imagination. The people who make use of the imaginative faculty for religious instruction in monotheistic religion are the prophets. The moral and spiritual virtues required of them in their role as prophets serve as guarantees that their use of the imaginative faculty will not involve gross manipulation of the masses' imagination.

Maimonides' critique of the imaginative faculty, as well as Spinoza's wider critique of it, are replete with inner tension. On the one hand, the imaginative faculty is the source of illusions with respect to the acquisition of the knowledge of causes. On the other hand, it is impossible to avoid making use of it in religious instruction directed at the masses.

## Projection and Errors in Idolatry and Religion

Psychologists, as well as people with common wisdom, see projection as a device for self-defense, for protection from beliefs that are difficult to bear. Thus, for example, it is difficult for a miser to believe that he is one, and so he "projects" his stinginess onto other people: misers tend to see more misers in their surroundings than do spendthrifts. In projection we discover the traits of the projecting person in what he imagines about others. Sometimes projection appears in reverse. If the mechanism of direct projection is the false attribution of one's own characteristics to others, then in reverse projection the person attributes to others characteristics which are opposite to the ones that he should have attributed to himself. Thus, for example, a weak person may use reverse projection to attribute omnipotence to some external force.

Xenophanes regarded the generation of religious concepts, or at least those of folk religion, as the result of direct projection, although he obviously did not use the word "projection" to denote this process. In principle he believed, as mentioned above, that man creates God in his own image.[15] Aristotle (*Politics* 1252b, 24–27) adds to Xenophanes' argument, claiming that people project onto the gods not only their form but also their ways of functioning. Thus they say, for example, that the gods have a king. They imagine that the gods conduct their lives like people. Direct projection is a transparent device, whereas reverse projection is a sophisticated mechanism. We are speaking here, of course, of self-illusion: these are not devices for deceiving others but mechanisms of self-deception.

We must note that this discussion of projection is subject to ambiguity between projection in the sense of the individual who projects his own particular traits onto someone else, and projection in the sense of human beings who generally project human characteristics, or those that the human race is capable of, onto the divinity, whether directly or in reverse. This at any rate is the view of modern religious critics, including Feuerbach, Marx, Nietzsche, and Freud.

Freud stresses the motivational character of reverse projection, whereas Feuerbach stresses the fact that it is an outstanding product of the human faculty of imagination.[16] According to Feuerbach, the imagination is a cognitive mechanism that serves the desires of the heart. Every thought involves abstraction, but the tendency to enliven abstract objects and to reify them as having independent existence is an outstanding activity of the imaginative faculty, which is applied to those abstractions that we are personally interested in. This tendency is central to the strategy of reverse projection according to Feuerbach, but the complexity of the projection mechanism prevents us from recognizing the phenomenon. This complexity is connected with the fact that religious projection, in Feuerbach's view, is a generic type of projection rather than the projection of the individual traits of a particular person.[17]

The religious Enlightenment, which we regard as being represented by thinkers as different as Xenophanes and Maimonides, attributed to the mass of believers anthropomorphic projections from themselves onto the divinity. In the view of these thinkers, a pure belief that has been refined of the dross of anthropomorphism is nevertheless possible. The thinkers of the secular Enlightenment, among whom we include its later disciples, such as Marx and Freud, considered this move of the religious Enlightenment as even more deceptive than the transparent beliefs of the idolatry of the masses. In cases where projection is gross and direct it is easy to uncover its illusionary character. A person who prays anthropomorphically to his idol is relatively easy to convince that he is really praying to himself. It is much more difficult to convince someone whose belief is cloaked in the abstraction of an omnipotent, omniscient, absolutely simple force that he is praying to himself. By praying to himself Feuerbach means that the person is praying to the human essence of man, not that the individual person is unconsciously worshiping his own individual personality.

The peak of monotheistic abstraction is the theory of negative attributes, which we discussed in Chapter 2. This is, in Feuerbach's view, also the peak of religious illusion. It expresses the believer's terror of existence, since every existence is limited and bounded, and uses reverse projection in the form of negative attributes to attribute to God a kind of existence without any limits or bounds.

## Abstraction as a Source of Error

A natural complement to the idea that the imagination is the source of idolatrous error is the claim that failure of abstraction is the cause of false beliefs. The imagination is a faulty substitute for abstraction. It is necessary to distinguish between two versions of the claim that the faculty of abstraction is limited: a radical version and a moderate version. The radical version says that the human race is incapable by its very nature of forging an abstract concept appropriate to the divinity. The moderate version says that the faculty of abstraction is limited not for everyone but only for some people. It is mainly the masses who are limited in their faculty of abstraction, while the elite can use their intellectual talents to form an appropriate conceptualization of the divinity.

We will distinguish three concepts of abstraction and see how each of them is relevant to the claim that the cause of idolatrous error is the failure of abstraction. It should be remembered that there were also people who considered an excess of abstraction to be an idolatrous error—not of mythological religion, to be sure, but of philosophical religion. An excess of abstraction creates the god of the philosophers instead of the God of Abraham, Isaac, and Jacob. The god of the philosophers is the god of philosophical idolatry. One sense of abstraction is pure nonobservational abstraction. The second sense of abstraction is concentration on one aspect—for instance, on the red color of tomatoes, fire engines, and blood to create the concept of red. The concept of red is abstract in this sense, yet it remains an observational concept. The third sense of abstraction is systematic unification.

The failure of abstraction in the first sense leads to idolatrous error, because the concept of God must be abstract in the sense of nonobservational. Since people with a limited faculty of abstraction are not capable of forming nonobservational concepts, they can think of the divinity only in observational terms, and this is the great error of idolatry. In a more refined version of this argument the claim is not that there is a total lack of ability to think in nonobservational terms but that there is an inability to think in the type of nonobservational terms required for the formation of the theistic concept of God. The concept of the number four, for example, is an abstract concept in the sense that it is not observational. The concept of electrons is also abstract in this sense. But whereas electrons enter into causal relationships in time and space, the number four does not enter into such relationships; it enters only into logical and mathematical relationships. The abstractness of God must be of such a nature as to permit a causal influence (at least in the direction from God to the world). On one hand, the abstractness of God is like the abstractness of the number four in the sense that God is not subject to time and space, but on the other hand, it is like the abstractness of the electron in the sense that it causally affects occurrences in time and space. Mental entities are abstract entities that do not exist in space (although they do exist in time), yet they have a causal effect on space. The failure of abstraction, in this view, is the inability to form a concept of the divinity as not being in time and space yet influencing occurrences there.[18]

If we shift our perspective from that of religious epistemology, which underlies the critique of idolatry, to modern anthropology, we reach the second sense of abstraction and find developmental claims stating that monotheistic religious conceptualization requires intermediate stages, such as the concepts of shadow and wind, in order to form our mental concepts. A shadow is visible yet impalpable, while the wind is palpable yet invisible. Through these concepts, as well as the concept of the soul, we reach the concept of the divinity. The religious epistemology underlying the critique of idolatry does not rely on the premise that abstraction is a product of learning from the concrete to the abstract. Some people are capable in a primary sense of forming an appropriate concept of the divinity.[19] The transition from idolatry to monotheism is not a necessary one. On the contrary, the primary concept that Adam had was the concept of monotheism.

The empiricist concept of abstraction as concentration upon a particular aspect is indeed related to the developmental conceptions of learning, but these are not part of the repertoire of religious epistemology underlying the critique of idolatry. After all, children are capable of acquiring the abstract concept "no" without concentrating on a particular aspect of things, so why shouldn't they be able to acquire the concept "God" the same way?

The third sense of abstraction, as systematic unification, is a sense that was used not against idolatry but against the monotheistic religions themselves. The claim changes from one against idolatrous error stemming from the failure of abstraction to a claim of excessive abstraction as a source of monotheistic error, transforming its philosophical version of the concept of the divinity into the concept of the philosophical divinity—which is a pagan concept.

### The Illusion in Abstraction

The critique of the failure of abstraction as a source of idolatrous error is a critique we attribute to the conceptual structure we have been calling the "religious Enlightenment." The secular Enlightenment, as paradigmatically represented by Kant, turns the spotlight on the cognitive tendency to abstraction—in the sense of formal, systematic unification—as a source of the typical religious illusion in the religious Enlightenment's own conception of God. The faculty of abstraction, in one of the important senses of this concept, is not only the source of a more refined conception of the divinity but also a source of cognitive illusions.

One of the flourishing industries in present-day science is the attempt to create a unified theory of all the physical forces: a theory that will unify the gravitational force, the electromagnetic force, the strong nuclear force, and the weak nuclear force. The dizzying success of the unification of the electric force with the magnetic force by James Clerk Maxwell was based upon impressive mathematical analogies in the theories of these forces, analogies that inspired the attempt to unify the two forces. But in the case of the other forces, whose descriptions are apparently very different from one another, what is it that inspires scientists to believe in the unification of these forces and leads them to try to discover a unified theory for them? What is so enchanting about the number one? Why not assume that there are indeed two, three, or four forces in nature that are different from one another?

If Kant had known of our example he would have said that human beings have a definite propensity for increasing unification.[20] This propensity is anchored in the idea that directs our investigations. The pull to unification is not a discovery about the state of affairs in the world but a rule for making discoveries, and as such it is vital and useful. The rule of unification is also liable to be a source of grave cognitive errors, as is attested by religious metaphysics, especially monotheistic metaphysics. We are subject to an illusion when we turn a methodological principle, such as the principle of unification, into a theoretical proposition about the world—when we turn the recommendation "Always unify" into the proposition "There is unity." The illusion is in transforming the rule from a principle organizing the description of reality into a proposition about reality. The monotheistic illusion is based on such an error. The scientific faculty of mind, which Kant calls the intellect, keeps us busy unifying our experiential impressions into general concepts. But this propensity to unification, which makes our cognition possible, continues to operate even when there are no impressions to apply concepts to. It operates on the concepts themselves in an attempt to unify them into a system, and it is this propensity that permits us to create systematic science. Although this ability of the understanding thus brings us an extra dividend, its price is the illusion that we are able to know things that are outside our experience.

The monotheistic illusion is a side effect of the mental faculty of unification.

What connects methodological unification with monotheism? We present this connection through the famous logical fallacy in which it is erroneously inferred that, because every effect has a cause, there must be one cause that is the cause of all the effects. (It is as if we inferred that because every girl is loved by a boy, there must be one boy who loves all the girls.) The propensity to this fallacy is a product of the search for the final cause—the cause of all the causes, the one unconditional source of all things. The search for the unconditional is a search for an explanation ("syllogism") with absolute premises, that is, premises that are not derived from more basic ones. The cognitive propensity to unification through the discovery of the unconditional is the same in principle as the propensity to religious unification in the form of monotheism. Kant's argument is not an argument against the truth of the idea of the monotheistic God. Rather, it is an argument against the cognitive justification for this monotheistic belief, which constitutes an illusion.

### Excessive Abstraction

Let us turn to the critique of abstraction from another direction. The abstraction of the concept of God transforms him from the God of Abraham, Isaac, and Jacob into the philosopher's God, which is an abstract and not vital God. This argument is also brought by philosophers with fideistic tendencies, such as Blaise Pascal and the twentieth-century theorist Miguel di Unamuno. According to the critics of the religious Enlightenment, the gods of the idolaters are actually closer to the abstract God of the philosophers than is the God of the monotheistic religions. In any case at least one fact cannot be denied: it was precisely in the idolatrous community in Greece that the philosophical concept of the divinity was invented; the thinkers of the religious Enlightenment only imported the concept from those idolaters. According to this argument, the God that appears in the Bible is a living God and not the abstract God of the philosophers, and the concept of an abstract divinity should not be inserted into the Bible. Just as it is ridiculous to attribute a belief in the existence of only one girl in the world to a boy who says to his girl, "You are the only one in the world, there is no one else but you," so it is ridiculous to read transcendentality and abstraction into biblical verses of the sort "Even the heavens to their uttermost reaches cannot contain you" (I Kings 8:27). The God of the historical monotheistic religions is not an abstract God, and he does not fulfill the characteristics that the scholars of the religious Enlightenment borrowed from philosophy. The abstraction of God is just as much an idolatrous error as the corporealization of him in an idol.

Searching for the causes of idolatrous error is part of understanding the arguments against idolatry. The point of view that interests us most is that of the monotheistic religions, especially of the trend that we call the religious Enlightenment. But our discussion also includes other points of view, especially that of the general Enlightenment, which considers the causes of idolatrous error to be the causes of religious illusions in general—monotheistic as well as polytheistic. We also include in this point of view those who aspire to present an "objective and scientific" viewpoint concerning religion, such as Feuerbach and Freud, since the liberating role they ascribe to the discovery of the causes of illusion is typical of Enlightenment thought.

We have already mentioned the idea that the act of searching for the causes of idolatrous error is a polemical act. It is based on the idea that the pagan viewpoint is so absurd that we should not bother to look for the reasons that brought people to hold it but instead should determine the causes or motives that led them to maintain this groundless point of view. The critique of religion in the general Enlightenment turned this very procedure against religion itself, where the justification for this step is the "Feuerbach thesis" (as it was aptly named by Bernard Williams). According to this thesis, if there is no God or gods, then there is no point in explaining the beliefs and it is only worthwhile to explain the believers. Explaining the believers must be done in terms of causes and motives rather than reasons.

A reason for a belief is a proposition whose truth implies the truth of the belief or whose truth makes the truth of the belief more probable. A motive for a belief is an interest that the believer has in its truth—an interest that is a cause of his belief, since otherwise the mere fact of the existence of such an interest is irrelevant to the truth of the belief. There are also causes—in the narrow sense—of belief:

for example, the explanation for belief offered by the fact that the believer had consumed alcohol.

The causes and motives for belief in idols are not exhausted by the imagination and ancestral custom. We have mentioned other factors, such as sexual license and fear, and later we will discuss additional factors, such as "stiff-neckedness." All these factors play an important role in the explanation of idolatrous error, but they can be subsumed under two basic factors: fear together with imagination and "stiff-neckedness" together with ancestral custom on the other.

The attempt to reduce the idolatrous viewpoint to its causes must also provide an explanation for the attraction of this viewpoint. Sexual license and promises based on the imagination have only paved the way for such an explanation. The polemics against idolatry lack any explanation for its attraction.

# 5

## The Wrong God

According to the view that idolatry is about false belief, the prototypical manifestation of idolatrous error is the belief in a "wrong" god in place of the "right" God. But how can we determine what is intended by the "wrong" belief? How can we distinguish one object of idolatrous belief from another, and how can we distinguish the objects of idolatrous belief from the object of monotheistic belief?

Augustine claimed that Varo, who was considered the most learned person in ancient Rome, believed that when people worshiped one god without the use of idols they were worshiping Jupiter.[1] But Moses certainly worshiped one God, without the use of idols: was he then worshiping Jupiter? Is Jupiter like the rose which "by any other name would smell as sweet"? Let us call the problem of the identification of the "right" God (the God of Moses) with a "wrong" god (Jupiter) Augustine's problem (even though it is really the problem of the idolater Varo rather than the monotheist Augustine). The reverse procedure, the identification of a "wrong" god with the "right" God, became Hegel's problem: in his lectures on religion Hegel describes a bitter controversy between two Catholic orders on the question of whether the Chinese, who worship a god whose name in translation is "Heaven" or "Lord," worship the right God.[2]

The church had been aware of this issue for centuries. The question confronting the church was whether it was permitted for missionaries to accommodate the

Chinese god to the Christian God as missionary camouflage. Pope Clement V disqualified what he saw as cynical accommodationism that blurred the identity of the right God. The question is whether the identification of one god with another is an objective matter or a matter of political judgment.[3]

It seems that not only Jesuit missionaries were faced with the problem: even Abraham, the father of monotheistic belief, had confronted it. At the end of the war of the four kings against the five kings (Genesis 14) the priest Melchizedek greeted Abraham with the blessing, "Blessed be Abram of God Most High [*El Elyon*], Creator of heaven and earth" (Genesis 14:19), where *El Elyon* was the name of the Canaanite god, whose title was "Creator of heaven and earth." Abraham then made the bold identification of this Canaanite god with his own God, swearing an oath to the king of Sodom with the words, "I swear to the Lord, God Most High, Creator of Heaven and earth" (Genesis 14:22), where "the Lord" is the personal name of Abraham's God. Did Melchizedek intend to speak of Abraham's God in his greeting to Abraham? Was Abraham a political accommodationist or a metaphysical believer? The attitude of the Bible and the sages is clear: Abraham is the father of belief and not the father of accommodationism. But the question remains: is the identification of one god with another a matter of metaphysics or of politics?

Rousseau believed that the issue was clearly a political one, and he ridiculed attempts to present it as an objective issue:

> How ridiculous is the scholarship in our day, whose only interest is to identify the gods of the various nations. As if it were possible for Moloch, Saturn and Chronos to be one god! As if it were possible for the Baal of the Sidonese, the Zeus of the Greeks, and the Jupiter of the Romans to be God Himself! As if fictional creatures with different names could have anything in common![4]

Rousseau thought that the idolatrous religions were civic religions, each nation with its own god, and that the identity of the gods was determined by the identity of the nations. Actually, in Rousseau's view, the identity of a god is like the identity of a national flag: just as the identity of a flag is determined by the nation it serves, so is the identity of a god determined by the nation it belongs to. Rousseau regarded the attempt to identify gods with one another as an activity of the Greeks, who considered themselves the masters of the world and so imagined that they saw their own gods everywhere.

But Rousseau was mistaken. The identification of gods with one another was not a Greek invention that was imitated by ridiculous contemporary scholars. The early Mesopotamians had already based their treaties on the identification of the gods of different nations; the gods were the guarantors of the treaties, which were signed by foreign cities and states.[5] This did not mean that each god should be responsible for the signatories on his side keeping the agreement—for example, that the Hittite god should be responsible for the Hittites and the Babylonian god for the Babylonians. Rather, it meant that the Hittite god and the Babylonian god were considered by the signatories to the treaty to be the very same god—and it was this god who was supposed to supervise the fulfillment of the treaty. The identifications that were accepted as a result of these treaties were sometimes far-reaching indeed—for example, the identification of the Hittite god Ra'am with the Egyptian god Amon. The question that remains open is how these legal identifications should be understood: do they express the metaphysical belief that they are really speaking about the same god under different names or merely a convenient legal–political convention not based on any metaphysical belief?

Our claim is that the identification of gods with one another, and sometimes even the identity of the gods themselves, do have political characteristics, but these are neither exclusive nor necessary. Rousseau's argument is nevertheless important, especially in the context of religious syncretism, which is often created by far-reaching identifications of the objects of worship and belief. This is especially blatant in the case of identifications based on a superficial similarity in the sounds of the gods' names, like the identification of Isis with Io. The accepted historical explanation for phenomena of syncretistic eclecticism is the political one, and it reminds us of the explanations for the arranged marriages between royal dynasties. However, syncretism can also serve as a religious viewpoint in its own right. In such a case the differences between the gods are perceived as differences between aspects of the divinity. The syncretism of Far Eastern religions often seems to have such a character.

From the point of view of the monotheistic religions, syncretism involving the right deity suffers from the idolatrous error of co-deification. But the question of who is worshiped in a syncretistic ritual is not simple. It is not clear how the identity of the "right" God is supposed to be preserved in such a form of worship. Evidence for this problem may be found in the strange story told in II Kings (chapter 17) about the "lion converts," those nations that were settled in Samaria by the king of Assyria in place of the Israelites of the northern kingdom, who had been exiled from there. These nations "did not worship the Lord; so the Lord sent lions against them" (II Kings 17:24), until a religious teacher was sent to teach them the proper worship of the God of Israel. The story describes in detail how each of these nations also worshiped their own gods in cult places they set up in Samaria: "The Babylonians made Succoth-benoth, and the men of Cuth made Nergal" (II Kings 17:30), for instance, each nation having its own gods, with the result that "they worshiped [literally, "feared"] the Lord while serving their own gods" (II Kings 17:33). The question is, did these nations worship the God of Israel in addition to worshiping their own gods, or did they worship the God of Israel by means of worshiping their own gods, or did they worship their gods and only fear the God of Israel? In any case the question remains as to whom they were really worshiping.

## Whom Do Idolaters Worship?

An important model of idolatry is the worship of the heavenly bodies. At first glance it would seem that there is nothing simpler than locating the object of worship of astral worshipers: the identity of their gods is the identity of the heavenly bodies.[6] A Japanese who worshiped the goddess of the sun and an ancient Egyptian who worshiped the god of the sun were therefore worshiping the very same entity—namely, the sun. At first blush there would seem to be no distinction between the statement that the Japanese and the Egyptian were both bowing down to the sun and the statement that the Japanese and the Egyptian were both shading themselves from the sun; it is obviously the same sun. It is possible that in each of these cultures people shaded themselves from the sun in different ways, say, the Japanese with parasols and the Egyptians with thatched roofs. In the same sense one might say that in spite of the different modes of ritual worship, the object of worship—the sun—is the same entity.

One of the attractions of idolatry is that its objects are visible to the eye and easy to identify. The idolater is characterized in the Bible as someone who "strays after the sights of his eyes," and it is thus no wonder that he chooses objects like the sun and the moon, which are easy to identify. It is this ease that leads him, in the view of the monotheist, to his great error: the error of confusing the creator and his creations. The visible object is merely the creation, whereas the creator is invisible. But in spite of the difficulty of identifying him, he and only he must be worshiped. The argument of the ease of identification of the objects of worship depends upon the assumption that the gods are identified with the heavenly bodies. The obvious question then is whether it is justified, on the basis of the sun worshipers' beliefs, to identify the sun with the god of the sun. In other words, does the sun worshiper believe that he is worshiping the sun or the god of the sun?

Frege asked why the identity statement "The morning star is the morning star" is trivial, whereas the identity statement "The morning star is the evening star" provides us with information that is not trivial at all, information that requires a knowledge of astronomy in order to ascertain its truth.[7] The linguistic expressions "the evening star" and "the morning star" denote the same heavenly body—the planet Venus—and the second identity statement transmits the information that the star seen in the west at twilight and the star seen in the east at dawn are the same entity. Frege's famous answer is that the representations of the star, once as "the evening star" and once as "the morning star," are different, and if we are told that these two different expressions represent the very same entity, then clearly we are being given information of great value. The nonmetaphorical interpretation of the concept of "representation" is formulated by Frege in terms of the difference between the sense and the reference of expressions. "The evening star" is an expression with a different sense from that of "the morning star," even though the reference of the two expressions is identical.

In light of the above we would expect that if the Greeks, for example, had found out that Hesperus (the evening star) and Phosphorus (the morning star) were identical, and they really identified their god with the star, then they would have identified the gods Hesperus and Phosphorus with each other and considered them to be one god. But if they continued to consider Hesperus and Phosphorus two different gods, as was apparently what actually happened, then this shows that they did not identify the star with the god. They were apparently not considered one god even though it was discovered that they were both "embodied" in the same star.[8]

If the star and the god cannot simply be identified with each other, then what is the relation between them? How can the relation between a star and a god be described? One solution that seems appropriate to us, even though it has an anachronistic ring, is to regard the god as an institution and the star as the building in which the institution is housed. The institution's building is often a convenient way of identifying the institution, but obviously the institution's identity will be preserved even if it is moved to another building. This is true of the god as well: it can move from star to star without affecting its identity in the least. There are different degrees of connection between a god and "its" star. Thus, for example, Venus, the Roman goddess of love, was closely associated with the planet Venus, while Aphrodite, who is identified with Venus, is perceived in Greek mythology as having a weaker connection with this planet. The stars are thus a means for identifying the gods but are not necessarily elements that constitute their identity. From this we may infer that the astral worshipers are not necessarily worshiping the stars any more than the worshipers of the God of Israel, who swear by the name of heaven and direct their prayers to heaven, are worshiping the heavens.[9]

Let us return to the comparison of gods with institutions. Imagine that archaeologists and historians of the fortieth century have found many artifacts from the twentieth century and are bothered by the question of what the label "Ford" denoted. They encounter the name in various contexts: many times on remnants of automobiles, and sometimes also on signs in offices and factories. Ford as a company is not an easy thing to describe. It has many labels, which are convenient to use, but the conditions of its identity are complicated. At any rate it is clear to those archaeologists that they must not identify Ford with the main office building whose ruins have been discovered. Analogously, the goddess of love may also be regarded as a company. Her identity, like that of Ford, depends largely on functional components and less on material components. The relation between this goddess and the planet Venus is analogous to the relation between Ford and its main office building, or perhaps its main factory.

An alternative model for the relation between a god and its associated star is the relation between the mind and the body, where the god is the mind and the star is the body. The god dwells in the star as the mind dwells in the body. The identification of the god through the star is like the identification of a person through his body. A person's identity is determined by his mind, but he is identified by his body: the body provides convenient signs for identification but not the criteria for identity. This is, of course, only one of the views of the personal identity of human beings, but even if one rejects it as a view of personal identity, it can still serve as a model for the relation between the god and the star. The crucial element in the idolatrous view as it is conceived according to the mind-body model is the conception of the gods as persons possessing will and mobility, while the stress on action or role is secondary. (In those cases where the role is crucial we find a division of labor among the gods. For example, while Helios is the god of the sun, the task of spreading the sun's light has its own god, Apollo, the god of light.) When a god is described as being fixed to a star, the fixed relation is generally a punishment for rebellion, which transforms the god into an entity lacking freedom and limited in the realization of its desires. More than one story has been told about gods, or active angels, or even human heroes, who were transformed into stars nailed into the firmament as a result of their hubris. But even in these cases, where the stars are the gods' prison cells, the relation between the god and the star is not like the relation between Lot's wife and the pillar of salt or between Lenin and his mummified body in the mausoleum. The star is perceived as a fixed manifestation of the god, as a limitation on its freedom of action, but not as its death.[10]

We have discussed three different models for the relation between a god and "its" star: the star as identical with the god, the star as the institution housing the god, and the star-god relation as analogous to the mind-body relation. Which of these models does justice to the beliefs of astral worshipers? In addition to this question we must also ask which model does justice to the observer's belief about the beliefs of these idolaters—with the recognition that not all observers of astral worshipers are alike. The anthropologist studying a tribal religion does not have the same beliefs as the missionary who is trying to convert the tribe. We can put it roughly this way: the view that the god of the sun is identical with the sun is the view that the monotheist attributes to the idolater. The view of institutional identity between them is the attribution of the neutral observer. But it is the view of the mind–body relation as the model for the relation between the god of the sun and the sun that is apparently closest to the view of the sun worshiper himself.

## Intentional Identity

An observer of astral worshipers is interested in stating propositions, such as the fact that the ancient Egyptians worshiped the sun god and the Japanese also believed in it, although such a god does not really exist. Propositions of this sort attest that the issue is one of intentional identity rather than actual identity. The task of the observer is not to discover the identity of the gods, as he does not believe in gods. His intention is to find and identify the thoughts and beliefs of astral worshipers and of idolaters in general.

Philosophers have discussed the issue of the intentional identity of fictitious names like "Sherlock Holmes," names that are considered both by their users and by neutral observers to be fictional. The situation we are dealing with is a different one. The observer of idolaters generally believes that the gods are nonentities and that their names are empty and fictitious, but this is not the opinion of the idolaters who use these names. The observer is aware that the reference of these names is not empty in the eyes of the believers. Thus the issue is one of intentional identity for the observer but actual identity for the believer. As observers we correctly attribute beliefs and intentions about the gods to their worshipers. We are interested in attributing the right sort of ontological commitment to the idolaters, without having any ontological commitments to these gods ourselves, as observers. This exceptional state of affairs must be considered a constraint on any account of intentional identity involving gods.

We now examine the suggestion, inspired by G. E. Moore, that is intended to fulfill the requirement of the attribution of intentional identity to idolaters by their observers.[11] According to this suggestion, the ancient Egyptians and the medieval Japanese worshiped the same sun god if and only if the following conditions obtain: (1) There is a causal relation between the descriptions attributed to the Japanese sun god and the descriptions attributed to the Egyptian sun god. (2) There is a substantial similarity between the descriptions of the two gods. (We must note that the causal relation may be a mediated one. If, for example, the descriptions of Astarte had a historical influence on the descriptions of Aphrodite, which in turn influenced the descriptions of Venus, then there is a causal relation between Astarte and Venus.)

A cursory inspection of the two conditions shows clearly that the sun god of the Japanese was different from the sun god worshiped by the Egyptians, since the causal condition does not appear to be fulfilled.[12] As to the similarity between their descriptions, the fact that the medieval Japanese spoke about a goddess while the Egyptians spoke about a god apparently attests that there is not enough similarity between the two. The difference between a god and a goddess is not necessarily crucial, and for the purpose of assessing similarity it may sometimes be considered superficial, but under normal circumstances it is nevertheless an important difference. Still, in spite of our cursory conclusion, we ought to pause for an additional and deeper clarification of both the causal and the similarity conditions.

### The Causal Condition

Our clarification of the issue of the causal relation between descriptions of the Egyptian god and the Japanese goddess relates to the question of whether the sun itself cannot serve as the one causal source of the two sets of descriptions. Couldn't the sun itself, in its daily journey across the sky from east to west, cause two cultures that have no historical connections between them to describe their sun god similarly? We must clarify whether the causal condition we require is a general causal condition, which includes the relation of inspiration from a common source, or a more narrow condition of historical causality. A historical relation is necessarily a causal relation but not vice versa.

Let us assume that in nineteenth-century Japan there developed, independently of Western science, a physics which was parallel in principle to the one that developed in the West, and let us further assume that this physics included among its elements the ether as a space-filling entity. Moreover, we assume that the ether in the Japanese view was considered a medium through which the forces of gravity, electricity, and magnetism travel, and that these forces affect other bodies even at a distance. Adding the assumption that there was no contact whatsoever between the Japanese physics of the ether and Western physics, we find that in such a case we could not say that "the ether itself" constituted the causal stimulus that brought about the creation of a parallel physics in the two places. The question that needs to be asked is whether the Japanese and the Western scientists intended the same ether. Let us put it another way: how can we evaluate a claim such as "The Western scientists believed that the ether filled space, and the Japanese scientists also believed that it filled space"?

To answer these questions and make some progress on the issue of the causal relation, we will employ the distinction between a singular description and an exclusive description. A singular description is a definite description whose reference is context-dependent. For example, "the president of the United States" is a singular description, as it refers to the incumbent president, whereas in the past it referred to other people. An exclusive description, in contrast, is a definite description that is not context-dependent. An exclusive description must be understood as a kind of conditional description: if the thing that is described by the description exists, then the description refers to this thing in every context.

When the subject of discussion is two cultures with no historical connections between them, and they have similar beliefs about something that they both describe with the same exclusive description, then there is an intentional identity between the foci of their beliefs; in other words, the beliefs are about the same thing. The ether in our story is an example of this; God under a certain interpretation may be another example. But let us leave God and return to the sun god. The upshot of our argument is that if the descriptions of the sun god are exclusive descriptions to both the Egyptians and the Japanese, then the sun god must be judged in the same way as the ether. If, however, the descriptions are singular but not exclusive, then the two cultures do not have the same intentional focus.

## The Similarity Condition

The other condition for intentional identity is the similarity condition.[13] Although both conditions for intentional identity were formulated from the point of view of observers of idolaters, we begin with the question of the similarity judgments of the idolaters themselves. For them the question of whether other believers worship their god is likely to have great significance. What degree of similarity in the descriptions is required in order for their answer to this question to be positive?

Within religious communities there are two opposing trends. One assigns great weight to common characteristics; the other assigns great weight to distinguishing characteristics. The first trend is dominant in religions that seek support for their belief far and wide, that consider themselves supported by the fact that people have reached the same belief in unexpected places, a sort of "great believers think alike" theory. The opposing trend is reflected in a religious community's tendency to exclusivity, in its tendency not to allow others to join its ideological heritage and to show its believers that there is something unique in their beliefs that is for their own exclusive benefit.

Similarity judgments are thus partly a product of the religious ideology itself, as it tells the believer how much weight to give to the common and to the distinctive. It is possible, for example, to imagine that the Japanese, living on an isolated island, might develop a consciousness of extreme exclusivity that would lead to profound insult at the very comparison of their sun goddess with the Egyptian sun god, as if they could be "the same thing." But the opposite reaction is equally possible to imagine: the Japanese might be imbued with a universal or ecumenical consciousness, and they might want support for their belief from the fact that others, especially early societies, also "saw the light" and believed in the same god. Such a consciousness would tend to lessen the weight of differences and find similarities between things that are far apart. It would assign very little weight, for instance, to the difference in the gender of the Egyptian sun god and the Japanese sun goddess.

Let us return to the issue of similarity judgments from the point of view of observers of idolaters. A "point of view" is a metaphorical expression whose meaning in the present context includes differences in ontological commitment and differences in emphasis and attention that are reflected in differences in similarity judgments. Attributing different points of view to observers of idolaters means attributing to them different ontological commitments and different similarity judgments. And indeed, a historian of religion is not the same as a scholar of comparative religion. It may be presumed that the historian will give great weight to the condition of causal-historical identity: he will refuse to identify clusters of descriptions as descriptions of the same god if there is no historical connection between them. The scholar of comparative religion, in contrast, will probably concentrate on the structural similarity between the descriptions and assign it decisive weight. For this scholar, the fact that Amon-Ra, the Egyptian sun god, traverses the heavenly ocean in a boat traveling from east to west does not distinguish it substantially from Helios, who according to Greek tradition traversed the same path in a chariot of fire instead. The east-west trajectory and the vehicle will be, for this scholar, the decisive similarity between the stories, and the difference between a boat and a chariot will most likely not seem particularly important to him.

In similarity judgments between gods it is their descriptions that are compared. We have mentioned that there is a similarity between Aphrodite-descriptions and Venus-descriptions. Aphrodite-descriptions do not require the name "Aphrodite" to appear in the description, nor do descriptions of any other god. "The scheming daughter of Zeus" is Sappho's Aphrodite-description. It is not, however, always easy in concrete instances to decide if a given description is an Aphrodite-description or a Venus-description. It would seem that we are caught in a vicious circle. In order to decide whether Aphrodite and Venus are identical we need their descriptions. But isn't it also true that in order to decide which is an Aphrodite-description and which is a Venus-description we need to know independently who Aphrodite is and who Venus is?

The error in this argument about the circularity of identification may be understood through Nelson Goodman's theory that a Venus-description should not be seen as a description of Venus. That a certain description is characterized as a Venus-description does not mean that there exists a Venus of whom it is a description.[14] In the expression "Venus-description" the term "Venus" has no independent meaning because the entire expression is one linguistic unit. In technical language we would say that "Venus-description," according to Goodman's suggestion, is a one-place predicate rather than a relational term. To determine what a Venus-description is, there is no need to identify Venus as a precondition. On the contrary, the determination of who Venus is and how she differs from Aphrodite relies on Venus-descriptions.

There is nevertheless a difficulty here: if the term "Venus" in the expression "Venus-description" has no independent meaning, then it must also lack independent meaning in the expressions "Venus-statues" and "Venus-paintings," and it is thus not evident how all three expressions are connected. It is clear that the relation among these terms is not like the relation (or, more precisely, the lack of relation) among the various appearances of "par" in the terms "party," "pardon," and "parsimonious." There is, of course, a very strong connection among Venus-descriptions, Venus-statues, and Venus-paintings. And our claim is that Venus's identity is determined partly by the commonality (say, golden hair) among the descriptions, statues, and paintings, rather than the reverse.

Another criticism of the determination of intentional identity on the basis of the similarity between descriptions is the following argument. During the history of any religion far-reaching changes occur over time in the descriptions of its God or gods. This is true of the idolatrous religions, and it is equally true of the monotheistic religions. The history of the Israelite belief, for example, is partly a history of changes and transformations in the descriptions of God. If God's identity depends on the descriptions, then who can guarantee that the biblical Moses and Moses Maimonides and Moses Mendelssohn all worshiped the same God? This is even truer of idolaters, as in the idolatrous religions the descriptions change at a much faster pace, because of the lack of sacred scriptures to guarantee a modicum of continuity in the descriptions. And if even within a given tradition the descriptions of the divinity undergo changes, sometimes even far-reaching ones, then how can we justify the claim that the focus of the beliefs in the tradition is preserved unchanged? And if this focus really is preserved unchanged, isn't that enough to disprove the claim that it is the descriptions that determine identity? Yes, but there is a more efficient method of preserving the continuity of intentional identity, and this is the continuous use of a proper name.[15]

## Definite Descriptions and the Tetragrammaton

A name is not shorthand for a definite description or cluster of descriptions. In the usual sort of historical transmission a name does its work by itself without accompanying descriptions that are liable to undergo noticeable changes. The work of a name is the preservation of the focus of intentionality of its users. The picture of the transmission of names in a historical chain of tradition is well known from Saul Kripke's theory. Kripke, however, was speaking about the preservation of the reference of a real name. The question here concerns the role of the chain of tradition of a name with intentional identity. From the perspective of a tradition of believers, the picture of the chain of tradition of a proper name is very tempting, thus we ascribe it to Maimonides. But from the agnostic observer's point of view the picture is not clear at all.

If there was a first use of the tetragrammaton as the name of God, whether at the time of Enosh ("It was then that men began to invoke the Lord by name," Genesis 4:26) or at the time of Moses, in the eyes of nonbelievers this was not a primary act of calling a real entity by name. The identity of a name's reference is partly dependent upon what is identified as its chain of tradition, but this is itself a problematic issue. There is an obvious sense in which Saul of Tarsus was closer to the sages of the Great Assembly than Moses Maimonides was, but the Jewish tradition does not regard Saul of Tarsus as belonging to it. On the contrary, he is regarded as someone who directed his worship toward an alien god, one of whose attributes is being the father of a son, and this put Saul of Tarsus outside the tradition of people who direct their worship toward the God of Israel. By contrast, Mohammed, even though he is not connected with Jewish tradition in the way that Saul of Tarsus is, nevertheless is regarded as someone who directed his worship toward the same God that the Jewish people worship. (This is, at least, the view of Maimonides.) An agnostic observer will therefore have his doubts about the picture of names transmitted by tradition as being guarantors of intentional identity. The use of names fixed by tradition cannot attest to anything but the fact that the people who regard themselves as belonging to this tradition intend the use of these names to denote whatever their predecessors in the tradition denoted by these names. This is not, however, a guarantee that they are actually intending the same object, if the accompanying descriptions have changed significantly.

Believers and agnostics obviously differ a great deal in their religious views, but they also differ in their semantic views. The agnostic is prepared to consider the use of proper names of God that are transmitted by tradition from one generation to the next as evidence that people within this tradition have the second-order intention to intend what their predecessors in the tradition intended. However, the agnostic does not think that what these predecessors believed necessarily has any clear sense. Those who belong to the tradition have a first-order belief that they are actually intending the same thing that their ancestors intended.

The question remains as to whether there is a difference in intention, whether first-order or second-order, between a name and a description. For this we turn, following Geach, to the interesting case of the senile believer.[16] Suppose that during an election we encounter a senile man who claims that he is a firm supporter of George Bush for president, because he always votes for the Democratic candidate and Bush is such a fine democrat. Aside from having been an excellent governor, Bush was a spectacular pilot during World War II and head of the CIA—and it's also nice that he's of Greek origin. In short, the man is hopelessly confused between the attributes of Bush and Dukakis. Moreover, he says that he will be voting for Bush as the Democratic candidate. In the face of this confusion, can it really be said that this senile man is a supporter of Bush?

Geach thinks that from the point of view of a believing Christian no members of any other religion can be considered believers in the true God, even improper believers. They must be considered like the senile voter, in that it is not clear what beliefs to ascribe to them or what they believe in. The senile man cannot be considered to be in error, since in order for a person to make a mistake there must be a focus for his belief, so that it can be considered false rather than meaningless.

Our question is whether there is a difference between the following two possible cases concerning the senile voter: the case in which he says he is supporting the Democratic candidate, and it turns out that he is ascribing to the Democratic candidate a cluster of attributes some of which describe Bush while others describe Dukakis; and the case in which he says he is supporting Bush, and it turns out that he is ascribing to Bush some attributes that describe him and others that describe Dukakis. Our opinion is that there is a difference. We would say that in the case where the senile voter uses the expression "the Democratic candidate" we have no idea which of the two he intends and we must state that he is hopelessly confused, while in the case where he uses the name "Bush" we would consider him to be in error about some of the attributes he is ascribing to Bush but we would nevertheless say that it is Bush he is describing. When proper names are involved we would tend to continue speaking about error rather than confusion. The difference, once more, is between someone who knows what he is talking about but is mistaken about what he ascribes to it, and someone who is so confused that he no longer knows what he is talking about. It is possible that the senile voter has knowledge of Bush from actual acquaintance with him but is confused about his attributes. This semantic intuition is, however, especially problematic when proper names of the divinity are involved, since the very idea of knowledge of God by acquaintance is vulnerable to the charge of idolatry.

## Idolatrous Error as Category Mistake

According to Maimonides the identity of the reference of worship is dependent solely on description. In the case of a false description in the worshiper's mind, a second-order intention of the worshiper to direct his worship to the God of Abraham, Isaac, and Jacob, would not save the worship from being a worship to a false God. What is crucial in constituting the identity is the description that is held by each individual worshiper. Paradoxically Maimonides' negative theology establishes severe constraints on providing such a description. What is the way to refer to God assuming on the one hand the importance of description and on the other hand the restrictions on description, and what is the role of God's proper name in such a case?

Although we introduced the subject of negative theology in Chapter 2, here we present a more daring version of the topic and its relation to Maimonides' thought. We must stress that negative theology represents only one possible interpretation of Maimonides' theory, and perhaps not even the most obvious one. We nevertheless believe that our radical interpretation is not only a possible interpretation but also an important one for understanding Maimonides' thought.

According to Aristotle's characterization, theological sentences are sentences that are about God. According to Maimonides they are all category mistakes.[17] Someone who utters such a sentence simply doesn't know what he is talking about. Someone who claims that Aristotle was blind is making a mistake, but it is a mistake of fact. In contrast, someone who claims that the wall is blind is making not a factual mistake but a category mistake. This is, at any rate, what Aristotle might have said and what Maimonides followed. Someone who says that the wall is blind is not saying something false but something meaningless, because walls do not belong to the category of things to which the expressions "seeing" or "blind" may be applied. Even though there is no syntactic fault in the sentence "the wall sees," it is ontologically disqualified: walls and seeing belong to categories that do not coincide. All this is true, of course, on the condition that we are speaking about the literal use of these expressions. If we use these expressions metaphorically, as in the sentence "The wall has ears," then we are not making a category mistake but expressing a different meaning.

Maimonides thought that sentences of the type "God is gracious" or "God is wise" in their literal sense have no cognitive meaning. The error in such sentences is worse than falsity, because false sentences have meaning while such sentences do not. This would seem to obliterate the distinction between idolatrous and monotheistic sentences, as any error in the literal ascription of a positive attribute to God is considered an idolatrous error. And if man's purpose is the true understanding of the divinity, then someone who adopts sentences such as "God is wise" in their literal sense is considered not a believer but a confused person—and perhaps even an irreparably confused person.

Maimonides discussed the example of a person who acquires information about an elephant that may confuse him irreparably. When he asks what an elephant is, he is told that it is a winged marine animal with one foot. Such a person, in Maimonides' view, lives under the illusion that he knows what an elephant is, but this is not true: if this is the information he has, then he has no idea what an elephant is. However, the person who asks this question about the elephant and receives this false information is not making a category mistake with respect to the elephant, since he is told that it is an animal. If he had been told that the elephant was a prime number, then his mistake would be a category mistake—and that is the sort of mistake that Maimonides is discussing. Therefore Maimonides' example is misleading.

The difference between falsity of the sort "The elephant is a marine animal" and category mistakes of the sort "The elephant is a prime number" is enhanced when these sentences are negated.[18] While "The elephant is not a marine animal" is not only a meaningful sentence but an obviously true one, the sentence "The elephant is not a prime number" remains meaningless, just like the original sentence it is negating. In the same way, the negation of a theological sentence that is a category mistake, such as "God is wise," yields the sentence "God is not wise," which is also meaningless. Nevertheless, in Maimonides' view there is an important difference between the original sentence and its negation. Among the two meaningless sentences, "God is wise" and "God is not wise," it is permitted to make use only of the positive form of the sentence; only this form creates within the person the proper attitude of respect for the deity, whereas the negative form creates an attitude of disrespect. The distinction between these two sentences is therefore didactic rather than cognitive. The phrase "God is wise" satisfies our conceptions of perfection. Even though these conceptions are not cognitively appropriate to the matter that the sentence is about, within the framework of our limitations this is the best we can do where the deity is involved.[19]

According to Maimonides theological sentences do not have a meaningful literal interpretation. They do not even have a meaningful analogical interpretation. There is no meaning relation between the word "wise" in the phrase "God is wise" and the word "wise" in the phrase "Solomon is wise." It is not only the case that "God is wise" is not analogical to "Solomon is wise," but there is no commonality at all between them, not even of polysemy. There is only homonymy here, without any meaning relation. In this radical interpretation the theory of negative attributes is not about an analogical or metaphorical understanding of theological sentences. A metaphorical interpretation of a theological sentence assumes that there are other theological sentences that can be used to paraphrase the metaphorical sentence, but then we would have to assume that the paraphrasing theological sentences are not themselves category mistakes, and this assumption contradicts Maimonides' view. Moreover, in the metaphorical interpretation of a sentence the literal meanings of the words in the sentence contribute to the understanding of its metaphorical meaning, while this is not true in cases of homonymy. If the word "stick" is a homonym for "piece of wood" and "cling," then the use of the word in the sentence "He threw the stick to the dog" does not help us understand the meaning of "stick" in the sentence "The stamp won't stick to the envelope." What then, in Maimonides' view, is the logical form of theological sentences? What is the correct analysis of a sentence such as "God is living" in light of this radical understanding of the theory of negative attributes, which bars any analogical, derived, or even metaphorical interpretation?

As a first step, it must be understood that God does not belong to the category of things about which one can say that they are living or dead: such attributes do not apply to God at all. The second step is to choose the term "living" in preference to the term "dead" because it expresses an appropriate attitude toward the divinity—in spite of the fact that one cannot consider it a description of reality. The third step in the analysis involves the realization that the ordinary meaning of the term "living" is not a guide to the understanding of the true meaning of a theological sentence, in which the term "living" applies to God in an exclusive manner that no other substance can share. When the sentence is given its correct logical form, the term "living" not only appears in a different meaning from the accepted one but also applies to a different syntactic category from the ordinary one: "living" is no longer an attribute but a name or to be more precise a title. We must explain both the lack of common meaning in the application of the term and the shift from attribute to name.

The definite description "the capital of West Germany" denotes the city of Bonn at the time this is being written. It is nevertheless easy to imagine that some other city could have satisfied this description—for example, if Adenauer had chosen Stuttgart as his capital instead of Bonn. In contrast, the definite description "the smallest positive even number" applies to the number two, but as opposed to the case of the capital of West Germany, it is unimaginable that another number could satisfy this description. The description applies necessarily, and not only exclusively, to the number two. At the same time the terms that comprise the definite description— "positive number" and "even number"—also apply to other numbers, and always with the same meaning. This, however, is not the case with respect to the term "living" in the sentence "God is living."

When it is being used theologically the term "living" not only must apply exclusively and necessarily to God it must also not apply in the same sense to other things.

We are thus confronted by two problematic conditions. (1) There is no meaning relation between the theological meaning of the term "living" and its ordinary meaning. (2) The theological meaning of the term "living" cannot be given an essential definition. The import of these two conditions is that the only candidate that can logically serve as the logical category of the term "living" in the sentence "God is living" is a proper name, or more precisely a title, and that the sentence is an identity statement. The second claim may be clarified by an example. "The White House" seems to be a definite description of that famous white edifice in Washington that houses the president of the United States. But actually "the White House" is not a description but the name of the building. The test for whether it is a name or a description is the attempt to describe what would happen if for some reason the building would be painted another color: would people then stop calling it "the White House"? If despite the change of color it would still be called "the White House," then we could say that this is the name or title of the building and not its description, where a title is a description that has degenerated into a name.[20]

Armed with the distinction between a title and an attribute, let us return to the claim that the logical form of the sentence "God is living" is not a predicative statement but an identity statement. The sentence "Samuel Clemens is Mark Twain" is also an identity statement, and not a predicative sentence that attributes to Clemens the odd property of being two fathoms deep (which according to legend is the meaning of the expression "mark twain"). Thus "Mark Twain" is Clemens's title, not a description of him. In the same way "living," like all the apparent attributes of God, is his title. And a title, from a logical viewpoint, is a name: to say that an expression is a title is just to gossip about its past and to hint that it developed out of a description. But from a purely logical standpoint a title is a name for all practical purposes.[21] If theological sentences are identity statements in Maimonides' view, then what sort of identity statements are they?[22]

"Samuel Clemens is Samuel Clemens" is certainly an identity statement, but it is totally uninformative, which is not true of the sentence "Samuel Clemens is Mark Twain." Similarly, the theological identity statement "God is living" is an informative identity statement. However, for Maimonides the model of a theological identity statement is actually a tautology. Moses asks God, "When I come to the Israelites and say to them 'The God of your fathers has sent me to you,' and they ask me, 'What is His name?' what shall I say to them?" (Exodus 3:13), and the famous answer he receives is "I Am That I Am" (Exodus 3:14). This is not an informative proposition but a tautology. To Maimonides it is an important tautology that shows—although it does not state—that God's existence is necessary, as both the subject and the predicate of the sentence denote existence in Maimonides' view. This famous sentence requires a separate chapter for itself in *The Guide of the Perplexed,* primarily because it is closely related to the theory of negative attributes. And that is indeed the reason for our interest in this sentence.

The sentence offered in answer to Moses' question about God's name is an existence sentence that hints at the tetragrammaton (which may have the literal meaning of "He Is" or "He Causes to Be"). We therefore believe that the key to Maimonides' theory of negative attributes lies in the names and titles of God. Among all of God's names the tetragrammaton is the name that denotes his essence, and this name is used without definition. When Moses asks for an explanation that he can give for the question about God's name, which in Maimonides' view is a request for an explanation of God's essence (that is, a definition), the answer he is supposed to give the questioners is that tautology, "I Am That I Am." This is not a substantive answer, as human beings are not capable of understanding God's essence. Nevertheless, the tetragrammaton succeeds in denoting God by direct reference, in a way that permits the use of titles or other names that are equal in reference to the tetragrammaton, by means of identity statements. In the sentence, "The Lord is mighty," "mighty" is not an attribute but a name or title: it denotes what the tetragrammaton denotes. This is true not only of other names of God, such as Shaddai or Tsur, but also of what are generally considered typical examples of attributes, such as "gracious," "compassionate," and "wise." The crucial question here is what guarantees the reference of the tetragrammaton in the first place, and the answer is Moses. He is the direct link in the sense that his knowledge was not mediated by descriptions. Moses' relationship with God does not guarantee any supernatural propositional knowledge, but it guarantees that the name by which God "revealed" himself to Moses has a reference. And from Moses the name was passed on by the chain of tradition. Maimonides strongly opposes magical uses of the tetragrammaton, but he believes that there is a difference among the various traditions in which the names of God were handed down. The purer the tradition, the more certain the connection to the reference of the name in Moses' speech. All the theological sentences that apparently ascribe attributes to God are thus identity statements, where the tetragrammaton is on one side of the copula, and the attributes, which are really titles, are on the other side, and all of them have the same reference.

There are three elements worth stressing in Maimonides' view as we are reconstructing it here: Moses' special status, the special status of the tetragrammaton, and the special role of "knowledge by acquaintance," which is a form of enlightenment, in an almost literal sense of the word (Maimonides uses the term "sparks"). The character of Moses presents us with a particular difficulty in our attempt to understand Maimonides. Was Moses the greatest philosopher in Maimonides' view—the person who attained philosophical understanding that even the great Aristotle was unable to attain? According to our interpretation of Maimonides, Moses was not the greatest philosopher but the greatest prophet. He attained an enlightenment that no other man attained, but not propositional knowledge that no other man attained. Moses' enlightenment brought him to something like a unique form of "knowledge by acquaintance" with God, and by virtue of this acquaintance his use of the tetragrammaton has a special status that guarantees the continuation of the reference of this name in the chain of tradition. This enlightenment was not a source of propositions about God but the source for the use of his name.

Maimonides uses the theory of negative attributes to criticize religious language even in its amended form. Religious language, even that of the elite, does not permit the formulation of divine cognitions. It is possible to avoid the errors of the masses, but it is impossible to formulate positive cognitions. Relative to the critique in the theory of negative attributes, the proofs of the previous, rationalistic stage do not really constitute proofs. They have some value in determining the limits of understanding, and they also have some social value in that religious understanding, which is achieved in relation to the semantics of the language of the elite, is necessary for the perpetuation of religious life in a community that observes the commandments and does not commit the sin of idolatrous belief. The rationalistic stage of providing proofs is for Maimonides a necessary step on the way to the stage of cognitive skepticism, which in its turn makes way for the fideism that is grounded in the last analysis in enlightenment, which does not consist in propositional knowledge. Any reference based on positive description will be false; God's proper name is the only secure reference independent of such a description.

We started with Maimonides' point that identity of reference depends solely on description. In Moore's terms what is crucial is the second condition for identity or similarity of description. What complicates the matter is that according to our interpretation of Maimonides' negative theology, there is no adequate description that will not be false. Therefore, the value of description is still maintained for identifying the wrong god. The right God can be identified only through his proper name.

## Idolatrous Discourse as a Language Game

In contrast to our attempt to locate the objects of idolatry by discovering the reference of names and descriptions that are supposed to denote these objects, there is a view that it is preferable to concentrate on the justifications offered by believers in one religion when in confrontation with another religion, or by one group of worshipers in confrontation with a rival group. It is not the identity of Aphrodite—whether intentional or actual—that should be sought, but the identity of the language game involving "Aphrodite" in Greece, by comparing it with the language game involving "Venus" in Rome and "Astarte" in Babylonia. This recommendation, say the critics, is also useful within a particular religion and culture, and not only in comparisons between religions and cultures.

What is to be sought is thus not the reference of the name "Aphrodite" in the speech of maidens versus its reference in the speech of prostitutes. Rather, the recommendation is to find out how maidens justified their use of the utterance "Aphrodite will find me a husband," and how, in contrast, prostitutes justified their use of the utterance "Aphrodite will give me the power to arouse desire in men." [23] Only by comparing these justifications is it possible to find out how similar are the rituals organized around the Aphrodite of the maidens and the Aphrodite of the prostitutes. In other words, it is not a semantic investigation that is needed here but a sociological investigation of the similar and the different in the "Aphrodite" language games of the maidens and the prostitutes. What is involved is the identification of social institutions rather than gods—not even gods as institutions.

The sharpest of the critics holding these views is Richard Rorty. [24] Rorty makes use of another issue we have discussed, namely, the issue of names that are recognized by everyone as fictional, such as "Sherlock Holmes." We have already pointed out that our case is different from the general case of fictional names in that the believers (as opposed to their observers) do not regard the names of the gods as fictional, and this must be reflected in any account of their language game. At any rate, in Rorty's opinion the question is not what religious speech, whether idolatrous or monotheistic, is about, but what sort of dialogues believers in one religion can conduct with believers in another religion, and especially what are considered legitimate and illegitimate moves in such dialogues. Thus, for example, Catholics can conduct dialogues with members of the High Anglican church more easily than with members of the Low Protestant church, and only with great difficulty can they conduct dialogues with Shiite Moslems. The contrasts between the types of understanding embodied in the two types of dialogue is all we need for our comparison. Easy flow of discourse in contrast to misunderstanding is a matter of convention: this is true in religion as well as in ethics and politics, and it is even true in science. While investigating the conventions of discourse it is possible to find out whether a particular misunderstanding is based on names or descriptions appearing in it. There are dialogues that create a feeling of solidarity and commonality within a community and others that create a feeling of division and alienation. If the use of the names "Zeus" and "Jupiter" does not hinder the flow of discourse between Greek and Roman believers, then there is no reason not to identify them or consider them fully parallel to each other. In contrast, one would expect an absolute barrier in a dialogue between a monotheist and a pagan believer: "Allah" and "Ahriman" are names that create a division between Shiites and Zoroastrians in Iran. "There's no such thing" is an expression of alienation and not necessarily an ontological declaration.

Such criticism of the sterile study of the semantics of the names and descriptions of gods is a criticism of vertical semantics, which is supposed to deal systematically with the relation between language and the world. Horizontal semantics, in contrast, deals with the relations between sentences of language, especially with the justifications that sentences provide for one another. Our argument against this criticism is that it is impossible to ignore the fact that a substantial part of a believer's picture of his belief is a matter of vertical semantics, of the relation between the names and the gods.[25] The believer who thinks that someone else's belief has no substance thinks that the reference of the names of the other person's gods is empty while the names of his own gods do possess a reference: vertical semantics is part of the believer's worldview. He does not perceive himself as worshiping God for the purpose of communal solidarity with his fellows. The sociology of solidarity does not give a proper account of the way believers perceive their own belief. Thus vertical semantics is essential to the understanding of religious discourse. As far as the advantages of horizontal semantics are concerned, we claim that the two conditions we provided for intentional identity, the causal condition and the similarity condition, are what justify the flow of religious discourse, if it is achieved, or explain its failure.

Our central claim in this chapter about worshiping the "wrong god" is that Moore's criterion, with its two conditions, is the best criterion for unifying the three points of view on idolatry: that of the believers, that of the critics, and that of the observers. We must clarify this claim by pointing out that we are not asserting that Moore's criterion actually guides believers and critics of idolatry. Rather, we are claiming that this criterion, which guides mainly observers of idolatry, is also appropriate for identifications that are made from other points of view.

Moore's criterion sheds light on the other side of the problem, which is how from the point of view of the monotheists the identity of the "right God" is established. Maimonides' emphasis on belief as the concept of God in the worshipers' mind gives priority to Moore's

second condition—similarity. Another approach from the monotheists, which opposes Maimonides' view, gives priority to
Moore's first condition—the causal. According to such a view the
reference to the "right God" is guaranteed by the tradition, by the
shared form of worship, and by the worshiper's intent to worship
the God of his fathers. The reference to God is fixed and independent
of the worshiper's own description; what matters is the proper worship and his participation in a common tradition. According to this
view (to which we return in Chapter 7), the problem of idolatry is
not the wrong concept of god in the worshiper's mind, but the
wrong form of worship.

# 6

## The Ethics of Belief

### Is the "Great Error" an Epistemic Issue?

We begin with the claim that idolatrous error is an error about the management of society (a political error) rather than an error about the management of the world (an epistemic error). Any idea can be a source of religious controversy if it can serve, under the appropriate social conditions, as a basis for the formation of a sectarian organization, whether within or outside religion, which threatens the central authority of the religion. The sin is thus not in the idea itself but in the organization around it. According to this line of thought it is a mistake to think that idolatrous beliefs are stamped as sinful errors only because they constitute a denial of monotheistic beliefs. Monotheistic ideas did not precede the struggle against idolatrous beliefs but were crystallized in the course of a political struggle against these beliefs. This struggle was not conducted on a metaphysical basis but by virtue of the fact that other religions and other sources of authority were involved. Thomas Hobbes expressed a similar idea when he said that if the elements of geometry had involved national interests, we would be arguing to this day about whether one or more straight lines connect two points.

In brief, any abstract idea, even if it is morally neutral and unlikely to arouse feelings or excitement, is liable to become the focus of a blazing controversy in the appropriate circumstances. This occurs when it constitutes a basis for the formation of an organization relying on an out-side authority. Yet an idea that seems alien on the basis of its content is likely to be tolerated as long as it does not involve the formation of an alien organization or the undermining of established authority. Alien ideas constitute a "superstructure," and the fact that they are denounced and vilified should not make us forget that the issue is not one of metaphysical error but of authority and interests. And since it is authorities rather than beliefs that are involved, the essence of the struggle is against idolatrous practice rather than idolatrous belief, as it is easier to identify worship than belief. Therefore it is worship rather than belief that is the outstanding sign of the strength of religious authority, as well as the outstanding sign of the under-mining of this authority.

This critical line of thought, according to which religious controversy is about authority rather than about belief or ritual worship, must provide an answer to the question of the scope of the authority. For if what is involved is nothing more than the authority to determine beliefs and rituals, then the entire issue becomes circular. In such a case it would be the critic's duty to explain why he is discussing authority rather than the content of the authority, that is, the beliefs and the ritual worship. But the critic's claim may be that even though the authority operates with respect to belief and worship, what is really at stake is something else—control over people. Supervising beliefs is important only as a manifestation of the wish to control people. There is no special importance to the beliefs involved—their content is secondary. A metaphysical error is great or small not because of some element of its content but because of its power to distinguish friend from foe, and because it is a reliable symptom of the undermining of an established authority.

We are now in a state of tension between two observations: on the one hand, metaphysical beliefs seem detached from real life, and it is difficult to see how they could arouse strong feelings of controversy. On the other hand, metaphysical controversies, especially of the theological sort, have always been at the center of the storm of social controversies that have often deteriorated into religious wars saturated with hatred and zealotry.

Let us introduce a concept that will make it easier for us to clarify the proper meaning of a "great metaphysical error." This is the concept of the ideological potential of a view. An ideology, in the present context, is a system of beliefs anchored in a society, which divides people into friends and foes according to whether they accept or deny it. The ideological potential of a view is thus its capability of becoming a doctrine that constitutes a focus uniting a community of believers, that is, a community of people who regard other adherers to the doctrine as friends and deniers of the doctrine as foes. A view has ideological potential when the basis for the division between friends and foes is the division between believers and heretics. The question of interest to us is not whether every metaphysical view, irrespective of its content, can divide people into friends and foes. After all, even competitive sport can do this under the appropriate circumstances. The argument of the ideological potential of meta-physical views claims that only a view which can promise something important to its believers and keep something important away from its deniers possesses ideological potential. A weaker sense of ideolog-ical potential may refer to a metaphysical view that does not con-stitute in itself a promise for its believers and a condemnation of heretics, but that is internally related to another view which is ideological in the strong sense and thus divides friends from foes. The purpose of the weak sense of ideological potential is to explain how it can happen that an apparently neutral view can become the focus of a deep quarrel.

Thus an error is a "great" one if it represents a deviation or a heresy with respect to a fundamental belief—a constitutive belief—of an ideology. (Religion in this context is a special case of an ideol-ogy.) Alternatively, it may be a denial of a belief that is not itself a fundamental belief but that is internally related to such a fundamental belief. Such an error represents a danger of undermining the authority of believers in the ideology, and especially of the formation of a deviant organization.

## A Viable Hypothesis

William James's concept of the viable hypothesis will help us expli-cate another conception of the "great error"—not as a social concept but as a personal concept. James's central idea is that the degree of liveliness of a hypothesis is a function of its connections with other beliefs.[1] Thus, for example, the hypothesis of the return of the Mahdi (the messianic deliverer who is guided by God) is not a viable hypothesis for a New England Puritan, because it has no connections with his system of beliefs. For an orthodox Sunni Muslim, however, even though he rejects this hypothesis in its Shiite form, it is still a viable hypothesis because it is part of a rich network of beliefs that partially overlaps the Shiite hypothesis.

Thus a necessary condition for a hypothesis to be a viable one is that it must be connected with other beliefs, where the required connection is the following: at least some of the other beliefs must be positively relevant to the hypothesis. A belief that constitutes evidence for a hypothesis is positively relevant to it if it increases the possibility that the hypothesis is true, in the eye of the believer. A Sunni Muslim's belief in the return of the Mahdi from the descendants of Mohammed is positively relevant to the "Shiite hypothesis." The Sunni may also hold other beliefs that are negatively relevant to the Shiite hypothesis, such as the belief that it is not plausible that the Mahdi who will be revealed is one who has been hiding for a thousand years and has been living for such a long time, or the belief that the Mahdi must have the name of the prophet Mohammed ben Abdullah, while the father of the Shiite Mahdi is named Hassan, and other beliefs of this sort that greatly decrease the plausibility of the Shiite hypothesis in his eyes. The viability of a hypothesis is a matter of degree and not absolutes. A Sunni Muslim possesses beliefs that are positively relevant to the Shiite hypothesis, even though he does not believe this hypothesis. Among the beliefs of William James, in contrast, there are no beliefs that support this hypothesis in the sense of being positively relevant to it.

The explication we are suggesting for James's concept of a lively hypothesis is not problem-free. According to this explication it turns out, for example, that someone who was born a Shiite but totally lost his faith is further from the "Mahdi hypothesis" than a Protestant who believes in the second coming of Christ, because the Protestant's belief positively relates to the hypothesis of the Mahdi as a messiah who is expected to arrive and redeem his people; moreover, in folk belief the Mahdi is sometimes identified with the Isa of the Koran, who is Jesus the son of Mary. Nevertheless, for someone who was brought up as a Shiite the mosque he doesn't go to is still the Shiite mosque, which is not true of the Protestant whose knowledge does not include a word about the hidden Imam. Our explication must therefore be refined, and conditions must be added to it that are not expressed only in terms of beliefs. But for our purposes the condition of positive relevance is in any case a necessary one. For the Shiite who has lost his faith we will not say that the Mahdi hypothesis is a viable hypothesis, but we will agree that it is likely to become such once more if his belief is renewed. The significance of the rabbinic saying that the temptation for idolatry has been killed is thus partly that the belief in idols has ceased to be a viable hypothesis.

So far we have concentrated on the explication of the concept of a viable hypothesis in belief but not in practice. But for James the essence of the concept of a viable hypothesis is its relation to human activity. A hypothesis is a lively one for James if actions supported by the hypothesis are performed decisively: "The maximum of liveliness in an hypothesis means willingness to act irrevocably" (*The Will to Believe,* p. 3). The difficulty in this characterization is that it is precisely the person who is within the range of influence of a viable hypothesis but does not believe in it, such as the Sunni in our example, who is prepared to go to battle against this hypothesis—as opposed to the Protestant, who does not perceive it as a threat. Thus a viable hypothesis is such not only for someone who is prepared to act decisively according to the hypothesis but also for someone who is prepared to act decisively against it, while it is not viable for someone who is indifferent to it.

We suggest an explication of the concept of the great error in terms of the concept of a viable hypothesis: an error is great if it denies a viable hypothesis, which for its part constitutes a major premise in a practical syllogism whose conclusion is the formulation of a major decision. Each phrase of this characterization is fraught with significance, and so our first task is to define a major decision and a major premise in a practical syllogism.

A "major decision" here does not mean a decision made by an important person, say a president or a military general, whose role gives the person the power to determine issues that are important for many people. Rather, we are referring to a decision that affects the person's own life first and foremost, and only derivatively affects the lives of others. An important characteristic of a major decision is its being significant and irrevocable for the person's life.[2] A person who joins a Catholic monastery has made a major decision, as opposed to someone who buys a new shirt. The decision to join the monastery is significant and irrevocable, which is not true of buying the shirt—even if we assume that the shirt is not returnable and that it is permissible to leave the monastery. The life of the person who has decided to join the monastery is likely to change in crucial respects, and his whole personality may be affected by this decision, while under normal circumstances nothing dramatic will change as a result of the purchase in the life of the person who bought the new shirt. Moreover, a major decision is a conscious decision. It is possible for people to undergo decisive changes in their lives without ever making even one major decision, if their lives consist of constant drift. In such a case they may find themselves at the end of the process in a fundamentally different state from the one they were in at the beginning. A major decision is not a sudden conversion, nor is it a "rebirth," if these are perceived by the person undergoing the change as having been compelled, in the sense of "I cannot do otherwise," as, for example, in the case of an experience of revelation.

A model for a major decision is Abraham's decision, when, according to the sages and the Koran, he had to decide if he would continue on the traditional path of idol worship or would break the idols in his father's house and become a monotheist. The Abraham of the Koran does not undergo conversion or drift: he is conscious of his decision and its price. In general, the life of a great believer can be accepted as the result of a great conversion—such as that of Paul on the road to Damascus—or as the result of a major decision. In contrast, the ordinary believer is not necessarily someone who has made a major decision, but rather someone who continues the tradition of his ancestors, perhaps by merely drifting or wandering about.

To define a major premise in a practical syllogism, let us look at a specific example. A person may be faced with a major decision in her life: for example, should she decide to be a musician or a mathematician? Let us assume that she ascribes great weight to both careers but is mistaken in her evaluation of her talents—she is very talented in mathematics but her musical talents are limited. In this case, if she chooses the musical rather than the mathematical career, then even though she is making a mistake in a major decision, her mistake is not a great error, because she is mistaken in the minor premise of the practical syllogism ("I am musically talented") and not in the major premise ("It is worthwhile for a person to become a musician if she is talented in this area"). The effects of the mistake may of course be tragic, but we are interested in the reasons for the error and not only in its effects. The concept of the major premise is taken by analogy from scientific explanations, in which the major premise is the one that formulates a lawlike statement, while the other premises formulate the initial conditions specific to the particular case. In the case of someone who is mistaken about her musical talents, we assume that she erred in the condition and not in the guiding principle, which states that both music and mathematics are worthy pursuits. Metaphysical or theological assumptions that concern what is worthwhile for a person to do in her life fulfill the role of the major premises in practical syllogisms leading to major decisions.

The idea that a syllogism leading to a major decision contains major metaphysical premises is not accepted by everyone. Existentialists claim that the deliberations that lead people to choice do not contain major premises, since what is supposed to appear as the major premise is something that the person adopts after rather than before the decision. Moreover, major premises are supposed to be held in common by many people, whereas an individual's major decisions derive from his life as an individual alone and not from an appeal to some essence that is common to himself and to others. Within the existentialist view it is possible to distinguish an even more extreme view about the status of major premises. This is the claim of the absurd, according to which major decisions, as opposed to minor ones, are not subject to reasoned choice at all. A major decision does express the freedom of the deliberating individual, but the decision is not based on universal reasons or on reasons at all. At any rate a major decision, even in the eyes of a religious existentialist such as Kierkegaard, is made not by virtue of a reasoned hypothesis, but by virtue of a "leap of faith."

These are criticisms that are worth discussing, but we are concerned with the explication of the great error as an error of belief. We consider an error "great" if it is inconsistent with a major premise in a practical syllogism whose conclusion is a major decision. By extension, "great" also applies to an error made by someone who allows himself to drift rather than come to a decision. In the case of the drifter the argument is that if the change in his life had been the result of a decision rather than drift, then the premise he would have been relying on is an erroneous major metaphysical premise. The moral argument against such a person is that he ought to be conscious of those of his actions and considerations that are of great importance for his life. Drift may be considered an extenuating circumstance in the case of a great error, but it does not exonerate the person from blame.

## The Great Error and the Teleological View

The natural framework for the explication of the concept of the great error is the teleological view.[3] The religions based on revelation, which believe in a God who created the world, naturally take a teleological view and also fulfill the Aristotelian recommendation that the way to find the purpose of something is to ask the one who made it (which is yet another manifestation of the assumption of the creator's knowledge). The revelation thus provides the creator's answer to the question of what the ultimate purpose is. The ultimate purpose may also be inferred indirectly, without revelation, and such inferences are the subject matter of natural theology. At any rate, whether we discover the ultimate purpose through revelation or through inference, it is clear that it is easier to discover the purpose of something that was created than of something that always existed. The ultimate purpose in the sense of the creator's plan fits a created world rather than a preexistent world (Maimonides, *Guide of the Perplexed,* 3:13). It is for this reason that Aristotle, who believed in the preexistence of the world, found it difficult to deal with the issue of the ultimate purpose of the world in the sense of a plan. He does speak of an internal purpose, but his model of purpose is taken from a creator's plan.

A great error in this framework is thus a mistake that someone makes with respect to his ultimate purpose, which is also his nature. Such a mistake about a person's natural obligations must be distinguished from a mistake a person might make with respect to something that he does in the framework of one of his roles. Being a doctor or a teacher are roles people take upon themselves, and they are judged as being correct or mistaken with respect to these roles. But beyond all these roles there is an attribute within which the person chooses all his roles: being human. Only with respect to the attribute "human" can a person commit a great error. This occurs when he does not understand what this attribute obligates him to do in the management of his life.

Aristotle was impressed by the fact that there are "errors" in nature itself in the sense of faults such as those we see in monsters (*De Caelo,* 271). Aristotle's explanation, which greatly influenced later thinkers, was that the source of errors in nature is in matter rather than in form, which is identified as ultimate purpose. Form is perfect, while matter is a source of imperfection, not because of some essential evil in matter but because many competing purposes are embodied in it. In speaking about the ultimate purpose of things in general, we tend to forget that the same material object can embody various purposes. When we speak about purpose in general, according to Aristotle, we mean the dominant purpose of a thing rather than its sole purpose. The dominant purpose of something is its most characteristic purpose. If a human being, for example, is defined as a rational animal, then being rational is his dominant purpose. Let us therefore correct our formulation and state that a great error is the error a person makes with respect to his own dominant purpose and to that of other things, where understanding this purpose properly is vital for the person's understanding of his life.

There are two types of purposes: defined and undefined. A person who wants to be elected to Parliament has a defined purpose, whereas someone who wants to advance the cause of women has an undefined purpose. The distinction is based on the degree of obviousness of the choice of means to be used for the achievement of the purpose. Undefined purposes characterize one's lifestyle rather than describe a particular goal that one must find the right means to attain. The ascription of a common purpose to people in general is vulnerable to the danger of involving an undefined purpose—for example, "to do God's will." With respect to a defined purpose one can speak of error, but it is much more difficult to speak of error with respect to an undefined purpose.

The religious enterprise, when it relies on the metaphysics of ultimate end, constitutes an attempt to turn an undefined purpose into a defined purpose in such a way that the undefined purpose—say, doing God's will—is detailed in terms of commandments whose function is to define what it is that God wants. Here we require the Aristotelian distinction between actions whose purpose is the action itself, such as playing basketball or listening to music, and actions whose purpose is detached from the action itself, such as playing basketball in order to earn money or listening to music in order to tune the piano. Following the commandments as constitutive of the purpose of obeying God's will, or doing philosophy as constitutive of the attainment of knowledge of God, are actions whose end is the action itself. In the religious realm there is a danger of confusion in the transformation of an action that is done for its own sake, an action whose end is the action itself, into an action that is not done for its own sake, an action whose purpose is external to it. If this transformation becomes a way of life, it constitutes a great error.

According to Aristotle, any person who does not live according to his dominant purpose is in a state of great evil (*Nicomachean Ethics*, 1096). But people in general have a common supreme purpose, which is the supreme good, and it is this purpose that gives all other things their value. The recognition of this purpose is vital for people's lives (1094). Thus anyone who does not direct his life according to its ultimate end is committing an error, and if he does not direct his life according to the supreme end, which is the supreme good, then he is committing an even greater error.

The connection between teleology and error has been limited so far to errors with respect to the ultimate purpose. In other words, correct metaphysical cognitions about man's nature and the nature of the world are required for the knowledge of man's ultimate purpose, and an error in this respect is a great error in the sense that it has crucial implications for the management of people's lives. But the connection between error and teleology is even stronger in a view that regards man's purpose as reaching knowledge of truths about God, knowledge with a propositional nature. This seems at first glance to be Maimonides' view:

> And the fourth type is true human perfection, which occurs when a person attains the intellectual virtues, that is, representation by concepts in order to derive truths about the divinity. This is the ultimate purpose which creates true perfection in man, and it is for him alone, in pure worship of the eternal existence. It is this that makes a person human. (*The Eight Chapters of Maimonides on Ethics,* chap. 5)

Man's purpose does not follow a formal plan. It is achieved not only with the intellect but also through the supreme cognitions and truths about divine matters that this unique ability gives us. Living according to the intellect is thus a necessary formal condition for achieving the ultimate human purpose, but only recognition of the truth can constitute a sufficient condition for attaining this purpose.

The problem we have been wrestling with in the last few sections is the problem of the great error. We suggested several different related explications of the concept of the great error, and these explications allowed us to see how idolatrous errors could be considered great errors. But idolatrous errors are not simply great errors: they are also sinful errors. The question now becomes how it is possible for an error to be considered a sin if belief is not a matter of will or decision.

## Will and Belief

The concept of idolatrous belief undoubtedly involves a negative moral evaluation. But although it clearly makes sense to censure someone because of his or her type of worship, one may question whether it makes sense to censure someone because of his or her beliefs. Underlying this question is the view that a person's beliefs are not subject to will and are not under the person's control. You are reading the book in front of you and you believe that there really is a book there. Could you, by a decision alone, change your belief, and believe that there is no book in front of you? The moral principle that makes it difficult to obligate belief is the Kantian principle that "ought" implies "can": you cannot command people to do what they are unable to do, and you may not praise or blame them for what they are unable to do. If belief is the sort of thing that is not under a person's control, then you can note the fact that someone holds an idolatrous belief, but you cannot blame the person for this fact.

But is it really true that belief is not subject to the will? An important argument states that not only is belief not subject to the will, but it is logic rather than facts that makes it necessary for belief to be nonvoluntary. The reason for this is that if belief were voluntary, then the conceptual relation between belief and truth would be severed. For if someone believes a particular proposition, then he or she believes that it is true, and if belief were subject to the will then truth as well would be subject to the will. After all, you, the reader, believe that the sun sets in the west: do you think that your wish not to believe this could change the direction in which the sun sets? If we accept this argument about the conceptual character of the involuntary nature of belief, then it differs from the involuntary nature of the heart muscles, for example, which is purely a matter of fact.

In contrast to those who argue that belief is involuntary, there is a respectable tradition of thinkers who claim that belief is voluntary. Descartes, one of the representatives of this tradition, actually regards the relation between belief and will as a conceptual relation. In his opinion there is a distinction between the intellectual act involved in understanding a proposition and the act of affirming its truth. We are able to understand propositions without taking a stand about their truth value, and this attests that understanding and assent (or dissent) are distinct: while understanding is involuntary, assent and dissent are under the control of the will.[4]

Even though the two schools of thought with regard to the voluntary nature of belief seem to be clearly divided, there is almost no controversy about the facts between the two schools. Everyone seems to agree that you, the reader, are unable to change, by virtue of your decision alone, your belief that you are now reading a book. Everyone also agrees that you are sometimes able to influence your beliefs indirectly, just as you can get your involuntary muscles to work by indirect means. (You can speed up your heart rate by running—that is, by using the muscles under your control.) The obligation to believe may therefore be interpreted as an obligation to adopt indirect methods that will bring you to believe. Praise and blame in this case would then be similar to the praise or blame we direct toward someone who has a predisposition to heart disease and adopts a lifestyle that either decreases or increases his chances of contracting overt manifestations of the disease. A person cannot will his heart to become healthy, but he can use his will to improve his situation or to make it worse, and for this he is worthy of praise or blame. Similarly, the adoption of a religious way of life, which embodies the right beliefs, increases the chances that the person who lives this way will come to believe in the true religion, while someone who adopts an idolatrous way of life is much more likely to adopt idolatrous beliefs as well. The command to believe can be understood not as a direct command but as an indirect command to adopt a way of life that will decrease the chances of wrong belief and increase the chances of correct belief. Pascal, a sworn voluntarist in matters of belief, thought that the implication of his wager could not be the voluntary adoption of beliefs but rather the recommendation to adopt a lifestyle that would lead to belief ("masses and holy water").[5] This view of the indirect nature of commands about belief does not necessitate the religious conception that practice is primary because it is only practice that can be commanded directly. It is definitely possible to hold the view that the ultimate purpose of religious life is belief, while religious practice is an indirect means for bringing about this belief.

In contrast to acts, beliefs are subject to evaluation, in our opinion, even when the principle that "ought implies can" is not fulfilled. The reason for this is that we have second-order beliefs about our first-order beliefs, and the gap between these two orders of belief enables us to judge beliefs morally even if they are not voluntary. The following example may help clarify the matter. The private diaries of the influential American essayist H. L. Mencken have recently been published. From these diaries it seems that the "Baltimore sage" unequivocally held strong anti-Semitic beliefs. However, Mencken (on some accounts) never admitted these beliefs in public, not even among his closest friends—neither in words nor in actions—so that these beliefs came as a total surprise to everyone. How should we judge Mencken as a result of what has been discovered in his diaries: is there something despicable about the man just because there is something despicable in his beliefs?

We must distinguish between the following two possibilities: in one case, Mencken was not at all disturbed by his anti-Semitic beliefs, but he believed that revealing them in public would hurt his public image, and so he concealed them in order to protect this image. In the second case, Mencken had the second-order belief that his first-order ethnic beliefs were invalid prejudices but he was unable to get rid of them. Moreover, he regretted having these ethnic beliefs and tried very hard not to act according to them. We would then say that there is a sharp moral difference between the two cases: it is justifiable to censure Mencken for his beliefs in the first case, while in the second case he is very likely praiseworthy. Although second-order beliefs are not any more voluntary than first-order beliefs, they are the beliefs that lead to a person's actions, and therefore they express his true personality.

The moral evaluation of beliefs is therefore independent of the question of whether beliefs are voluntary. The evaluation can be based on second-order beliefs, as well as on second-order desires about first-order beliefs and desires. It seems that the tension between the two orders of belief is one of the signs of modern religious consciousness. The religious believer is often in a state of hazy doubt concerning his first-order beliefs. He believes that it is good to believe, and he longs to return to a state of "second innocence," that is, to the state of innocent first-order belief that he lost during the course of his life. He conducts his life in a religious framework and in the company of believers, in the hope that his belief will return. He lives the life of a believer, not out of hypocrisy but out of longing for a second innocence. This religious type is not so rare nowadays, and he can be judged morally even if his first-order religious beliefs are not under his control.

### The Indirect Approach to Belief

Let us return to the obligation of belief as the obligation of adopting indirect methods that may increase the chances of coming to believe. Isn't there a fundamental flaw in the indirect method, in that it involves self-deception? Of course, self-deception is not necessarily involved in the fact that you now believe "p" and you bring yourself to believe "not p" after some time. We are not claiming that every change of belief, even if it is a result of one's desire to change the belief, is born of self-deception. For example, if the desire to change one's belief is accompanied by exposing oneself to new justifications for the opposite belief and against the original belief, then the newly acquired belief is not necessarily a product of self-deception. The acquired belief is not merely the product of one's will but is brought about by the new justifications as well. Nevertheless, if a belief is the product of the adoption of an indirect approach that does involve self-deception, is the belief thereby invalidated?[6]

We can imagine states of affairs in which changing one's beliefs at will is justified even if it does involve self-deception. This is the case with self-fulfilling prophecies or beliefs in which the very act of belief significantly increases the chances that the beliefs will come true, even if their chances of being true at the outset were very small. The priest in Hugo's *Les Miserables* believed that Jean Valjean was a thief. He also believed that if he could bring himself to believe that Valjean was not a thief he would greatly increase the chances of rehabilitating him. The priest could not simply pretend to believe this, because the escaped prisoner was very intelligent and would notice the pretense. Given all this, should the priest have tried to bring himself to believe that Valjean was not a thief, when he actually believed that he was one? We think that in the case of a self-fulfilling prophecy there are good reasons for changing one's belief voluntarily, even if there is a stage of self-deception in the process.

William James, proponent of voluntary change of belief in the case of self-fulfilling beliefs, was mistaken in thinking that belief in the existence of God is of this type. The existence of God is not dependent on whether people believe in him or not. James apparently confused people's need to fulfill themselves through belief with self-fulfilling beliefs. It is necessary here to distinguish between the requirement to believe certain specific propositions and the requirement to believe propositions that are acquired by a specific procedure. The former requirement of belief is not concerned with the question of how the belief was acquired, as long as one believes what is worthy of belief because of its content. In contrast, the requirement to adopt beliefs only on the basis of an appropriate procedure, like the requirement of rational belief—"Believe only what you have sufficient evidence for"—disqualifies the adoption of beliefs by means of faulty procedures, even if the beliefs are actually true and important. The requirement for religious belief is first and foremost a requirement to believe certain specific contents, and so the procedure by which the believer acquires his belief is secondary. It is preferable for the believer to reach his belief by a tortuous path, even if it includes self-deception, than to remain in error.

## Acceptance and Heresy

The voluntary nature of religious belief does not constitute an evaluative difficulty for the view that what is required of us is not belief but acceptance. Acceptance, in contrast to belief, is within our control.[7] We must distinguish between two concepts of acceptance that are relevant to our discussion. According to the first concept accepting a proposition means acting as if it were true, even if the person does not believe that it is really true. The good salesperson accepts the proposition that the customer is always right even if he or she does not believe it. The salesperson is obligated to act as if it were true. It is obviously not a religious ideal that the religious person should only accept the principles of belief in this sense of acceptance, without actually believing them. The religious believer is not supposed to be a salesperson. But the requirement of belief may nevertheless be understood as the minimal requirement of acting resolutely and decisively according to this belief, even without subjective conviction of its truth. (What is especially confusing in the relation between belief and acceptance is the fact that among the commandments of some religions is the obligation to accept the propositions of the form "I believe with total faith that . . .")

The second meaning of acceptance is phenomenologically closer to a description of the reality of religious life, and it especially suits the simple believer. Such a person believes both in the truths of the sacred scriptures and in the religious authorities as interpreters of these scriptures. This does not mean, however, that such a person fully or even partially understands the propositions of his or her belief. The situation is similar to that of a person who receives a message in code. For external reasons such a person may believe, even without knowing the code, that what is written in the message is true. Acceptance in this sense—the acceptance of the truth of propositions that are not understood—is no more voluntary than belief in the propositions themselves. There is nevertheless much more freedom in accepting interpretations of the sentences that are believed to be true.

So far we have discussed the voluntary nature of belief. But what about the voluntary nature of disbelief? An accepted explanation for disbelief is stubbornness. But is this conduct in matters of belief actually a voluntary act? To answer this question we must first understand the concept of heresy as it relates to stubbornness. This is heresy in belief rather than heresy in practice. Heresy is rebellion, that is, the undermining of religious authority. There are many manifestations of heresy. It can even be expressed in extreme orthodoxy, such as in the adoption of exaggerated poverty, if this constitutes an undermining of the relative weight that the religious authorities ("the church") assign to religious values—even if it does not constitute an undermining of the values themselves. The root of the word "heresy" comes from a Greek word meaning "choice." The way to understand this meaning relation is that it is forbidden for people to make their own judgments in matters of belief—they must rely upon the religious authority whose source is the divinity.

Heresy may be partial or total: the partial heretic is the unbeliever who denies some of the truths of the religion without denying its basic principles, while the total heretic denies all the principles that constitute the religious belief, and in extreme cases even denies that there is anything that these principles are about. Both types of heretic differ from the infidel, in that they are expected to believe because of the opportunity they have had to learn the principles of faith.

Now we can address our question as to which heretics are the ones toward whom the complaint of being voluntarily obstinate is directed. Our answer is that this complaint may be directed only against heretics whose sin is disbelief by omission—those who do not listen, out of negligence or refusal to hear, to the teachings of the religion in spite of the fact that they are available to them, or those who do not exert the necessary and possible effort to be exposed to the belief. (This is, by the way, the category that includes those people who claimed "We didn't know" or "We couldn't believe it" in connection with the Nazi atrocities.) Stubbornness in the sense of "they stiffened their necks and would not pay heed" (Jeremiah 17:23) applies both to those who do not listen out of omission and to those who actively refuse to listen.

In the case of positive disbelief, where a person is exposed to the belief under the proper conditions and nevertheless denies it, this person cannot be accused of voluntary stubbornness. Calling such a person stiff-necked is an expression of despair rather than an explanation. This is similar to our reaction when we have presented someone with a proposition that seems obviously true, and have added a clear and convincing explanation for believing it, yet the person nevertheless continues to deny the proposition. "You refuse to believe" or "You won't allow yourself to listen" might be expressions of despair and impatience in the face of what seem to us manifestations of irrationality, but they do not constitute explanations of the person's behavior. This type of stubbornness is like that of a mule. It is not voluntary stubbornness but an involuntary behavioral tendency.[8]

# 7

## *From Idolatrous Belief to Idolatrous Practice*

Whereas in the previous three chapters we discussed the sin of idolatry as an error of belief (either because erroneous practice causes erroneous belief or because it reflects such belief), in this chapter we consider the problem not in terms of metaphysical belief but in terms of actual religious practice. According to this view, opposition to idolatry does not necessarily involve the presentation of an alternative metaphysical picture. What is involved is the prohibition on worshiping any object other than God, and sometimes the prohibition of certain ways of worshiping God himself. Such approaches reflect a totally different understanding of idolatry and the gravity of the sin involved, and they dissociate idolatry from error. The pagan / nonpagan controversy thus concerns not a worldview but the criteria of worship. This shift is of great importance within the monotheistic tradition because the philosophical concept of unity has never been preserved in all its purity, and a "mythic" worldview has always penetrated deeply into the monotheistic community.

The term "unity" is a "portmanteau word" that serves as a short expression into which different ideas about the deity are packed. Two complex conceptions of unity that exist within the nonpagan camp—organic unity and hierarchical unity—narrow the metaphysical gap between the pagans and the monotheists. In the conception of hierarchical unity the picture of the divine world closely resembles that of a royal court with its entourage, or a pantheon headed by a chief god. In the conception of organic unity the picture is one of a system with many different aspects that are connected to one another by the relations of emanation and absorption. In these two conceptions there is more than a tinge of polytheism, and thus the distance between them and the more sophisticated versions of paganism are limited to issues of idolatrous practice rather than idolatrous belief. It was Julian, the fourth-century pagan emperor, who articulated the hierarchical conception in a manner that is close to the formulations of some adherent antipagans: "Our writers say that the creator is the common father and king of all things, but that the other functions have been assigned by him to national gods of the peoples and to gods that protect the cities, everyone of whom administers his own department in accordance with his own nature."[1] Nine centuries after Julian, the great rabbinic authority of Spanish Jews Nachmanides wrote in the same tone about the other gods: "It is known that some of them have rulership over the peoples, as it is written, 'the prince of the kingdom of Greece the prince of the kingdom of Persia'" (Nachmanides, Exodus 20:3). Nevertheless, even without an alternative metaphysical picture the nonpagans maintain the ban on idolatry as essential to their self-definition.

One of the most important and instructive examples for our purposes is the kabbalistic tradition. There are a number of senses in which this tradition blurs the metaphysical distinction between paganism and monotheism by rejecting the conception of "simple unity." As a result of this difference in the concept of unity the question of what constitutes idolatry acquires a new meaning. We therefore use this tradition as an example of the alternative conception and discuss the way it identifies idolatry as a sin relating to worship. Another perspective that shifts the emphasis in idolatry from error to worship is the approach that regards every deviation from the accepted method of worship as a form of idolatry, even if it is God himself who is being worshiped. According to this understanding of idolatry, a form of worship can be idolatrous even if no idol or false god is being worshiped. The writings of R. Judah Halevi serve as an example of this view of idolatry as a form of worship. Halevi's approach also connects this conception with the controversy about the status of philosophy in religious life.

The shifting of the center of gravity from idolatrous belief to idolatrous practice also makes it important to discuss the concept of worship. What is worship? How is worship to be distinguished from other types of acts? Is every gesture toward an idol considered worship? Does intention determine the characterization of an action as an act of worship? What is the relation between intention and worship? In the context of an approach to the prohibition on idolatry that stresses the exclusivity of the mode of worship of God rather than his metaphysical exclusivity, the question of what is considered worship acquires a crucial importance.

We begin with a simpler question: do those who forbid the worship of other gods deny their existence, or do they admit their existence while forbidding their worship? Various biblical scholars claim that the original biblical belief was monolatry, that is, a belief that does not deny the existence of other gods besides the God of Israel but only forbids their worship. In the opinion of these scholars the biblical belief was a belief in a jealous god who forbade the worship of other gods. It did not present a new metaphysical picture in opposition to the syncretism practiced by the pagans; rather, it determined that ritual worship must be directed to the one God of Israel.[2]

Some biblical verses may be read as proof that there is a polytheistic belief in the primary layer of the Bible. In the song after the crossing of the Red Sea the Israelites praise God by saying: "Who is like You, O Lord, among the gods" (Exodus 15:11). In Deuteronomy the following is written: "And when you look up to the sky and behold the sun and the moon and the stars, the whole heavenly host, you must not be lured into bowing down to them or serving them. These the Lord your God allotted to other peoples everywhere under heaven" (4:19). The other peoples are permitted to worship other gods, whose existence is not in dispute, while the Israelites are forbidden to worship them because God has chosen them to be his own people. Jephthah says to the king of the Ammonites: "Do you not hold what Chemosh your god gives you to possess? So we will hold on to everything that the Lord our God has given us to possess" (Judges 11:24). And as David tells King Saul, "they have driven me out today, so that I cannot have a share in the Lord's possession, but am told, 'Go and worship other gods'" (I Samuel 26:19). One of the most blatant expressions of this conception in the Bible occurs in the Psalms. In Psalm 82 God is described as participating in a conference with many gods. These gods are judging "perversely," and the psalm denounces them and calls upon God: "Arise, O God, judge the earth, for all the nations are [literally: "will be"] Your possession" (82:8). In other words, now there are various gods who judge the different nations, but in the future all the nations will be God's. These verses describe an almost geographical god whose kingdom encompasses one particular piece of land, accompanied by other gods whose kingdoms are other pieces of land.

According to the monolatrous view, the ban on idolatry exists even in the primary layer of the Bible, but idolatry is forbidden not because of a different metaphysical picture but because of a monolatric attitude. The God of Israel has an additional attribute, that of jealousy. He admits the existence of other gods but forbids their worship. There is no dispute between the pagans and the non-pagans about the existence of gods other than the God of Israel: the dispute between them is over whether it is permitted to worship these other gods.

Kaufmann totally rejects the monolatrous viewpoint. In his view (which we discussed in Chapter 3), biblical belief is imbued with the monotheistic idea in all of its layers, in both story and rites. The Bible knows nothing of the wars of the gods, of the early myths that describe the families of the gods, and of their histories, in which much that happens to the gods is in the hands of fate. All the verses that hint at the existence of many deities are nothing but remnants of things that had already disappeared from the historical consciousness of the Israelites. Even if there are some divine beings other than God himself, they are only faded echoes of living gods. The God of Israel does not fight them, Israel's worship is not addressed to them, and the Bible is completely imbued with the idea of monotheism.[3]

The claim of the scholars who accept the assumption of monolatry is that monotheism is a much later phenomenon than it seems, and that the prohibition on idolatry was historically and conceptually prior to the belief in universal monotheism. This claim thus frees the prohibition from necessary dependence on a monotheistic worldview. Besides monolatry there are sophisticated versions of monotheism that allow for the existence of other powers next to or within God, such as the notion of plurality as a hierarchy or as different aspects of one power. These views narrow the metaphysical gap between monotheism and polytheism, and they turn the issue of idolatry from a matter of a worldview to a matter of an attitude toward a worldview.

### Unity, Hierarchy, and the Christian-Pagan Controversy

Monotheists can be similar to pagans in perceiving the divine world as a hierarchy. Both agree that there exist divine beings headed by one supreme deity. The subjugation of the will of these divine beings to that of the supreme being is the condition for monotheistic belief. Unity is conceived of here as a kind of institutional unity of a system subjugated to the God who heads it. An outstanding expression of the divine world as a hierarchical world built on the model of a royal court is the *Hekhalot* (literally, "palaces") literature. The ascent of the mystic in this literature is through gates and the angels that watch these gates, and the mystic must always preserve the correct hierarchical order between the ministering angels and God. The angels are not just blind forces or agents; they have a will of their own and sometimes are perceived by the mystic as independent rebellious powers, as the stories of the angel Metatron attest. Sometimes the angels, like other bureaucrats, do not rebel directly but rather act slyly for their own purposes.[4]

Claims of similarity between a hierarchy and a pantheon were raised in the Christian-pagan controversy in the direct context of a debate on idolatry. In this controversy, which was conducted during the second and third centuries, the enlightened pagans shared the Christians' metaphysical view of a hierarchically ordered pantheon. The pagans in the controversy claimed that their religion was described literally and thus distorted by the Christians, and that a deeper investigation of the pagan belief would reveal that the Christians had unjustified metaphysical pretensions. Celsus, as quoted by Origen, claims that the Christians had not introduced any novelties into religious belief, and Porphyry, the third-century pagan, claims that it is impossible to distinguish the Christian angels from the pagan subordinate gods.[5] As we saw in the context of the allegorical reading of myth in Chapter 3, there were pagans who interpreted Homer or other pagan texts allegorically. Powers which are aspects of one entity are personified in allegorical literature, and this is how, in the opinion of the enlightened pagans, the pagan texts should be read. Moreover, it seems that the pagans were stricter than the Christians in avoiding corporealization. They did not literally believe in a mythological story about the birth, death, and resurrection of a son of God, while the Christians were unable to give their myth an allegorical interpretation. Although the Christians gave themselves the right to interpret the Bible metaphorically in order to save God from corporeality, they denied this right to the pagans with respect to Homer's writings. The question raised by Celsus is how this can be justified, especially since the Bible is a text that also includes laws that cannot be given an allegorical interpretation, whereas Homer can be interpreted allegorically throughout.

As claimed by E. R. Dodds, the controversy between the pagans and the Christians was not about metaphysics.[6] At that time such controversies cut across lines and did not distinguish between Christians and pagans. The controversy was partly about the issue of the pluralism of pagan worship, as opposed to the monolithic Christian worship. The Christians, according to Origen, claimed that it is better to worship the God at the top of the ladder, and also that it is possible that the pagans were worshiping evil spirits. In the latter argument the Christians are imputing a dualistic viewpoint to the pagans in order to denounce a rival form of worship, but actually the pagans themselves did not have a dualistic viewpoint and did not believe that the forces they worshiped were forces of evil. Origen argued that it is preferable to placate the good God, who is able to defeat the forces of evil, rather than try to placate the evil forces. He did not deny the existence of these forces; he only rejected the strategy of placating them.[7]

The question of how monolithic worship should be was the topic of another controversy related not to metaphysical issues but to attitudes toward the state. Emperor worship, which the enlightened pagans considered nothing more than an expression of loyalty to the state, like anthem singing or flag waving, was rejected by the Christians as idolatry. This raised suspicions that the Christians were not sufficiently loyal to the state and that in times of need they would not rush to defend the empire. This suspicion was particularly significant at a time when the Roman empire was being threatened by external forces. Tertullian's stringent interpretation of the laws concerning idolatry, and their extension to a view of all pagan entertainment and sport activities as acts of idol worship, made it all the more difficult for the Christians to demonstrate their identification with the general Roman public.[8] The restrictions of monolithic worship created a social divisiveness, which became the focus of the controversy between the pagans and the Christians at that time.

We are faced with a prohibition on idolatry in cases where there is no metaphysical difference between the worshipers and those who prohibit the worship. This stage is more sophisticated than the stage of monolatry, which also involves a concept of idolatry without an alternative metaphysics. At this later stage the plurality of forces is perceived as different aspects of a single reality or as organized in the hierarchy of a pantheon, rather than as equivalent forces that divide up nations and territories among themselves, as was the view in monolatry. The zealotry of the monotheists in this controversy is expressed rather in the insistence on the worship of one God than on the existence of one God who is identifiable as most sublime. The center of gravity thus shifts from metaphysics to worship.

With its insistence on one exclusive way of worshiping God, Christianity eventually succeeded over the syncretistic paganic confusion. It instilled in its followers the type of assurance that comes from zealotry for a single way of life, an assurance that could not be provided by pagan pluralism. The opposition to idolatry based on dogmatic maintenance of the metaphysical principle of one God gives way to the orthodox insistence on one form of worship, to one object and in one way. This is the source of the intolerant nature of the monotheistic tradition.

## Correct Worship according to R. Judah Halevi

The Christian-pagan controversy centered on the issue of whether or not there must be an exclusive object of worship, which must be the God at the head of the system of forces. In addition to the question of the object of worship, there is the question of what constitutes the correct form of worship even with respect to the given and proper object. If there is one right way to worship God and all other forms of worship are alien and forbidden, there can be idolatry even in the worship of God. Thus R. Judah Halevi, the twelfth-century Jewish thinker and poet, in his book *The Kuzari* explains the sin of the worship of the golden calf in the desert as a form of improper worship of God. In his view, the Israelites did not, in their worship of the golden calf, deny the God who had taken them out of Egypt. Rather, they were looking for a picture that would provide them with a special and wonderful presence of God, so that they could address as a deity something that symbolized God for them more than anything else—like the holy ark in the temple, which contains the tablets of the law and has the cherubim on top of it and which is addressed as a representation of God. The Israelites' sin in making and worshiping the golden calf was in making a type of picture that was forbidden to them and in ascribing divine power to something they made by themselves of their own will without being commanded to do so by the deity:

> This sin was not on a par with an entire lapse from all obedience to the One who had led them out of Egypt, as only one of His commands was violated by them. God had forbidden images, and in spite of this they made one. They should have waited and not have assumed power, have arranged a place of worship, an altar, and sacrifices. This had been done by the advice of the astrologers and magicians among them, who were of the opinion that their actions based on their ideas would be more correct than the true ones. (*Kuzari*, 1:97)

The sin was in the Israelites' choice of their own symbol, without waiting for a command, as the form of worshiping God must be determined by God himself. In Halevi's famous allegory, the Israelites were like a fool who hands out medicines to ill people without realizing that a medicine that can help one ill person can kill another. In contrast, there are pictures that God has commanded to be made, such as the cherubim. Halevi, who defends the Israelites in the commission of this sin and claims that they did not worship an alien god but rather worshiped God in a way that they were not commanded to, interprets the prohibition on making pictures as a prohibition relating to the method of worship. The ban is on making pictures of one's own choice, like the fool who pretended to be an apothecary.

The difference between idol worshipers and worshipers of God is related mainly to the right method of worship. In the words of Halevi's Kuzarite king: "The theory I had formed, and the opinion of what I saw in my dreams you now confirm, namely, that man can only merit divine influence by acting according to God's commands. And even if it were not so, most men strive to attain it, even astrologers, magicians, fire and sun worshipers, dualists, and so on" (*Kuzari,* 1:98). In this list the Kuzarite king includes prototypical idol worshipers such as fire worshipers and sun worshipers. What characterizes these worshipers, whose intentions are acceptable, is that they do not perform actions prescribed by the deity. The object of the worship is not the decisive factor, since their intent is to worship God to the best of their understanding. The decisive factor is the method and nature of the worship. Only through direct revelation from God is it possible to know what the true and proper worship is.

Halevi wrote *The Kuzari* in the form of a dialogue initiated by the king of Kuzar as he sought to find the true religion. After unsatisfactory discussions with a philosopher, a Christian, and a Muslim, the king was convinced by a Jewish sage to convert to Judaism. In the introduction to the book Halevi describes the event that motivated the king of Kuzar, an idol worshiper, to begin the spiritual search that led to his conversion. An angel appeared in a dream to the Kuzarite king, saying: "Your intention is acceptable but your acts are not acceptable." This message, which was received by the Kuzarite king while he was still worshiping the Kuzarite gods, could not be imagined by someone who insisted on the strict identity of the object of worship. How could his intention be acceptable if he was bringing sacrifices to a worthless god? The king's dream leads to his search and his sudden interest in clarifying the question of the right religion. It thus turns out that already in the dream, which is the starting point of the book, it is not the object of worship that constitutes the central problem, but the method and nature of the worship.

Indeed, when he discusses the controversy with the Karaites, who are apparently equivalent to the rabbinic (non-Karaite) Jews from the standpoint of the object of their worship and differ in their methods of worship, Halevi equates them with idol worshipers. He says: "Did we not state before that speculation, reasoning and fiction about the Law do not lead to God's pleasure? That otherwise dualists, materialists, worshipers of spirits, anchorites, and those who burn their children are all endeavoring to come near to God? We have, however, said that one cannot approach God except by His commands" (*Kuzari,* 3:23). The Karaites resemble idol worshipers in that they too worship God in ways of their own choosing and not on the basis of the tradition handed down from Sinai. The chasm between the Karaites and believers in dual divinity is fathomless when the focus is upon the object of worship, yet Halevi nevertheless equates them because their intention of worshiping God is acceptable but their acts are not.

This emphasis on the proper method of worship is connected with Halevi's battle against philosophy. There is a transition here from the model of error, which asserts that the proper object of worship is the one described by the philosophers and that this is the decisive factor, to a model of proper worship of an object determined in general by the intention, sincerity, and seriousness of the worshiper. This transition reflects to no small extent the dispute about philosophy. The emphasis of the religious philosophical tradition on the proper object of worship undermines the more traditional conception in two senses. One sense is that if the central issue in worship is the proper object, then the issue of the worship itself becomes secondary. The same object may be worshiped in many ways, and the essence of the question is whether the object is the right one and not whether the worship is of the right kind. Philosophy's weak point, in Halevi's view, is that its ethics and worship are relative.[9] Philosophers believe that the goals they are interested in achieving may be achieved in many different ways. In contrast to this philosophical religion, Halevi asserts that the proper way is determined by revelation rather than by reason. Just as the object of worship can be alien, so can the method of worship.

The second sense in which the standpoint of philosophical religion toward error is disturbing to Halevi relates to his view that even the proper description of the object of worship is determined by tradition rather than by philosophical reasoning. If the object of the proper worship were determined by the intellect using some metaphysical method, then every act of performing a commandment would have to be preceded by an intellectual discussion. According to those who view idolatry as error, it is forbidden for anyone to worship God until he knows exactly what the object of his worship is, since worship of the wrong object, even if it is done in the proper manner, counts as idolatry. Halevi asserts that the object of worship is determined by tradition and thus liberates the halakhah from the necessity of making use of philosophy as a prerequisite. Tradition, not philosophy, determines the right object of worship according to the halakhah.

At the end of the fifth section of *The Kuzari,* after discussing the various claims of the philosophers and asserting that anyone who deals with them will end up a heretic, Halevi explains his opposition to the views of the Karaites, who believe "that a complete knowledge of God must precede worship of Him." The truth is that God's command is "to imitate one's fathers and ancestors in their belief in the God of Abraham, Isaac and Jacob." A complicated investigation of the proper object of worship, which is required by those who identify idolatry with error, is not necessary. According to Halevi the knowledge of truths about the deity does not have priority over worship of the deity. Moreover, this knowledge is attained by tradition rather than by investigation. In the complex relationship between revelation and reason, the claim of the importance of the proper object tips the scales toward reason, which is given the right to determine the object of worship. Reason is thus granted a priority which entails that all of revelation without reason might become the worship of an alien god and that the simple believer who clings to tradition might become an idolater. Those who attempt to defeat reason in its battle with tradition assert that there is no real importance to exactness in anything but the worship itself, since the object of worship is determined by the revelation that is handed down by tradition.

According to Halevi, the question of the proper worship puts the other monotheistic religions together with the idolatrous religions on one side, in opposition to Judaism on the other side. This is implied many times in the course of the book; neither the idolatrous religions nor the other monotheistic ones have the proper form of worship—as opposed to Judaism, which continues according to Halevi to transmit the revelation that showed the true path. Halevi's attempt to free tradition from the hold of philosophy shifts the center of gravity from the proper object of worship to the proper form of worship. He emphasizes proper worship as transmitted by revelation and the understanding of idolatry as an alien form of worship rather than as the worship of an alien god.[10]

## Nachmanides' View of Idolatry as Rebellion and Witchcraft

A detailed conception of the sin in idolatry that does not involve the metaphysical issue may be found in the writings of Nachmanides.

Nachmanides believes that idolatry is the worship of real forces, and that it is perhaps for this reason that it was forbidden. In Nachmanides' view the issue is the appropriate attitude toward the metaphysical worldview rather than the metaphysical worldview itself. He emphasizes not only the proper form of worship but the proper attitude. Nachmanides presents us with a systematic viewpoint of what might be called "sophisticated monolatry," that is, monolatry with a metaphysics of plurality involving a hierarchy of forces rather than equipotent forces.

In his interpretation of the verse "You shall have no other gods besides Me" (Exodus 20:3), Nachmanides distinguishes three categories of idolatry that were customary among the idolaters (Nachmanides, Deuteronomy 18:9, Leviticus 17:7). The first is the worship of separate intelligences, or angels. The Bible calls this type of worship the worship of "other gods" because angels are called "gods." This worship has substance, in Nachmanides' opinion, "because it is known that some of them have rulership over the peoples, as it is written, 'the prince of the kingdom of Greece, the prince of the kingdom of Persia.'" The second category is the worship of the heavenly bodies—the sun or the moon or one of the constellations—and this category had its false prophets, about whom Nachmanides says: "Now all these groups had false prophets who foretold them future events and informed them through the arts of sorcery and divination some of the things that were to come upon them. The constellations also have lords who abide in the atmosphere as the angels do in the heavens, and know the things that are to come." The third category is worship of demons and spirits, as Nachmanides says: "Some of them too are appointed over the peoples to be masters in their lands and to harm their beleaguered ones and those who have stumbled" (Nachmanides, Exodus 20:3).

Nachmanides describes idolatry as the worship of various elements in the hierarchy of forces—angels, constellations, demons. The implication is that these forces are real ones, that God gave the constellations dominion over the gentile nations, and, moreover, that it is possible to foretell the future by means of witchcraft and divination. Israel is forbidden to worship these forces principally because the constellations have no dominion over them, as the Israelites are God's portion and property. Idol worship is thus not an error, and this idea stands out clearly in Nachmanides' daring interpretation of the sending of the scapegoat into the desert on Yom Kippur:

> Now this is the secret of the matter. They used to worship other gods, namely, the angels, bringing offerings of a sweet savor to them . . . Now the Torah has absolutely forbidden to accept them as deities, or to worship them in any manner. However, the Holy One, blessed be He, commanded us that on the Day of Atonement we should let loose a goat in the wilderness to that "prince" [power] which rules over wastelands, and this goat is fitting for it because he is its master, and destruction and waste emanate from that power . . . Now the intention in our sending away the goat to the desert was not that it should be an offering from us to it—Heaven forbid! Rather, our intention should be to fulfill the wish of our Creator, who commanded us to do so. (Nachmanides, Leviticus 16:8)

What is unique about the sending of the scapegoat, in Nachmanides' view, is that this ritual involves addressing a power that is generally worshiped by idolaters. The scapegoat is sent into the desert, which is the fiefdom of the minister of ruined places, and the minister is worthy of receiving this gift because he is the lord of the place, as his power creates ruin and desert. What distinguishes the sending of the scapegoat from idolatry is that this act is done at the command of God. The gap between idol worshipers and their opponents is thus narrowed in the extreme. Not only do monotheists and idolaters agree on their worldview, but in this important though exceptional case they actually address the same power. The difference is that the nonpagan does this at the command of God, who orders him to bring a sacrifice to one of his servants.

This distinction clarifies a profound issue in Nachmanides' view of what idolatry is. Idolatry is rebellion and the attempt to impose a different order on the world through the use of various powers. This is the source of the closeness between idolatry and witchcraft, which is especially salient in Nachmanides' interpretations of the verses dealing with the ban on witchcraft.[11] In Nachmanides' opinion witchcraft is effective because God made the higher beings—the stars and constellations—rulers of the lower beings. Reality is constructed in the form of a hierarchy, in which each level influences the level below it. Thus the constellations influence events occurring below them, and so burning incense to a particular constellation at a par-

ticular time can influence future events for good or for evil. Idolatry
is thus the attempt to attain this sort of influence on states of affairs.
After asserting the effectiveness of witchcraft Nachmanides justifies
its prohibition: "in order to let the world continue in its customary
way, in the simple nature which is the desire of its Creator"
(Nachmanides, Deuteronomy 18:9). Witchcraft is a denial of the
hierarchy of forces, a forbidden attempt to impose a change on
reality by violating its natural order. There is a hierarchy of forces
from the first emanator down to the constellations and demons, and
the witch breaks into a particular level of the hierarchy and employs
his power in isolation from the other elements and from the primary
wish of God. Nachmanides perceives a direct connection between
witchcraft and idolatry, and in his description of idolatry in the
passage cited above he says: "Now these are the people who began
making the many forms of graven images, *Asheirim* and the sun-
images. They would make the forms of the constellations in the
hours of their strength according to their rank" (Nachmanides,
Exodus 20:3). The making of statues and pictures is thus connected
with the attempt to influence the constellations at the proper times
with the appropriate pictures. Idolatry is forbidden precisely because
it is not an error but an attempt, which is sometimes successful, to
intervene in the order of things as God wants them to be.

Nachmanides, who was a prominent kabbalist, held the view that
the hierarchy of forces according to which the world functions exists
not only in the levels between God and the world but also within
the divinity itself. This daring view of the godhead had among many
other implications an impact on the redefinition of idolatry in kabbalistic tradition, as we will discuss in this and the next section.
From the twelfth century onward one of the central preoccupations
of the Kabbalah was the articulation of God as a network of attributes known as *sefirot,* which are linked to one another in a branched
arrangement of emanation and influence. God's faculties flow from
the hidden aspect of God known as the *Ein-Sof.* When they reveal
themselves they take the form of the *sefirot,* the active powers of the
divine, which enjoy complicated relations of giving and receiving,
of tension and sympathy. One of the most significant tensions
within the structure of the godhead takes place between the attribute
of judgment, which is the divine aspect that establishes limits and
boundaries, and the attribute of love, which represents the endless

and unlimited bounty of God. The role of man according to the kabbalists is to secure the unity of this teeming divine structure, and he accomplishes this by fulfilling the commandments of the Torah. Man becomes responsible for the equilibrium within the godhead, for the delicate divine balance that is always on the verge of upsetting itself, and he secures the affinity between God and world that keeps the world in existence. Idolatry according to the kabbalists is the extreme opposite of what is achieved in adherence to the Torah; instead of unity, idolatry creates division within the godhead. Worshiping one of these aspects of the divinity, such as the characteristic of justice, and separating it from the totality of the *sefirot*, constitutes idolatry in the mystic sense. The expression used for this in the kabbalistic literature is "cutting the plants." The "cutting" generally takes place through the separation of the lowest *sefirah*, dominion, from the *sefirah* of splendor, which connects it with the rest of the system of *sefirot*. This "cutting" (which is described extensively in the thirteenth-century text *Ma'arekhet ha-Elohut*, in the section "On Destruction") causes the world to be cut off from the abundance flowing from splendor *(tif'eret)* to the lowest dominion *(shekhina)*. It also causes the evil forces of Satan to cling to the *shekhina* and prevent it from functioning, which allows harsh decrees to come down upon the world.

Nachmanides offers a kabbalistic explanation for the sin of idolatry. Using this esoteric explanation, which he calls "the interpretation according to way of truth," he analyzes the verse "You shall have no other gods besides Me" in the following way: "According to the way of truth, you will understand the secret of 'face' [*panim*] from that which we have written that the Torah warned about the revelation: 'Face to face [*panim be-phanim*] the Lord spoke to you' (Deuteronomy 5:4). And you will know the secret of the word 'other' [*acheirim*]." Besides the simple sense of "other gods" as constellations and idols, it is apparent that there is an esoteric understanding of what "other gods" are. Nachmanides hints that the esoteric interpretation of "other gods" refers to the *sefirot* of the divinity itself when considered separately. According to this interpretation, which is related to the kabbalistic perception of the divinity, idolatry is worship of one of the *sefirot* in isolation from the divinity as a whole. In explaining the sin of the golden calf, Nachmanides says: "Thus they transgressed the prohibition, 'You shall have no other gods besides Me' (Exodus 20:3), as I have hinted there, and you will understand this" (Nachmanides, Exodus 32:4). This explanation of the sin of the golden calf clarifies the esoteric point hinted at in Nachmanides' interpretation of the earlier verse:

> Now Aaron's intention was as follows. Because Israel was in the wilderness, a desolate wasteland, and destruction and everlasting desolation come from the north, as it is written, "From the north shall disaster break loose upon all the inhabitants of the land" (Jeremiah 1:14), the reference being not merely to the king of Babylon, as can be seen clearly from what is written, but rather that the attribute of justice comes to the world from the left, to requite upon all the inhabitants of the land according to their evil; and since in the account of the divine chariot it is said, "each of the four had the face of an ox on the left" (Ezekiel 1:10), therefore Aaron thought that the destroyer was a guide through the place of destruction where his great power is centered. (Nachmanides, Exodus 32:1)

Nachmanides explains why he sees the calf as the symbol of the characteristic of justice. He says that the divine chariot, which is a widespread symbol for entire system of *sefirot,* has the face of an ox on its left side, and the left side is the characteristic of justice in kabbalistic symbolism. Aaron addressed the characteristic of justice specifically because the Israelites were in the desert, which is its domain. The Israelites' sin was that they displaced the power of the characteristic of justice from its position in the system of the *sefirot* and worshiped it alone, on the assumption that in Moses' absence this was the *sefirah* that would lead them in the desert, the place of justice. Nachmanides specifically refers to this sin as "cutting the plants" in his interpretation of the verse "your people have acted destructively" (Exodus 32:7):

> God said to Moses, "My people have done a twofold wrong" (Jeremiah 2:13). One is that "your people have dealt destructively." The meaning of the term *hashchatha* is the destruction of a structure, similar to that which is written, "each with his club [*mashchetho,* literally, "his weapon of destruction"] in his hand" (Ezekiel 9:1) . . . And the meaning of "destruction" here is what our Rabbis called "cutting the plants" [by seeking to undermine the principle of the Unity].

In the next section we discuss the kabbalistic conception of idolatry extensively. What is important at this point is that there is an analogy between idolatry in its exoteric meaning and idolatry in its esoteric meaning—between the ordinary, exoteric meaning of the verse "You shall have no other gods" and the kabbalistic meaning. To have other gods, according to the simple meaning, is to worship one of the lower powers, such as the angels, and to use them to change the order of the world. The motivation is opposition to the existing order and the wish to impose a new order. In the esoteric sense "cutting the plants" is not only meddling in the cosmic order but also disturbing the very balance among the various manifestations of the divinity itself. It is thus a denial of the divine hierarchy from within. Instead of worshiping the divinity as a whole, the worshiper addresses only one of the *sefirot* and thus isolates it from the rest of the system of divine forces. This constitutes intervention within the internal hierarchy of the divinity and distorts the whole system.[12]

Idolatry in and of itself is not an error, even though it may stem from an error—from a one-sided view of the total system of forces. Those who reject idolatry do not offer an alternative metaphysical picture to that of the idolaters—monotheists and idolaters share the same metaphysical picture. Both of them believe in the existence of forces that can be influenced by ritual, both admit the existence of ministers who rule over the nations of the world and demons who have been granted dominion over ruined and desert places. Moreover, those who "cut the plants" and those who consider them sinners and heretics do not differ about the metaphysical picture of the *sefirot* with their internal dynamic balance; it is the attitudes of the two groups toward this metaphysical picture that are totally different. The main sin in idolatry is not that it is based on an incorrect and misleading worldview—perhaps it is entirely correct—but that it involves breaking into the picture in a concerted attempt to isolate one aspect of reality and influence the world through it. When this "cutting of the plants" takes place at deeper points in the hierarchy, the sin becomes more severe, because the worshiper is attempting to affect the inner layers of the divine order. We are faced with an approach that identifies idolatry as an act of rebellion and destruction rather than as an error.

To clarify the notion of "cutting the plants" and the concept of the divinity that arises from it, we turn to a discussion of organic unity and idolatry in the kabbalistic tradition, as an example of the separation of the issue of idolatry from the metaphysical problem and its transformation into an issue of worship.

## Organic Unity

In various kabbalistic traditions the symbols of divine unity are organic symbols. The divinity is symbolized as the primordial man, or as a tree, whose various aspects are connected with one another through a ramified system of emanation and absorption. From the hidden aspect of God, the "infinite," his powers emanate and are revealed in ten *sefirot* related as givers and receivers, which maintain a dynamic system of tensions and balances among the various aspects, such as will and wisdom, justice and mercy. The various symbols of the *sefirot* and the relations between them describe the inner life of God, which is nourished from within itself, in its multiplicity of different aspects. The "infinite," which is the hidden God, reveals itself in the *sefirot* that are nourished by it, in such a way that there is a duality in the relationship between the hidden, unknown, undefined aspect—the "infinite"—and the system of *sefirot* nourished by it.

In addition, the *sefirot,* which are different aspects of God's rulership, constitute within themselves a multiplicity of oppositions, including that between justice, which is the narrowing and limiting aspect, and mercy, which is the infinite and unlimited abundance of the divinity. What preserves the unity of the whole system is a process similar to the one that preserves the unity of organic systems: the organism is unified by connections of nourishment and growth, its various aspects depending for their existence on the functioning of other parts of the system. This is not a simple unity in the philosophical sense, but a complex organic unity.

The unity of the divine system was described at the first appearance in the Kabbalah as the image of "a flame attached to a burning coal." [13] The purpose of this image was to strengthen the unity between the *sefirot* and the infinite. In this image it is the relation of continuous causal dependence, in spite of the fact that the flame and the burning coal are two different entities, that preserves the unity of the system. In addition to the continuous causal dependence, the image provides a feeling of the realization of things that were already latent in the infinite, and the continuity also provides a concept of unity for the system.

Gershom Scholem considered this change in the concept of unity one manifestation of the return of myth into the heart of the monotheistic tradition. In Scholem's view the myths that had once been rejected by the monotheists had become central to Judaism, and their return could be seen in the mythic symbols of the *sefirot* describing the inner life of the deity, such as the masculine symbols of splendor and foundation and the feminine symbol of the *shekhinah*.[14] In addition, some kabbalists ascribed to evil an ontological source within the divinity, a view that may pose a danger of tending toward dualism, in which evil has a parallel ontological status to that of the forces of good. The conception of the commandments also adds a mythic dimension to the kabbalistic view. The reasons for the commandments in the Kabbalah are theurgic—that is, through the performance of a commandment it is considered possible to affect the divinity. The commandments serve to patch up the tears between the various aspects of the divinity, which sometimes become separated from one another. In this conception of the commandments as a "higher need," the relationship between God and man is not the relationship of commander and fulfiller: God is perceived as dependent upon the actions of man. Thus the Kabbalah becomes closer to the mythic view in which magic is involved in ritual worship and the deity is in a state of mutual dependence with its worshipers.

This kabbalistic conception of the deity and the commandments fulfills the conditions we used to characterize myth in Chapter 3. The various aspects of the divinity provide the characters for the divine drama, which is the first condition for myth, and the theurgic conception of the commandments provides the sacrament, which is the realization of the divine drama in the life of the believer and in the ritual worship.[15]

This brief description of the concept of organic unity leaves out the various streams within the kabbalistic tradition and the differences between the more philosophical kabbalistic approaches and the approaches that are known for their mythic daring. The author of the *Zohar,* with its wealth of mythic symbols, is not the same as Gikatila or Cordovero, with their philosophical leanings. Side by side with those who considered the *sefirot* as constituting the essence of the divinity, there existed kabbalists who considered the *sefirot* created vessels or instruments for divine action. The latter group gave less weight to myth; they perceived a complete unity within the divinity itself and viewed the *sefirot* existing outside God as intermediaries between God and the world.[16] A more radical criticism within kabbalistic circles of the mythical element of the *sefirot* was raised by Abulafia, a thirteenth-century kabbalist from the ecstatic school, who rejected the Kabbalah of the *sefirot* as confused and heretical. He adopted a Maimonidean view of the internal unity of the godhead and rejected the theosophy of the organic unity of the *sefirot* as a theosophy of polytheism.[17] The mythic idea created by the theosophy of the *sefirot* aroused internal tensions within kabbalistic circles regarding the proper formulation of the relationships between the *sefirot* and God. That mythic element drove some kabbalists to an overall criticism of the way of the *sefirot*.

This is not the place for an extensive description of the various transformations of the symbols and views of the theory of the *sefirot*. In our brief survey we have seen that a mythic motif became deeply intertwined with the tradition, so that with the spread of the kabbalistic tradition the problem of idolatry turned into a problem within Judaism. The sworn enemy—clothed in a halo of the esoteric—infiltrated into the very camp, captured hearts, and won itself a permanent place in the Jewish tradition. How, then, does the kabbalistic tradition, with its outstandingly mythic tone and its concept of organic unity, understand the prohibition on idolatry? This question is related to the main argument of this chapter—that different visions of the divinity create different conceptions of idolatry. The mythic tradition as well, inasmuch as it is a part of the Jewish tradition, must distinguish itself—at least from its own viewpoint—from what it defines as idolatry. What is idolatry for those who describe the divinity as the primordial man? What god can be "other" for the kabbalistic God to whom elements of myth are attached?

The denunciation of the Kabbalah as sullying the pure monotheistic tradition was expressed early on by R. Meir ben Simon. He described the kabbalists as follows:

And they say that one must pray at day-time to one created god and at night to another, who is above him but who is created like

him, and on holidays, to yet another . . . They are an abomination
to all flesh; the worm of their folly will not perish, and the fire of
their nonsense will not be extinguished. For they have chosen
many gods and they say in their unreason that they are all connected with one another and all is one . . . If they say that He is
one, why do they then divide their prayer between one of the day
and one of the night?[18]

According to R. Meir ben Simon the practice of praying to different
*sefirot* on different occasions is an outstanding sign of the polytheistic
heresy of the kabbalists. Such formulations of addressing prayers to
the *sefirot* had existed among the kabbalists in the twelfth century, as
R. Isaac the Blind said: "For there is no way to pray except through
limited things. One is accepted and raised in thought to the
infinite."[19] In a later text, one written by a kabbalist, the attitude
toward those who pray to the various *sefirot* is described even more
sharply:

All those who pray to any entity except God are heretics and rebels
against the kingdom of Heaven. Their honor will be given to
others, for they pray to a god who cannot help them. And even
though there are some new-fangled kabbalists who have strayed
from the right path—one prays to the crown, one to wisdom, and
one to understanding; one makes his requests of greatness and one
pleads with splendor and the following *sefirot* . . . I will answer
them shortly and say that no one should be seduced by this, no
clever person should outsmart himself by following his own
understanding, because he will come to deny God and to substitute
the servant for the master, God forbid. This will happen to those
who are seduced by their opinions, who stray from the straight
path to walk on the path of darkness and worship gods besides
God . . . But God forbid that anyone should pray to any *sefirah* or
to any of God's characteristics, for there is no greater heretic than
one who worships other gods and the number of his gods is the
number of his fingers. He deserves to be torn apart like a fish on
Yom Kippur, which occurs on the Sabbath.[20]

Here the plurality of objects of intention in prayer is called absolute idolatry. The intentions of the kabbalists, who address the different *sefirot* at different times and with different prayers, constitute
the worship of other gods. Their worship loses its exclusive object,
and this is the root of idolatry. The danger of idolatry stemming

from the plurality of the *sefirot* and the prayer intentions addressed to each *sefirah* led some kabbalists to hedge these intentions and to interpret them differently. They explained the custom of addressing different *sefirot* at different times and under different circumstances as meaning that the one God should adopt the characteristic of justice or the characteristic of mercy, rather than being a prayer to these characteristics, even as intermediaries.[21]

These explanations of the prayer intentions, which avoid the independent worship of the *sefirot,* are not the literal interpretation of the kabbalistic instructions for the intentions. These instructions imply that the worshiper is addressing a particular *sefirah,* and his intention goes up in a secret unity to the "infinite." The "infinite," since it is unknowable and impersonal, is not an object of prayer and worship: prayers address the *sefirot,* through which they rise and then cling to the "infinite." The multiplicity of divine aspects existing in the model of organic unity harbors the danger of worship of these aspects, and this already constitutes a dangerous narrowing of the gap between worshiping God and worshiping other gods. With the slightest deflection of thought and intention the worship of God can be transformed into idolatry, and only a hairbreadth divides the true worshiper of God from one who prays to a God who cannot help him. This danger exists if the prayer is not uttered according to the exacting instructions that limit the independence of the *sefirot.* Indeed, according to the critics many worshipers are actually addressing an alien god in their prayer. Here idolatry infiltrates into the very heart of Judaism, and the struggle against idolatry becomes an intrareligious struggle between various factions that consider themselves traditional.

Idolatry in the context of the image of organic unity is the worship of an aspect—the separation of a part from its unity and the worship of that separated part. This is the language in which the kabbalists themselves warn their followers against prayer to specific *sefirot* independently, in sharp warnings calling such prayer idolatry. From the mythic worldview of divine organic unity, in which man can act and cause a separation between the elements of the unity, the concept of idolatry as "cutting" was created. This is idolatry that has real substance, as it destroys not only the soul of the worshiper but also the very delicately balanced structure of the divinity, thus separating the world from its source of vitality.

## What Is Worship?

Since the center of gravity has shifted to the concept of worship, it is important to clarify what worship is. The first question is whether worship is constituted by intention—whether worship reflects belief and an internal relation to the object of worship—or whether it is completely defined by ritual actions, with no importance attached to the intentions accompanying the act of worship. In this analysis we make use of examples taken from the discussions of worship in the Talmud and the medieval commentators on the Talmud.

The Talmud describes a number of cases that seem to contradict one another on the subject of the relation between worship and intention. Attempts made by medieval commentators to reconcile these cases with one another reflect various attitudes toward the relation between intention and worship. The first case appears in the Mishnah, Tractate *Sanhedrin* chap. 7: "If someone relieves himself before Ba'al Pe'or, this is the way it is worshiped; if someone throws a stone to Mercury, this is the way it is worshiped." According to the Mishnah, anyone performing one of these acts has committed idolatry, because this is the way these two idols, Ba'al Pe'or and Mercury, are worshiped. The Gemara, in its commentary on the Mishnah just quoted, says: "'If someone relieves himself before Ba'al Pe'or, this is the way it is worshiped.' Even if he intended to mock it. 'If someone throws a stone at Mercury, this is the way it is worshiped.' Even if he intended to stone it." [22] The Gemara asks why the Mishnah saw fit to single out these instances of idolatry from all other idolatrous acts. After all, these are the ways in which the idols called "Ba'al Pe'or" and "Mercury" are worshiped. The Gemara deduces from this that anyone who performs these acts is liable to punishment, even if his intention was to mock the idol by relieving himself before it or by throwing stones at it. According to the Gemara, the Mishnah mentioned these cases, in addition to the general rule that it is forbidden to worship idols in the customary manner of their worship, in order to teach us that this rule applies even if the person intended to mock the idol. Worship, even if it constitutes a mockery of the idol, is forbidden because it is the accepted ritual for worshiping the idol. The definition of the act as worship thus depends not on the intention of the worshiper but solely on the question of whether the act he performed fits the observational criteria for the customary worship of that idol. It is the context that provides the meaning of the act as worship.

The second halakhah pertaining to the relation between intention and worship is the one asserting that idolatry is a prohibition which must not be transgressed even at the cost of one's life. That is, if a person is threatened to be killed if he does not commit idolatry, he must refuse to do so and allow himself to be killed.[23] This halakhah implies that even though he was coerced the act is considered idolatry, and he must sacrifice his life. Thus according to this halakhah as well it turns out that it is not the person's intention that determines the nature of his act, since a coerced person obviously has no intention of worshiping the idol.

The third example, which contradicts the two examples above on the question of whether intention is a condition for worship, is Raba's view: "If someone worships idols out of love or out of fear, Abbaye says that he is liable to punishment, but Raba says that he is exempt from punishment. Abbaye says he is liable because he has performed an act of worship, while Raba says that he is exempt—if he accepted the idol as a god, then he is liable, but if not, then he is exempt."[24] According to the interpretation of most medieval commentators, Raba's opinion is that a person who worshiped an idol because he was afraid of another person, or because he wanted to appease him, is exempt from punishment. Raba's reason for this is that this worshiper did not accept the idol as a deity, but only worshiped it because of external pressure. According to Raba—and this is the opinion that is accepted in practice—"acceptance as a deity" is necessary in order to make the worshiper liable for punishment for idolatry: the act alone is not sufficient.

Medieval commentators on the relation between worship and intention attempted to reconcile these contradictory examples. To understand their attempts we must distinguish between two sorts of intentions. One is the intention defining an action, and the other is the intention defining an action as a sin. Let's say that a person happens to be standing in front of an idol, and he bends down to take a thorn out of his foot. It then appears as if he is bowing down to the idol, but in such a case even those who claim that intention is not needed for worship will agree that he did not worship the idol. The intention that is lacking here is that required for the definition of the action under the description of "bowing down" rather than "bending down"; the intention that defines the action as "worship" is therefore not even under consideration. Another example is that of a person who bows down in the synagogue on Yom Kippur, when this action is prescribed by custom. In such a case intention is necessary in order to define what this person is bowing down to. He is supposed to be bowing down to the invisible God rather than to any visible object in front of him, but we would have to know his intention in order to determine that he is not actually bowing down to the picture of the lion on the curtain covering the holy ark. This is not the intention that determines whether one is performing an act of worship. It is a second sort of action-defining intention, in the sense that it defines the object of the bowing down.[25] In the first example the intention differentiates between bending down and bowing down, whereas in the second example it defines the object to which the person is bowing down. In neither of these cases is the intention of the sort that defines worship, meaning, "I hereby accept as a deity this idol that I am bowing down to." Rather, it says, "I am bowing down rather than bending down," or "I am bowing down to the idol rather than to some other object." It is the sort of intention necessary for describing the observed act as bowing down to an idol, rather than that necessary to define the act as idolatry in the opinion of those who claim that idolatry requires intention.

There are, however, times when the intention of accepting the object as a god is necessary for the definition of the action itself. Such a case occurs when the observational data do not determine whether the action is idolatry. For example, let us assume that bowing down is a gesture that is performed by one person for another to demonstrate respect. When someone bows or curtsies before the Queen of England, there is no reason for anyone to think that this is worship—it is most likely a gesture of respect. In such a case the definition of the act as worship would be dependent on the intention of the person performing the act to accept the Queen of England as his deity. The observational context of the act does not provide its meaning as worship, because in general people who bow or curtsy to the Queen of England are not worshiping her but are simply offering a gesture of respect.

In the case of bowing down to an idol that is ritually worshiped, the context and the fact that this idol is one that is religiously worshiped define the act as an act of worship rather than a gesture of respect, independently of the intention of the person performing the action. When, however, such a context is lacking, and this object has never been worshiped by anyone else, what defines the act as worship can only be the intention of accepting the object as a deity. There is no external context that can define it as such, since the gesture may be interpreted in various ways. Those commentators who claimed that idolatry is in principle independent of intention offered the following interpretation of Raba's claim that idolatry does depend on intention: Raba was referring only to a case in which intention is required for the very definition of the act as worship, and not to a case in which intention is required for defining an act of worship as a sin. One example of this view is the opinion of the Tosafists, who perceive a contradiction between the halakhah that one must sacrifice one's life rather than commit idolatry and Raba's claim that one who worships out of love or fear is exempt from punishment.[26] They resolve the contradiction by emphasizing the context and accepted practice. In Raba's case the intention of worshiping a deity is required, because without this intention there is no context to provide the meaning of the act, as in the example of bowing down before the Queen of England. But in a case where there is such a context, that is, where this idol is worshiped by a community, then the act is idol worship even without intention. Intention is not required as a necessary condition for determining that the person has performed an idolatrous act, because in the case of unwilling worship, such as worship under the threat of being killed, the act performed is an established idolatrous act, as in the case of someone who performs the rituals peculiar to the worship of Ba'al Pe'or or Mercury with the intention of mocking them. Intention is required in a case where there is no external context independent of the intention that can define the act as an act of worship, as in the case of an object that is not generally worshiped. Raba requires limited intention, according to this view, only in cases without a context. Intention is required on an elementary level to determine what action is being performed and what criteria we use to describe it, but not as an essential part of the definition of the sin. This approach claims that worship is essentially an observational event, but sometimes the context does not provide the meaning of the event, and in such cases intention becomes important. This approach thus contrasts with the view that worship is an internal event by definition.

Most of the medieval commentators followed Nachmanides' conclusion that intention is necessary for the definition of an act of worship as a sin. As Raba maintained, to commit idolatry one must accept the object as a deity. Cases in which it is obligatory to allow oneself to be killed rather than commit an idolatrous act reveal the obligation of sanctifying the name of God. As Nachmanides says in his commentary on Tractate *Shabbat,* if a person is threatened with death unless he bows down to an idol, he must sacrifice his life—not because he will be committing idolatry if he does not sacrifice his life, but because he is obligated to sanctify the name of God by his opposition, to demonstrate his opposition to idolatry even at the cost of his life.[27] Indeed, if he worships the idol and does not sacrifice his life, he may not be sentenced to death as an idolater, since he did not intend to accept the idol as his deity. In such a case he is considered one who failed to sanctify the name of God rather than an idolater. These commentators thus believe that the act committed under the threat of death is not considered worship under compulsion; rather, it is not worship at all, as worship is dependent for its very definition on internal intention. The person who is exempted from the death punishment in the case of bowing down under the threat of being killed is exempt not because he was compelled to perform the act but because the act is not considered an act of worship at all. This is how these commentators resolve the contradiction between Raba's dictum that acceptance of a deity is required for idolatry and the obligation to die rather than perform an idolatrous act.

The second case the medieval commentators attempted to resolve concerns the law that a person is held liable when he intends to mock an idol such as Ba'al Pe'or or Mercury by performing the act that is the customary way of worshiping this idol. This case is different from the case where one is obligated to forfeit one's life rather than perform the idolatrous act because in this case the act itself is performed voluntarily, although for the purpose of mockery. The same commentators—those who claim that worship requires the intention of acceptance of a deity—assert that in the second case, despite the person's intent to mock the idol, he is considered to have worshiped it because this is the way of worshiping that idol. That is, even though he understands the meaning of his action as mockery, he intends to worship the idol by means of this mockery.[28] According to these commentators, in a case where he intends to mock the idol but not to worship it he is exempt from punishment, because worship requires the intention of acceptance as a deity. Worship is an internal event that requires intention, and the external context is not sufficient to define it as such.

Another question to be discussed is which gestures are considered forms of worship. Is any gesture addressed to an idol considered worship of the idol, on the assumption that it is accompanied by the intention of worship, or are there some specific gestures that are defined as worship according to various criteria? This question is important because our lives are filled with rituals demonstrating respect toward individuals or institutions, such as saluting the flag or standing up in honor of an important person. When do such acts become idolatry? The full significance of this question will be clarified in the next chapter. Here we address the performance of gestures in a clear ritual framework.

The Mishnah in Tractate *Sanhedrin* and the section of the Talmud dealing with the definition of idolatry establish a number of criteria for worship. The first criterion for idolatry is worshiping an idol in the way its worshipers do: such worship is called "customary worship." The second criterion is worshiping the idol with the acts that are defined as worship of God in the holy temple and are called "temple worship"—animal sacrifice, incense burning, libation, and blood sprinkling. When someone performs one of these acts in worship, even if this is not the customary worship of the idol, he is considered an idolater and the act is called "worship that is not customary." The third criterion is the act of prostration, or bowing down with at least one's knees and head touching the ground. Prostration, although not an inner act of worship in the temple, is always defined as worship, even if it is not the customary way of worshiping the particular idol. We therefore are faced with three types of idol worship—customary worship, temple worship, and prostration. In contrast to these acts of worship are such acts as embracing, kissing, honoring, sprinkling water for, anointing, and clothing the idol. A person who performs one of these acts is deemed to have transgressed a negative commandment, but he is not subject to the death penalty as an idolater. These acts are considered acts of honoring the idol, but they are not acts of idolatry unless they are the customary way of worshiping the particular idol. They are not considered acts of idolatry even if the person performing them intended by them to accept the idol as a deity, because intention, even according to those who believe that worship requires intention, is not a sufficient criterion for worship; it is also necessary to perform an act that is interpreted as worship.

To clarify the conditions under which a particular act is interpreted as worship, we must describe in more detail the last two kinds of worship we mentioned. Prostration is considered worship in any context, whether or not it is the customary worship of the idol. The very gesture of prostration includes its meaning within itself. Prostration may be defined as the universal language of worship, and thus the person performing this act before an idol is always liable to punishment (on the condition that he performed the act with intention, according to the medieval commentators cited above), whether or not this is the customary worship of the idol. In contrast, all other forms of worship are dependent on convention. If they are considered worship by those who perform them, then they are acts of worship, even if they appear to be acts of mockery, such as relieving oneself before Ba'al Pe'or or throwing a stone at Mercury.

Temple worship may be explained as acts that constitute a paradigm of what is considered worship in general—for example, animal sacrifice. In this sense they are similar to prostration, which is, as we have seen, a type of worship that is not dependent upon the conventions of the worshipers of the particular idol. Such an explanation is implied by Rashi, who explains why other acts of worship associated with the temple, such as putting the blood of the sacrifice into a receptacle or bringing it to be sprinkled, are considered acts of worship for the purpose of various other laws but are not considered acts of idol worship if performed for idolatry. In Rashi's words, "We have not seen idols that are worshiped by putting the blood into a receptacle or bringing it to be sprinkled."[29] According to Rashi not all acts of worship performed in the temple are considered acts of temple worship for the purpose of defining idolatry; only those "classic" acts of worship that are generally performed for idols.

Another way of explaining temple worship is to say that it involves worshiping idols by doing acts that are supposed to be performed only for God. It is because these are acceptable conventions for the worship of God that performing them for idols is forbidden. Acts of temple worship are always considered worship because of the prohibition on performing for idols acts that are unique to the worship of God. According to the second explanation this category is different from the category of prostration, because even if these acts of temple worship were not considered acts of worship any-where else—even if they were not "classic" acts of worship—they would still be considered idolatry since they involve acts that are supposed to be unique to the worship of God.[30]

## Idolatry and Lifestyle

The place of metaphysical error in the sin of idolatry is over-shadowed when the stress is shifted from the object of worship to the method of worship. The relevance of belief to idolatry is decreased even further when the degenerate lifestyle of the idolaters is seen as the worst aspect of idolatry. This view has its roots in certain biblical passages that equate idolatry with licentiousness (Leviticus 18:27). The trend is continued in the Talmud, which describes a direct connection between sexual license and idolatry, with sexual license being considered the motive for idolatry.[31] In Tractate *Avodah Zarah,* which (in spite of its name) does not deal with idolatry but rather with the determination of the proper rela-tions between Jews and idolaters, one finds a harsh picture of idola-ters, who are suspected of incest, adultery, and murder. These suspicions have various halakhic ramifications connected with the obligation of caution and keeping one's distance in dealings with these lawless people, who are capable of any crime. It is forbidden to be alone with them in a room or to walk with them alone on an unfrequented road, and there are various other laws that highlight their image as lawless people.[32] In addition there are metaphorical extensions of idolatry in the Talmud, such as the homiletic interpre-tation in Tractate *Shabbat* of the verse "You shall have no foreign god among [literally: within] you" (Psalm 81:10), which interprets the expression "within you" as referring to someone who is enslaved to his evil desires, as if he had a foreign god within himself that he was enslaved to.[33]

But although a degenerate lifestyle was associated with idolatry and idolaters, a degenerate lifestyle is not a definition—and certainly not a halakhic definition—of what constitutes idolatry. According to the sources mentioned, the picture of a degenerate lifestyle is attached to idolaters, whether justifiably or not, but in none of these sources is there any hint of the more interesting converse assertion that, since idolatry is a degenerate lifestyle, therefore people who live in a well-ordered, law-abiding society, even if they believe in a plurality of gods, are not idolaters. It was only much later, in R. Menahem Ha-Meiri's writings on Christianity in the thirteenth century, that idolatry was identified with lifestyle and defined halakhically as a sinful one.

A few words about the Jewish attitude toward Christianity in the Middle Ages will provide the background for our discussion of Ha-Meiri's writings. Tractate *Avodah Zarah* set limits to the relations between Jews and idolaters. It was forbidden to do business with idolaters three days before or three days after their holidays. It was forbidden to derive any benefit from idolatry or to provide it with any benefit. Thus it was forbidden to participate in any sale if the taxes on it would be transferred to a place of idolatry, and there were many other restrictions connected with this prohibition.[34] During the Middle Ages these restrictions created many difficulties in the economic life of the Jews who lived among the Christians. Unlike the Muslims who were considered by Jews as pure monotheists, the Christians were perceived as apparent idolaters because of their belief in the Trinity and the incarnation of God in his son and because of the presence of images in the church. The most important rabbinic authorities, including Maimonides, held the opinion that the Christians counted as idolaters for all considerations. The application to dealings with Christians of all the prohibitions concerning business dealings with idolaters prevented the Jews from doing business with Christians at all. If Sunday is the Christians' holiday, and it is forbidden to trade with them three days before and three days afterward, there are no days left on which to do business with Christians. This difficulty was augmented by other restrictions on entering into partnerships with gentiles, living in a city of gentiles, attending their trade fairs, and so on.

In practice Jewish communities simply did not observe the prohibitions prescribed by Tractate *Avodah Zarah*. They traded with the Christians before and after their holidays, and they did not observe the other prohibitions on selling objects used for ritual worship or on trade in which part of the profits would be used for the church. The medieval rabbinic authorities, especially the Tosafists, considered the Jewish community a holy community and therefore considered it their task to justify the acts of the community as being in accordance with the halakhah. Thus they devoted much effort to explaining these practices, which apparently contradicted the halakhah, and some of their discussions concern the status of Christianity and the definition of idolatry.

The attempts to reconcile the practices of the Jewish communities with the halakhah are discussed extensively in Jakob Katz's book *Exclusiveness and Tolerance*.[35] Three approaches to resolving the problem can be identified. The first approach is a local resolution of the problem. For example, some of the Tosafists suggest a new interpretation of the talmudic passage containing the restriction under discussion, limiting the restriction without changing the status of Christians or Christianity in any way. A specific example is R. Tam's explanation of the prevalent Jewish practice of trading with the Christians before and after their holidays. He claims that the prohibition of trade applies only to what might be used as a sacrifice for idolatry, and not to other, ordinary sorts of business.[36] In other words, it is forbidden to sell, say, incense that may be used as part of an idolatrous ritual, but buying and selling other things is permitted. Although R. Tam bases his opinion on one of the passages in the Tractate, he does not in any way change the definition of Christianity as idolatry or of the Christians as idol worshipers. The only thing he changes is the extent of the restrictions placed on the relations between Jews and idolaters.

The second approach at reconciliation of halakhah and practice involves changing the status of the Christians without changing the status of Christianity. This step is based on the saying of R. Jochanan: "Gentiles outside the Land of Israel are not idolaters, but they are merely following the customs of their ancestors."[37] Basing his opinion on this saying, the eleventh-century rabbi Gershom Meor Hagolah permits trade with Christians even on the day of their holiday.[38] To R. Gershom and other authorities with similar opinions it was important to maintain Christianity as an idolatrous religion, especially in view of the Jews' continual struggle against it, but they had to ease the restrictions on business dealings with the Christians in order to preserve the economic life of their communities. They therefore claimed that the Christians were not devoted adherents of their religion but were simply following the customs of their ancestors.

There is no change in the status of Christianity as an idolatrous religion; only the status of the Christians as loyal practitioners of this religion changed. This opened the door to the easing of many other restrictive prohibitions.

The third approach is a change in the status of Christianity itself. The only one of the medieval rabbinic authorities who extensively changed the status of Christianity as a religion, as Katz has pointed out, was R. Menahem Ha-Meiri.[39] The point we want to emphasize here is that the change in attitude toward Christianity stemmed not from the claim that the Christians have monotheistic metaphysical beliefs but from a renewed understanding of idolatry as a lawless lifestyle. This understanding superseded the local attempts at reconciling the practices of the Jewish community with the halakhah. Instead of distinguishing between monotheists and idolaters, Ha-Meiri creates a new distinction between nations that are law-abiding and nations that are not, and this leads naturally to a new interpretation of the nature of idolatry. Using these new categories, Ha-Meiri distinguishes the Christians from the idolaters to whom the laws in Tractate *Avodah Zarah* and in other parts of the Talmud apply. According to Ha-Meiri, the idolatrous nations that the Talmud speaks of are nations that are not law-abiding. In Ha-Meiri's description, "They are polluted in their practices and disgusting in their moral traits . . . but the other nations, which are law-abiding, and which are free of these disgusting moral traits and, moreover, punish people with these traits—there is no doubt that these laws do not apply to them at all."[40] In the other sources we have discussed idolatry was accompanied by a degenerate lifestyle but was not defined by it. In Ha-Meiri's view this is *the* definition of idolatry. Thus the issue is not the metaphysics of the community one is trying to define but its lifestyle, and this issue had far-reaching implications for the Jewish attitude to Christianity.

Ha-Meiri differs here from the tradition of Maimonides—by whom he was influenced in many other areas—not only in his halakhic opinion on the status of Christianity but also in his attitude to idolatry.[41] For Maimonides it is the object of worship, the theology, that defines worship as idolatrous, whereas for Ha-Meiri it is the lifestyle that is the deciding factor. Ha-Meiri distinguishes between barbarians and civilized people, and therefore he considers Christianity a nonidolatrous religion. The Christians insist upon a moral lifestyle, they prohibit murder, thievery, incest, and adultery, and so they are considered a law-abiding people. In contrast to Ha-Meiri, many rabbinic authorities distinguished between Islam and Christianity. Since Islam's theology contains no trinity or incarnation, they claimed that Islam is a monotheistic religion for all purposes, while Christianity is not.[42] The definition of idolatry as a lifestyle rather than a theology accompanied by a lifestyle thus creates, for Ha-Meiri, a new boundary between monotheists and non-monotheists—the distinction between law-abiding and non–law-abiding nations. In Ha-Meiri's approach the transition is not from alien belief to alien worship, but from alien belief to alien lifestyle.

# 8

## Idolatry and Political Authority

### The Kingdom of Heaven as an Exclusive Political Kingdom

This chapter deals with the sin of idolatry within a political rather than a marital framework, as we discussed in Chapter 1. Religious language is replete with metaphors of political sovereignty speaking about God. God is described as king, master of the universe, and savior; the Hebrew word for God, *Elohim,* is itself connected with rulership; and the Israelites are often described as being subjects of God. God performs common political tasks in the Bible—he is the legislator and the commander-in-chief.

God's political role is emphasized even more by those scholars who believe that the various covenants between God and Israel were modeled on covenants between kings and their vassals. In the covenants between God and Israel the vassal's obligation of political loyalty is transmuted into an obligation of loyalty toward God on the part of Israel. For example, the book of Deuteronomy has the general structure of such a covenant, and it contains all the constituents that characterize covenants between kings and vassals. Deuteronomy begins with the historical tale that is the basis of the vassal's obligation to the king. This tale is followed by the laws that the king has decreed, and the book ends with provisions for blessings if the covenant is kept and curses if it is disobeyed. The covenant is then placed as evidence in the sanctuary before God, who is the guarantor of its fulfillment.[1] Analogously to the case of the metaphor of family relations, the basic concepts for defining religious obligation are taken here from the political arena, and the political model plays a central role in determining these patterns in the Bible.

In the marital metaphor God is the husband, and the other god is the third side of the triangle—the lover. In the political model the threatening third party is the human political institutions that demand a competing political loyalty from people. What is God's relationship to the system of human dominion? Is the relationship of political loyalty to God so exclusive that any other political loyalty is considered a betrayal, and therefore a form of idolatry? It should be noted that on the face of it the marital metaphor creates a tie of loyalty that is more exclusive than that created by the political metaphor. An erotic relationship, according to the sexual morality of monogamy, is not transferable. (The biblical law prohibits a woman to marry two husbands, although a man is permitted to have many wives. Israel is therefore represented as the wife.) A man may not grant his friend the intimate right to sexual relations with his wife. Such an act would contradict the essential exclusivity of the marital tie. Political authority, in contrast, is transferable by its very nature. Political authority is divisible, and a sovereign often grants his right of political dominion to a third party. There can be no partial marriage, but there definitely can be partial slavery.[2] Marital relations are inclusive and exclusive, which is not necessarily true of political relations. The transition to the political metaphor transforms the metaphorical image of the interpersonal relationship between man and God into a much more complicated one.

Much of the tension between various political theories may be grounded in the issue of the exclusivity of political sovereignty. The similarity between political relations and marital relations raises several issues, including the relation between God's political leadership and human institutions that demand loyalty. How does God relate to his political rivals? Does he demand such exclusive political sovereignty that any other political loyalty is considered idolatry? These questions are of great importance for our discussion of the relation between theology and politics and the degree to which the monotheists permit political activity that is not authorized by the one God.

The starting point for the prohibition of idolatry is the exclusivity of the worship of God—the ban on worshiping other gods. The discussion of idolatry and politics leads us to an extension of this exclusivity from ritual worship to the relationships of political loyalty and sovereignty. How far is the exclusivity of the worship of God extended to his exclusivity as a political sovereign? In other words, how far is the prohibition against worshiping other gods extended to the issue of political loyalty? Our analysis of sources later in this chapter is not intended to be a comprehensive historical survey of the issue. These sources, which are taken mainly from the Jewish tradition, constitute an example of political tensions, and in discussing them we will deepen our conceptual clarification of the issue.

## Idolatry and Deification

There is an important difference between the marital and the political metaphor. In the political metaphor there is no need for a third party to create a situation of disloyalty. The subject does not have to transfer the sovereignty of God to another person—he can take it for himself. Thus we arrive at the problem of deification.

The heads of the great powers in the geopolitical arena of the Bible are described as people who have dared to cross the boundary between the human and the divine. Isaiah is the source of this description. In his prophecy the following is written about the king of Babylonia:

> How are you fallen from heaven, O Shining One, son of Dawn! How are you felled to earth, O vanquisher of nations! Once you thought in your heart, "I will climb to the sky; higher than the stars of God I will set my throne. I will sit in the mount of assembly, on the summit of Zaphon: I will mount the back of a cloud—I will match the Most High." Instead, you are brought down to Sheol, to the bottom of the Pit. They who behold you stare; they peer at you closely: "Is this the man who shook the earth, who made realms tremble?"  (Isaiah 14:12–16)

Ezekiel describes the prince of Tyre as follows:

> The word of the Lord came to me: O mortal, say to the prince of Tyre: Thus said the Lord God: Because you have been haughty and have said, "I am a god; I sit enthroned like a god in the heart

of the seas," whereas you are not a god but a man, though you deemed your mind equal to a god's . . . Assuredly, thus said the Lord God: Because you have deemed your mind equal to a god's, I swear I will bring against you strangers, the most ruthless of nations. They shall unsheathe their swords against your prized shrewdness, and they shall strike down your splendor.   (Ezekiel 28:1–2, 6–7)

Ezekiel also describes the pharoah, head of Egypt, the third great power: "Thus said the Lord God: I am going to deal with you, O Pharaoh king of Egypt, mighty monster, sprawling in your channels, who said, 'The Nile is my own, I made it for myself'" (Ezekiel 29:3). The death of the kings who are drunk with power is the end of the illusion that they can cross the divide between the upper beings and the lower beings. The tendency of powerful political leaders to arrogate divine attributes to themselves clashes with the principle of exclusivity of God's political leadership.

There were times when these kings directly challenged God's leadership. Rabshakeh, the Assyrian king's emissary at the time of the siege of Jerusalem, says to the Israelites:

Beware of letting Hezekiah mislead you by saying, "The Lord will save us." Did any of the gods of the other nations save his land from the king of Assyria? Where were the gods of Hamath and Arpad? Where were the gods of Sepharvaim? And did they save Samaria from me? Which among all the gods of those countries saved their country from me, that the Lord should save Jerusalem from me?   (Isaiah 37:18–20)

The war of Assyria with Israel becomes a struggle against God's power. God answers Rabshakeh's challenge thus:

Whom have you blasphemed and reviled? Against whom made loud your voice and haughtily raised your eyes? Against the Holy One of Israel! Through your servants you have blasphemed the Lord, because you thought, "Thanks to my vast chariotry, it is I who have climbed the highest mountains, to the remotest part of the Lebanon, and have cut down its loftiest cedars, its choicest cypresses, and have reached its highest peak, its densest forest" . . . Because you have raged against Me, and your tumult has reached my ears, I will place My hook in your nose and My bit between your jaws; and I will make you go back by the road by which you came.   (Isaiah 37:23–24, 29)

The direct threat to God's political rulership here encounters a sharp response. God will lead Assyria back to its land the way an animal is brought to its place. From the standpoint of the exclusivity of political leadership, two points arise here: God is the only king who is permitted to be a deity and who is worthy of this role. Other leaders who are not able to withstand the temptation of power and who have pretensions of becoming like the supreme being are punished, and they learn the lesson of their mortality bitterly. The Bible thus speaks about political leaders' tendencies to self-deification, where this tendency cannot be reconciled with God's exclusivity as a political sovereign.

## The Israelite Monarchy and Deification

In the political context the problem of rival political authorities as idolatry is of central importance, both for the very existence of the institution of monarchy in Israel and for the character of this institution and the method by which it is formed. The demand for the establishment of a monarchy in Israel is directly connected with the problem of God's exclusivity as Israel's sovereign. Gideon's response to the people when they offered to make him king reflects the principle of God's exclusivity as the nation's sole ruler: "I will not rule over you myself, nor shall my son rule over you; the Lord alone shall rule over you" (Judges 8:23). This standpoint fits the character of the judges' regime, which lacked the outstanding characteristics of the institution of organized monarchy, as the Book of Judges attests: "In those days there was no king in Israel" (18:1).[3]

In the light of this exclusivity of the kingdom of heaven, it is not surprising that God's agreement to allow the coronation of a king, when it is finally given in the days of the judge Samuel, is interpreted as a waiver of his exclusive political role. The transition from the political system of rulership by judges to a kingdom encountered many difficulties relating to this exclusivity, and it involved struggle, surrender, and the establishment of restrictive conditions. God agrees to function as a sovereign through the agency of a human king in Israel, in spite of the fact that he sees the very request as a rejection of his exclusive rule. This is how he explains the request to Samuel: "For it is not you that they have rejected; it is Me that they have rejected as their king" (I Samuel 8:7). Later, in his words of reproach to the nation for their request, Samuel says: "you said to me, 'No, we must have a king reigning over us'—though the Lord your God is your King" (I Samuel 12:12). In these verses there is a distinct sense of rejection, of the people's refusal to belong exclusively to God's leadership—and this is how the people's demand is interpreted by God himself. Samuel is disturbed by the nation's demand, and God comforts him with an interesting analogy that teaches us a great deal about the connection between idolatry and disloyalty to political leadership: "Like everything else they have done ever since I brought them out of Egypt to this day—forsaking Me and worshiping other gods—so they are doing to you" (I Samuel 8:8). To comfort the dejected Samuel, God says that Samuel should not take the nation's rejection personally. This has been Israel's way in the past, and they have forsaken God many times to worship other gods. The ingratitude shown toward the leader of the community is compared to idolatry, and Samuel's feeling of being betrayed is described as a feeling that God has already gotten used to.

Although God waives his exclusive political sovereignty in response to the nation's demand for a king, he makes this waiver conditional on both the king and the people understanding that they are still subject to God and that the king is nothing but an agent: "if both you and the king who reigns over you will follow the Lord your God, [well and good]. But if you do not obey the Lord and you flout the Lord's command, the hand of the Lord will strike you" (I Samuel 12:14–15). The political metaphor allows for the division of authority—not every demand for loyalty to a human political institution is like idolatry. God waives his right to be the community's direct leader, and he bestows some of his power on another authority. Unlike the marital metaphor, the political metaphor allows for agents, but this agency is conditional on the clear and continued dependency of the human leadership upon God.

Although a monarchic regime is entirely natural in Israel's political environment—as the Bible itself stresses when it adds to its anticipation of the nation's demand the phrase "as do all the nations about me" (Deuteronomy 17:14)—this regime encounters many difficulties when Israel tries to copy it.[4] These difficulties must be understood against the background of another innovation in Israel's environment—the monotheistic idea. The rejection of the worship of other gods and the exclusivity of the worship of God is extended here beyond ritual worship to the realm of exclusivity of sovereignty and political loyalty. The prohibition against worshiping other gods is more general and broader than the narrow sense of ritual, and it involves other areas, such as reliance upon a regime. This is the source of the many difficulties in the transition from judgeship to kingdom.

The connection between idolatry and politics arises not only during the formation of the institution of monarchy and the struggle surrounding it, but also in the character of the monarchy once it has been accepted. There are fundamental differences between the conceptions of the institution of the monarchy in Israel and those in Egypt and Mesopotamia of the same time, as Henri Frankfort has clearly demonstrated.[5] Frankfort points out that the conceptions of monarchy in Egypt and Mesopotamia were connected with the king's responsibility for the social order, as a reflection of his unique status in the cosmic order. In Egypt the king was one of the gods, while in Mesopotamia he was their representative on earth and sometimes their incarnation as well. In the biblical conception, by contrast, the monarchy is not an institution rooted in the cosmic order, and it is not part of the primordial structure of the world. Monarchy in the Bible is an institution that developed relatively late and only because the people demanded it—much later than the consolidation of the people into a nation. This institution is not essential for the existence of order in nature or in the political sphere. The gap between the king and the cosmos also is expressed by the fact that the Israelite king has no special role in divine worship, and he is not responsible for the rainfall or the success of the crops.

The rules concerning the king in Deuteronomy are intended to limit his power, primarily to prevent the pride that comes with the concentration of power: "Thus he will not act haughtily toward his fellows" (Deuteronomy 17:20). This is mentioned in connection with the prohibition on amassing many horses or much gold and silver. The biblical problem with a powerful person is how to prevent the tendency to self-deification. Therefore the rules concerning the king in Deuteronomy consist of conscious limitations on the concentration of power in his hands.[6] A similar command to limit Israel's military power was given to Gideon when he gathered the Israelites for battle: "The Lord said to Gideon, 'You have too many troops with you for Me to deliver Midian into their hands; Israel might claim for themselves the glory due to Me, thinking, "Our own hand has brought us victory"'" (Judges 7:2). Gideon reduced the number of his troops so that the people would not claim the victory for themselves but would ascribe it to God, a reduction in the spirit of the command in Deuteronomy: "He shall not keep many horses" (17:16).

The political model of God as king does not require absolute exclusivity. Monarchy is an authority that can be granted to others, unlike marital status. However, the model fixes clear boundaries for the character of the earthly monarchy, both in the definition of the king's role and in the understanding of the danger in the concentration of power in the hands of one person. This is the source of the unique character of the political debate in the Bible on the issue of monarchy, and it is also the source of the difference in the institutionalization of the monarchic regime in Israel.[7]

## "Either You or I in the Palace"

As Weinfeld has shown, the book of Deuteronomy, whose basic structure is the political metaphor, describes the worship of other gods as rebellion against a master. The description of the sin in Deuteronomy is accompanied by elements such as "inciters" and "seducers" to idolatry, and false prophets who call upon the nation to worship other gods. If there is even a rumor of a rebellion of this sort, the people are obliged to ascertain its truth and then fight the rebels. The political aspect of the sin also involves the motif of pride in idolatry. The source of the great metaphysical error is in the cumulative illusion of power that blurs the boundaries between the human and the divine and traps the powerful person in the myth of his own power. The marital metaphor we analyzed in Chapter 1 locates the source of the sin in whoredom and nymphomania. The political model, in contrast, presents pride and political power-drunkenness as the sources of the creation of gods and the sin of idolatry. The connection between idolatry and hubris may be found in the words of Isaiah: "Their land is full of silver and gold, there is no limit to their treasures; their land is full of horses, there is no limit to their chariots. And their land is full of idols; they bow down to the work of their hand, to what their own fingers have wrought" (Isaiah 2:7–8). Isaiah makes a connection between idolatry and pride, between man's haughtiness and his bowing down to the work of his hands and turning himself into a deity. According to some readings, the original story of political idolatry is the story of the Tower of Babel (Genesis 11). At this tower, which was the collective effort of an entire society, the first rebellion of civilization against God was declared. This is how the *Midrash Genesis Rabbah* describes the sin of the building of the tower:

> R. Elazar said, "Which is worse, the person who says to the king, 'Either you or I in the palace,' or the person who says, 'Neither you nor I in the palace'? The one who says 'Either you or I' is worse. Thus the generation of the flood said, 'Who is God that we should worship Him?' but the generation that built the Tower said, 'Will he choose the upper world for Himself and give us the lower world? Therefore let us make a tower for ourselves and put an idol at its top and put a sword in its hand, so that it will look as though it is making war on Him.'" (38:11a)

This midrash explains the sin of the Tower of Babel in the context of idolatry. It interprets the expression "to make a name for ourselves" (Genesis 11:4) as meaning "to make an idol."[8] The midrash distinguishes between the sin of the generation of the flood, which was the denial of God, and the sin of the tower builders, which was the pretension to usurp his throne. In this context idolatry is not betrayal or error and forgetfulness, but war: "let us make a tower for ourselves and put an idol at its top and put a sword in its hand, so that it will look as though it is making war on Him." Man wants the upper world—the lower world is not enough for him: "I will mount the back of a cloud—I will match the Most High" (Isaiah 14:14). Besides pride there is the motif of jealousy: "Will he choose the upper world for Himself and give us the lower world?" It is man's jealousy of God that leads him to declare war. The political aspect adds the dimension of rebellion to the analysis of the sin. The rebellion is motivated by the subject's jealousy of his lord, and the illusion of his relative power turns him into a pretender to the throne.

Idolatry is a challenge to God's exclusive position as king, and the sin represents a crisis in a political system. The political model provides us with a different understanding of the sin of idolatry. Instead of whoredom and nymphomania, instead of the forgetful woman who loses her identity, it uses the image of a rebellious slave who becomes a pretender to the throne when he is driven insane by jealousy and a craving for power.

## Family and Politics

The discussion of the connection between politics and idolatry brings us to another problem: the third party in the arena of international politics. The prophets denounced Israel's treaties with Assyria and Egypt. Isaiah's comment on the treaty with Egypt against the threat of Assyria is a typical denunciation:

> Ha! Those who go down to Egypt for help and rely upon horses! They have put their trust in abundance of chariots, in vast numbers of riders, and they have not turned to the Holy One of Israel, they have not sought the Lord. But He too is wise! He has brought on misfortune, and has not canceled His word. So he shall rise against the house of evildoers, and the allies of the workers of iniquity. For the Egyptians are man, not God, and their horses are flesh, not spirit; and when the Lord stretches out His arm, the helper shall trip and the helped one shall fall, and both shall perish together. (Isaiah 31:1–3)

Those who go down to Egypt for help forget that Egypt is man, not God. The reliance upon Egypt is perceived as a deification of that nation. There is a theological dimension in the relation of political protection because Israel is supposed to request political protection only of God. The treaties with the Egyptians and with the Assyrians are described by Jeremiah as the abandonment of God:

> See, that is the price you have paid for forsaking the Lord your God while he led you in the way. What, then, is the good of your going to Egypt to drink the waters of the Nile? And what is the good of your going to Assyria to drink the waters of the Euphrates? Let your misfortune reprove you, let your afflictions rebuke you; mark well how bad and bitter it is that you forsake the Lord your God, that awe for Me is not in you—declares the Lord God of Hosts. (Jeremiah 2:17–19)

Ezekiel too, as we saw in Chapter 1, associates political treaties with idolatry. Israel has betrayed God with idols and afterward with neighboring nations: "In your insatiable lust you also played the whore with the Assyrians; you played the whore with them, but were still unsated" (Ezekiel 16:28). The political treaties are described in terms of marital relations. Israel is compared to a woman, and the relation between God the king and his nation to a relation of husband and wife. The request for political protection addressed to powerful neighboring nations is perceived as adultery. The transition to the family metaphor strengthens the impression that political relations are exclusive. There is no place for the division of authority accepted in many political systems. The political third party is described as a lover, in order to reject any possibility that an intermediary political power could be involved. There is no agency in erotic relations, and therefore the reliance on Egypt and Assyria constitutes betrayal.

This image stands out particularly boldly because there are other places where the prophets recommend the acceptance of the conditions put forward by a foreign ruler, including subjugation to his rule. For example, Jeremiah calls upon the Israelites to subjugate themselves to the king of Babylon: "I also spoke to King Zedekiah of Judah in just the same way: 'Put your necks under the yoke of the king of Babylon; serve him and his people, and live! Otherwise you will die together with your people, by sword, famine, and pestilence'" (Jeremiah 27:12–13). The king of Babylon is not described as a lover whom it is forbidden to serve. King Nebuchadnezzar is God's emissary, as Jeremiah puts it: "I herewith deliver all these lands to My servant, King Nebuchadnezzar of Babylon; I even give him the wild beast to serve him" (27:6). The king of Babylon is God's servant, and God is the king who grants his servant authority. The use of the master-servant metaphor creates the justification for agency. In this case God does not demand direct exclusive sovereignty but grants some of his authority to his servant. Thus Jeremiah does not think that surrender and subjugation to the Babylonian king constitute betrayal and adultery. When, in contrast, the prophets are attempting to reject the possibility of political agency, they strengthen their rejection by describing political relations in terms of marital metaphors: the nation is married to its king and political treaties with foreign powers constitute forbidden sexual relations because of Israel's being a married woman. The different images of the relationship between God and Israel change the quality of the exclusivity that is being demanded.[9]

## Deification and the Exclusivity of Political Attributes

Our discussion of the relation between idolatry and politics confronts us with the issue of how to accept human political authority that demands a political loyalty rivaling God's. Unlike relations in the marital metaphor, political relations are transferable. Political authority can be divided and granted to another. The king of Israel can be God's servant, and so can Nebuchadnezzar. There is a tension between the demand for exclusivity in God's direct political authority and the possibility of agency—between Gideon's unambiguous statement and Samuel's compromise.

We have seen that as God's exclusive political attributes are given a broader range, the rule of any social authority that is not anchored directly in God's authority is undermined. The reason for this is that the transfer of these exclusive attributes from God to human authorities is considered idolatry. As the range of uniquely divine attributes and gestures becomes more inclusive, their ascription to people or to human institutions comes to be regarded as idolatry. The question is thus how broad this range is. This question has far-reaching implications for the very possibility of constructing a social hierarchy and for the extent of such a hierarchy. For example, if one person is afraid of another because the latter has the power to do him harm or good, does this constitute idolatry? If because of this fear one person tends to flatter another, is this an idolatrous form of worship? If the power to do harm or good is an exclusive power of God's, then the first person has deified the second by fearing him. If, on the one hand, the practice of flattery based on fear is a form of worship that may be directed only toward God, then it constitutes idolatry when addressed to one's fellow human being. On the other hand, one might say that in order for a relation to a deity to be created it would be necessary for one person to ascribe additional attributes to another, such as eternal existence or far-reaching influence on the cosmic order.

Two questions arise in the political context: which attributes and gestures, when required by a rival political authority, constitute a deification of that authority? And when is subjugation to that authority considered "worship"? The term "deification" here requires clarification. It is possible that a particular act or the ascription of a particular attribute will be perceived as deification by monotheists or other observers, while the worshipers themselves do not perceive it that way. Alexander the Great, who was influenced at the outset of his career by the regal behavior at the Persian court, demanded that his Greek subjects prostrate themselves before him the way the Persian subjects did before their king. The Greeks considered this an improper gesture because it was exclusive to the gods and not appropriate to mortals, and thus many of them opposed performing it. The Greeks believed that the Persians regarded their kings as gods because of these gestures. But from what we know about Persian politics it is clear that the kings were not regarded as gods. They were never given the names of gods and were considered merely servants of the gods. At most the prevalent attitude toward the kings in Persia was rather similar to the Greek attitude toward heroes or to the Christian attitude toward saints.[10] The question of which gestures are exclusive to the man-god relation is thus often dependent upon one's point of view. Our interest is mainly in the monotheists' viewpoint on what is considered deification. We discuss several possible answers to this question.

One might say that deification depends not on the ascription of attributes to a particular power but only on the ritual acts that are addressed to it. According to this approach, if one burns incense and brings animal sacrifices to the emperor, then it does not matter what attributes one ascribes to him—the very act of sacrifice to him is an act of deification. If we have a clear definition of which gestures are considered "worship," then we can easily define what is considered a deity. Such an approach stands in opposition to the ones we discussed in the previous chapter, which assert that in order for an act of ritual worship to be considered idolatry it must be accompanied by the intention of "acceptance as a deity." We assume that this requirement of intention implies not only that the worship is performed voluntarily but also that the worshiper has a certain inner attitude toward the object of his worship.

Ritual acts performed toward someone or something, even if they are voluntary, are not always a clear sign that these acts are accompanied by the internal intention of accepting a deity. The Greeks worshiped their heroes with ritual acts that were customarily addressed to the gods, but they did not define these heroes completely as gods. The heroes were worshiped at their monuments and not at temples built in their honor, and they did not have a priesthood. There is a difference between a private household ritual to the spirit or demon of an ancestor and ritual worship of the gods in a public temple with an organized priesthood. The Romans had a god whose entire role was watching over the threshold of the house, and the members of that house would worship it, but does this constitute the acceptance of a deity? The Romans certainly called it a god, and from their point of view it was a god, but can one really say that they accepted it as a deity if its entire role was that of a watchdog?

In addition to the problem that ritual worship does not supply the content of "acceptance of a deity," in case it is demanded, there is a problem of circularity in the attempt to characterize something as a god according to a collection of gestures exclusive to the gods that are performed for it. If, for example, people bring animal sacrifices to a certain king, there are two opposite conclusions that we can draw from this act. We can say that the king is considered a god because a gesture exclusive to the gods is being performed for him, or we can say that the bringing of animal sacrifices is not a gesture exclusive to the gods, since it is performed for kings as well. An actual case of two such opposing interpretations is our earlier example of the different interpretations offered by the Greeks and by the Persians themselves to the gesture of prostration before the Persian kings. Defining deification solely by means of exclusive gestures involves circularity. We thus return to our previous understanding of deification: it is assumed that ritual worship alone does not define people's attitude toward something as an attitude toward a god, partly because the very definition of an act as ritual worship requires that it be an act performed toward a god, and partly because an intention toward a deity must accompany the act. The issue, therefore, is what such an intention involves.

If the narrow definition of divinity on the basis of gestures is rejected, then the question of which attributes are unique to a deity must be discussed. From the point of view of the pagans the question is complex. The space between gods and humans is filled with powers having the complicated status of demigods and deified humans. In Egypt deification was not something that occurred to a king at his death—he was a god even while he was alive and always had been. In Rome, however, kings acquired the title of gods and were worshiped as such only after their death. What happens, then, when someone is deified? (Aside from the question of which attributes are ascribed to kings in the process of deification, the question is whether the subjects or the kings themselves really believed in the attributes they ascribed to the kings. This is an important issue with regard to the deification of the Roman emperors; there are some historians who claim that this deification was not taken seriously but was only a political tool.)[11]

There are instances of deification that occur through the identification of the person's origin in a divine source, as in the myth of Alexander's having been sired by Dionysus, who impregnated his mother while in the form of a snake. Sometimes there is an external identification, when the name of the king is spoken and written in a manner that is unique to the names of gods. The ascription of immortality is also a necessary element, but it is clear that it is not a sufficient condition—if it were, then the belief in angels or immortal humans would be a belief in a plurality of gods. It seems that immortality must be accompanied by influence on natural and historical processes, and even more important than influence or power is sovereignty. Angels, even though they have influence and ability, do not acquire the status of gods because they are subordinate. They are considered first and foremost servants doing God's bidding and lack autonomy, which is at least as important as ability. Immortality must be joined with power and a certain measure of sovereignty in order to turn something into a deity and in order to transform the attitude of the believer into the characteristic dependency of a people on a deity.

Another important element is the ability to have symbolic presence, the ability to have not only power but also omnipresence. One may make requests and even offer prayers in the presence of a king who has not undergone deification, one can request forgiveness or favors—after all, it is well known that the modes of prayer to deities are constructed according to the modes of address to kings—but this can be done only in the king's presence or through an intermediary who transmits the request to the king. In contrast, powers that have undergone deification also have symbolic presence, and one can pray to them not only in their actual presence but also in a variety of temples and sanctuaries. They are not tied to a place in the sense that mortal beings are, and so they have a ubiquitous presence. Any simultaneous presence in many places, or even the possibility of such presence, is an essential attribute of a deity, perhaps even the most important attribute.

The divine attributes that we have enumerated in this partial list-ing, such as immortality, power, autonomy, and omnipresence, do not all appear together in every instance of deification. Indeed, one of the important aspects that varies from one theology to another is the combination of attributes that uniquely defines divinity. A thinker like Nachmanides believed that the ascription of the attribute of creator, and the power to change the order of nature, are neces-sary for the definition of divinity.[12] In contrast, Maimonides believed that one may speak of divinity without the attribute of creator.[13] In such a "Spinozistic" picture God is the necessary being, while all the rest of existence contains merely possible entities. Asking whether the world was created or has always existed is thus equivalent to asking not whether there is a God or not but which of the two attributes, wisdom and will, is worthy of being ascribed to God. There are some thinkers (such as the contemporary Israeli philosopher Yeshayahu Leibowitz) who claim that the question does not depend on the metaphysical ascription of attributes but rather on a special relationship.[14] What characterizes God is not an ontological proposition, an exclusive collection of attributes, but the attitude of unconditional obedience to him. In this view the deification of the state would thus be unconditional and uncritical obedience to its dic-tates, which constitutes idolatry. Deification is the transformation of something into a supreme value rather than a supreme ontology.

Beyond the tensions between the various standpoints on the essen-tial attributes of the divinity, there is another question that touches upon the reverse side of idolatry. The description of someone as an idolater entails that the worshiper ascribes to the powers he worships attributes that are essential and exclusive to God. Without such ascription it would be difficult to speak of people as worshipers of an alien god. Of course the worshiper must omit some of the essential attributes of God, or else he would not be worshiping an alien deity and would simply worship God himself. For example, the worshiper might ascribe the attributes of omnipotence and omniscience to a certain material entity. The question is which attri-butes are such that their ascription to a nondivine power constitutes deification.

In this context a distinction between the narrow and the broad senses of deification should be made. The narrow sense is that deifi-cation occurs only when nonpolitical divine attributes are ascribed to a political power, and it is such attributes that transform the political power into a deity. In the Egyptian conception, which is a prototypical case of the deification of kings, the pharaohs were considered not only the founders of the social order but also possessors of influence on natural processes. The pharaoh was the power of fruitfulness; it was he who caused the Nile to overflow its banks, and his influence was not limited to society. Hence the Egyptians granted their king nonpolitical attributes that are characteristic of gods and made no clear distinction between society and nature: the force that stabilizes the social order is also the key to the natural order.

The broad sense of deification is that this process occurs in the very act of ascribing political attributes, or ascribing them in too extensive a degree, to a human power, without granting this power nonpolitical divine powers. An example of this is the ascription of the title "king," where the claim is that only God is worthy of this title. Another example would be when an earthly king ascribes his power to himself and does not consider himself an agent. In the Mesopotamian conception the king was not a deity but an agent of the gods. This agency distinguished him from all other people, but since he was considered the gods' agent, he could not be considered a god. In the context of political deification what makes the difference may be the claim of absolute sovereignty. In addition to absolute sovereignty, one of the central strategies of deification in political contexts is the assertion that the leader is infallible. The leader is thus raised to the status of a prophet. Mao and Stalin were regarded as leaders who held the key to history and were therefore able to foretell its processes completely. The ability to be the creators of the processes they foretold transformed them from prophets into gods.

In the narrower thesis, deification occurs only when nonpolitical metaphysical attributes are ascribed to political systems. The ascription of political attributes does not lead to deification unless additional ontological attributes are added. The problem in deification is not political authority itself but the enhancement of politics into something that it really is not. According to the broader thesis, politics itself is a realm that is exclusive to God, who possesses the central political role, and there is no need to add other attributes to a political system for it to constitute deification.

There is an interesting example of the connection between the unique attributes of the divinity and the sin of idolatry in a debate recorded in the Babylonian Talmud, Tractate *Sanhedrin,* and the various interpretations given to this debate by the medieval commentators. The debate is between the scholars Abbaye and Raba, who differed as to whether someone who worshiped idols out of love or fear is liable to punishment for idolatry. The expression "love or fear" is itself ambiguous and has been given various interpretations, which we discussed extensively in the preceding chapter. Rashi explains that "love or fear" means that a person worships an idol out of love or fear of another person. According to Rashi and many other medieval commentators,[15] the debate in the Talmud is about whether this person is considered an idol worshiper even though his motivation for worship is not the powers he ascribes to the idol but the desire to please or to pacify another person.

For Rashi, the debate is about intention. Maimonides has a different interpretation, which is relevant to the present discussion. Maimonides claims that the "love or fear" mentioned in the Talmud refers not to another person but to the idol itself.[16] In his *Code of Jewish Law,* in the section on the laws concerning idolatry, he writes:

> If someone worships an idol because he finds its shape desirable, because of its very beautiful workmanship, or if he worships it out of fear, lest it harm him—as its worshipers imagine that it can cause benefit or harm—then if he accepted it as a deity he is punishable by stoning. But if he worshiped it in the customary way of worshiping this idol, or in one of the four types of worship that define idolatry, and if this was done out of love or fear, then he is exempt from punishment.

According to Maimonides, the attribution to an idol of supreme esthetic value or the power to cause harm does not constitute the acceptance of this idol as a deity. The power of causing good or harm does not define divinity, and someone who worships an object because he believes that it has such power has not turned this object into a deity. Therefore such a person is exempt from punishment for idolatry. In Maimonides' view the worshiper would have to add attributes such as eternity to his description of the idol in order for the idol to be defined as a deity. Thus a person who is afraid of a particular official who has the power to cause him good or harm has not deified this official by ascribing this power to him. And if he flatters him regularly by minor rituals like bringing him coffee, he still is not considered to be worshiping him. Maimonides' opinion about the debate between Abbaye and Raba thus directly concerns our discussion of what constitutes deification.

Some of the medieval commentators differed with Maimonides on this issue. R. Menahem Ha-Meiri responded to Maimonides' argument this way:

> Their claim does not seem plausible, as anyone who worships out of the fear of punishment or in order to change his fate, even if he worshiped a star in this way, it constitutes the acceptance of a deity. Because if the star can have a harmful influence on him and so he prays to it, there cannot be any clearer acceptance of a deity.

Maimonides' view does not make sense to Ha-Meiri because the worship of a star or idol out of the belief that this worship can affect one's fate is precisely the meaning of acceptance of a deity.[17]

Let us return to the political sphere and to the issue of the exclusivity of God's rule. The issue of the possible limits of the acceptance of a foreign political authority is well reflected in the controversy between the Perushim and the Zealots in the final days of the Second Temple period, and in the Christian-pagan debate at the beginning of the rise of Christianity. The controversy between the Perushim and the Zealots was focused on the question of whether it was permitted for the Jews to subjugate themselves to Roman rule. The Zealots believed that the acceptance of such subjugation was an affront to God's dominion. Josephus Flavius articulated this view: "They consider their God alone as their leader and ruler, and they are willing to accept all sorts of strange forms of death upon themselves, and acts of vengeance against their relatives and friends, rather than call any man their lord."[18] In this view God is the exclusive political leader, and the act of subjugating oneself to another power constitutes idolatry, so that one must accept death rather than commit such a sin. The political consequence of this standpoint was the revolt that led to Judea's ruin. The Zealots, as Josephus relates, refused to pay taxes to the Romans and called for a revolt.[19] The Perushim, in contrast, believed that the payment of taxes did not constitute the acceptance of a foreign authority as a deity in a way that detracted from God's dominion. Both groups believed that worshiping the caesar constituted idolatry, that burning incense to an idol of the caesar, for example, was forbidden because incense burning is a gesture performed exclusively to God. The debate concerned the payment of taxes: does such payment constitute an affront to God's exclusivity? The Zealots claimed that the Perushim, by agreeing to pay taxes to the Romans, were "worshiping the Romans instead of God."[20] The Perushim, in contrast, believed that paying tax to the caesar and accepting his dominion did not constitute worship of the caesar.[21]

This controversy between the two Jewish groups directly involves the distinction we suggested between deification in the broad sense and in the narrow sense. In the opinion of the Zealots the very ascription of political attributes to a power constitutes deification, and obedience to the ordinary authority of a government, such as the collection of taxes, is worship in the religious sense. The standpoint of the Perushim, in contrast, is that of the narrow sense of deification. That is, the mere ascription of political attributes does not transform a particular power into a deity, and so ordinary political gestures toward such a power do not constitute worship. Only when other, nonpolitical attributes are ascribed to the political authority and the gestures toward this authority are drawn from the practice of ritual worship is the attitude toward this authority transformed into idolatry. The question of God's exclusivity as a political leader was thus a fateful question for Judea at the end of the Second Temple period.

In the Christian-pagan controversy the rites addressed to the caesar acquire central importance. E. R. Dodds describes the controversy as not being mainly about beliefs.[22] On the issue of rites addressed to the caesar, the pagan elite was of the opinion that the caesar was not a deity and that the intention of the rites was not to recognize him as a deity but rather to express loyalty to the state and the caesar. What was involved, in their view, was a civic religion with symbols and obligations, like flag waving or marching. The deification of the caesar was often the result of doubt concerning the existence of gods at all: if there are no gods, then why not call the caesar a god? If this was really the case, then the Christian opposition to the rites addressed to the caesar made the Christians suspect of disloyalty to the empire, a disloyalty that occurred at a time when the empire was weak and thus needed its subjects' devotion more than ever. The Christians who opposed the rites paid dearly for this, but they were willing to do so because they believed that the rites involved gestures that were exclusive to God and should not be transferred to any other being. The ban on idolatry here rejects aspects of civic religion whose purpose is the expression of loyalty and solidarity with the state. Approaches that expand the range of gestures exclusive to God limit the possibility of a "ritual" attitude toward a political entity. It was this range of gestures that was at the focus of the difficult struggle between the pagans and the Christians at this time.

The attempt to define which gestures are exclusive to the religious realm, so that performing them for some power constitutes ritual worship, is connected with the question of what "worship" is. The mishnah in Tractate *Sanhedrin* attempts to define worship; it distinguishes between acts constituting the worship of an idol, such as bringing animal sacrifices and burning incense, and acts constituting the honoring of the idol, such as hugging and kissing it (as we discussed in the previous chapter). The problem is also expressed in the question of how far a system that prohibits idolatry is able to accept the ritual symbols of a civic religion, as exemplified by the dilemma of the Christian communities in the pagan Roman empire.

In moving to a discussion of the relation between idolatry and politics we take the idea of God's exclusivity out of the realm of ritual worship and into broader areas. The breadth of the range of God's exclusive political authority profoundly affects the political power of human institutions. The idea of exclusivity associated with the rejection of idolatry contains anarchic dynamite in that it determines theological limits to the possibility of subjugation, whether to a king of Israel who has become overly proud, or to a gentile king who attempts to impose his authority. If one accepts the more inclusive definition, then the possibility of involving the community in the realpolitik among the nations of the world vanishes from the theological standpoint. Defensive treaties with various powers in the region that guarantee the political existence of the nation are prohibited, and thus the community's ability to survive among the great blocs in the region is directly prevented.

It was the tension between the political ideal of the kingdom of heaven and the realpolitik that brought the Israelites to demand of Samuel, at the end of the period of the judges, that he give them a king so that they could be like all the surrounding nations. The nation was no longer able to bear the burden of holy politics according to the political ideal represented by Gideon: "I will not rule over you myself, nor shall my son rule over you; the Lord alone shall rule over you" (Judges 8:23). And the kings that followed did indeed make treaties again and again with the great powers in the region, in spite of the opposition on the part of the prophets, who regarded such treaties as a betrayal of God's dominion. The conception which asserts that God has an exclusive status as the political sovereign of the community, and that any other political obligation is necessarily idolatry, limits the potential for constructing human political authorities that can participate in playing the game of earthly politics. The failure of the politics of the prophets is inherent in the uncompromising requirement of God's exclusivity in the political realm, and this results in the nation's repeated need for some mediating agency.

# Conclusion

Our discussion of idolatry has been an attempt to understand a community's self-definition through its idea of what is excluded and through its notions of "the other." The prohibition against idolatry is the thick wall that separates the nonpagans from pagans. It is supposed to be the wall that constitutes the city of God, leaving the strange gods outside and marking the community of the faithful. We found that the location of that dividing wall is not fixed, and that opposing conceptions of idolatry define the outskirts of the city of God differently. Some leave out, as belonging to the pagan camp, some quarters that others consider part of the city. It is essential for the self-definition of nonpagans to share the general concept of idolatry, but they do not share a specific definition of what is idolatry and what is wrong with it. Changing conceptions of God create different ideas about what is idolatry. The converse holds too: the notion of the alien, or false, god shapes the concept of God. Our central aim in the book has been to capture the mutual effect of these concepts on each other.

This is not a book about paganism, its description or its merits. It is not about how pagans describe themselves, or how anthropologists and historians of religion describe paganism. It is a book analyzing how paganism is viewed mainly in Jewish sources, which is a vantage point of those whose negation of paganism is the most primary and central feature of their self-identity. From the point of view of practitioners, anthropologists, or historians of different pagan religions, the very general category of paganism—a category that includes an enormous variety of religious phenomena—seems empty. Mesopotamians and Egyptians would not have described themselves under the supercategory of pagans. They were Mesopotamians or Egyptians, each group forming a distinct religion. The only perspective from which the category of paganism makes any sense is the nonpagan perspective, and it is this perspective that we have tried to explore.

The subject of idolatry is rich in connections to a variety of philosophical issues which we have focused upon. These include the nature of representation—linguistic or imagistic—causes and types of great metaphysical errors as well as the importance or nonimportance of metaphysics, the relations between willing and believing, the identity of other gods, intention and action in worship, and sovereignty and its limits. Situated within the life and thought of communities in conflict, their own discourse on idolatry was not marshaled in what is recognized as a philosophical argumentation. Instead, it was a polemical and hostile discourse, but it is exactly that position of importance in the life of those communities that makes these problems urgent and complex.

Four different conceptions of idolatry have been outlined and discussed. The first, the biblical, views idolatry as betrayal and rebellion. Through the root metaphor of marriage, God's relationship to Israel is construed by the prophets as exclusive. Within the marriage metaphor God is the jealous and betrayed husband, Israel is the unfaithful wife, and the third parties in the triangle—the lovers—are the other gods. Idolatry, then, is the wife's betrayal of the husband with strangers, with lovers who had no shared biography with Israel, the other gods whom Israel never knew. The notion of idolatry as rebellion arises in the Bible out of the conception of God as the exclusive political leader and protector. The covenant between God and the people is modeled on a treaty between a king and a vassal. Such a covenant is inherently political, and it portrays God as a sovereign. Within this political picture idolatry is connected with challenges to God's exclusivity as sovereign, such as signing protective vassal treaties with foreign parties like Egypt and Assyria, or appointing a king, an act that is viewed by Samuel as a demand to dethrone and replace God. Both notions of idolatry, as betrayal and as rebellion, are deeply embedded in the anthropomorphic views of God. The sense of idolatry as sin is explained and evoked through analogies to human institutions and relationships that create demands of exclusive obligation and loyalty, obligations that are breached in the worship of other gods. The deep layers of anthropomorphism are manifested not only in the metaphors used to construct the source of Israel's obligation but in the rich and complicated emotional life attributed to God, the raging husband caught in the internal contradictions of his own jealousy.

The second view of idolatry we have discussed is idolatry as a great metaphysical error. Maimonides, the main exponent of this approach, equates worshiping other gods with having a wrong concept of God in the mind while worshiping. The main mistake about God is the anthropomorphic conception of God, the very conception that made sense of idolatry in the biblical approach. This grave mistake, according to Maimonides, is caused by a projection of human qualities onto God, a projection that is due to a lack of power of abstraction and to the inherent limitations of human language. Idolatry here is not the religion of the other nations, or of the Israelites who worship in the temple of the Ba'al. Rather, idolatry is the religion of the masses who are controlled by their imaginative faculty, and are unable to form the correct opinion about God. With idolatry defined as having a wrong concept of God in the mind, idolatry can be performed in the synagogue while praying to the God of Israel. Idolatry is thus internalized; it is an event that happens in the mind and in the midst of the community. The criticism of idolatry is the criticism of superstition and its allegedly damaging effects on human life and society. Uprooting idolatry is chaining the imaginative faculty, and eradicating its role in the formation of the metaphysical picture of the world and its impact on the political behavior of the multitudes.

The influence of Greek philosophical culture is crucial in the formation of this Maimonidean concept of idolatry. The Aristotelian vision of God as a nonanthropomorphic being, detached from the fluctuating life of the emotions and the finitude of the body, portrays the false god as the anthropomorphic god, the product of the imagination. It is an interesting dialectical move in which a conception of God which originated outside the Jewish tradition and was assimilated into the tradition, at least by Maimonides and his school, redefines the boundaries of the tradition, leaving outside some elements that had been within it. This is the reason for Maimonides' complaint that a straightforward reading of the Bible is one of the causes of the mistaken conception of God. From Maimonides' perspective a necessary condition for overcoming anthropomorphism is the radical reinterpretation and allegorization of biblical language—a task that

Maimonides attempts to accomplish in *The Guide of the Perplexed*. The religious enlightenment locates the wall of idolatry on the border between abstract nonanthropomorphic views of God and the other gods, including among them the very anthropomorphism that made sense of idolatry within the biblical tradition.

The view that idolatry is an error has implications for another domain of idolatry, the domain of representation. The prohibition against idolatry not only refers to the worshiping of other gods but also includes a prohibition against representing God himself in pictures and images. The biblical tradition seems to make a sharp distinction between pictorial and linguistic representations of God. While linguistic representations of God are allowed in the Bible—including linguistic descriptions of God's own image—pictorial representations are prohibited. We have suggested some explanations for this distinction based on the assumption that although God has an image which is described, he may not be represented in icons and pictures. The problem with iconic representations according to this approach is not that they are mistaken representations but that they are improper representations. The view that idolatry is a mistake perceives image making as something that might lead to a mistaken idea of God; since God has no image, he should not be represented in images. If this is the logic of the argument against pictorial representations, there is a strong argument to extend the prohibition to linguistic representation as well. Like pictorial representations, linguistic representations might also lead to a mistaken notion of God. It is as dangerous to say that God has a hand as to paint God's hand, and much of Maimonides' *Guide of the Perplexed* is devoted to the claim that linguistic representations are as problematic as pictorial ones. Since the view that idolatry is an error aims to break the images of the mind, linguistic representations become a target for iconoclasm as well.

The third sense of idolatry that we have discussed is connected to the common yet problematic opposition between monotheists and polytheists. Monotheism—if it means the assertion that only one divine power exists—is just one version of nonpagan religion. Many of those who viewed themselves as nonpagans held nonmonotheistic views about the divine world. We have identified two conceptions that diverge from the idea of pure monotheism, yet whose proponents still consider them a rejection of idolatry. The first describes the divine world as a hierarchy of powers with God at its top. In this hierarchical worldview other powers exist and have a certain degree of autonomy, including demonic powers. The second conception that departs from pure monotheism is the view, held by many kabbalists, that God himself consists of a multiplicity of aspects and powers which are connected and unified through a complex, virtually organic, relationship. These two conceptions of the divine world, the hierarchical and the organic, blur the distinction between polytheism and pure monotheism, and consequently approach the problem of idolatry as something other than an issue of a metaphysical worldview and error. Pagans and nonpagans may share essentially the same metaphysics about the divine world and yet differ radically in their conceptions of worship.

This third position on idolatry, explored through the writings of Nachmanides, is idolatry as the worship of an aspect, or the worship of an intermediary. On this approach, idolatry is prohibited because it is effective: it is a form of high magic in which the idolater isolates one power from the hierarchy of divine powers and effects this power through worship, thus violating God's given and desired order. The view of the godhead or the divine world as a multiplicity of powers therefore produces a shift from the concept of idolatry as a mistake to the problem of its being a form of worship, that is, a shift from metaphysics to ritual.

The fourth position on idolatry is related to the ambiguity of the rabbinic term for idolatry, *avodah zarah*. Literally this means alien worship. But the strangeness of worship can be understood in two ways. The first refers to the strangeness of the subject of the worship, meaning worshiping another god or worshiping a mistaken idea of God. The second refers to strangeness in the worship itself, meaning worshiping God—even the right one—in the wrong manner. This view of idolatry, which we have identified as Halevi's view, plays down the question of what concept of God is in the worshiper's mind, and it undermines the priority of metaphysics that is prominent in the second position. The problem is to worship God in the right, revealed way. The wall that separates the idolatrous from the nonidolatrous marks the boundary between those who have the right revelation and those who have the false one, and not between those who have correct beliefs about God and those who have false beliefs about him.

\*       \*       \*

These four approaches to idolatry constitute four different sets of oppositions between idolatry and nonidolatry. The first opposes the alien gods, the "other" gods, to Israel's own God, the God who took Israel out of Egypt. In the anthropomorphic biblical terminology the opposition is between the adulterer and the husband, the rebel and the sovereign. The second approach to idolatry opposes the false and mistaken god to the true and right God. The opposition here is thus between the product of the imagination and the product of reason. The third approach to idolatry opposes an aspect of God, or an intermediary power, to the supreme God. Shifting the emphasis to worship, the fourth approach opposes the alien worship of God to the right worship of God. Although the prohibition against idolatry is essential to the self-definition of nonpagans, the four different articulations of what stands for the opposition between idolatry and proper worship suggest that it is a mistake to articulate an account of what is the essential content of idolatry. Our approach is therefore not to try to formulate one definition of idolatry that will capture its essence, but to show how diverse and problematic the concept itself is. The boundary drawn by the prohibition against idolatry marks different territories, which depend simultaneously on different ideas of God and on different ideas of idolatry.

Idolatry, as discussed so far, is a complementary concept to some notion of a proper God; both God and idolatry are codependent conceptually and in the lives of the faithful. This codependency is shifted and broken in some of the modern discourse on idolatry, which is the subject of the rest of the Conclusion. Our aim is to outline the different modern extensions that arise from the powerful yet fluid opposition between idolatry and nonidolatry.

What distinguishes some instances of modern rhetoric of idolatry is, on the one hand, its use of terminology from the religious critique of idolatry and, on the other hand, its attitude to what stands against the idols and what is supposed to complement them. The complementary concept to idolatry is no longer a proper God but something else. Thus the category of idolatry is maintained, while what it is in opposition to changes. A second, more radical modern use of the language of idolatry occurs when the category of idolatry is extended to include any competing opposite, even what was supposedly conceived as the right God himself. According to this view, any candidate for opposing the idol is by definition an erection of a new idol. A third way in which the rhetoric of idolatry is applied in modern use is to accept the basic oppositions between pagans and nonpagans but to invert the value assigned to them, namely, to attach the positive value to the pagans and the negative to the non-pagans. These three modern forms of the discourse of idolatry—replacement, extension, and inversion—are best explained with examples.

One of the first and most powerful examples of replacement is Francis Bacon's fourfold description of the idols of the mind: "The formation of ideas and axioms by true induction is no doubt the proper remedy to be applied for the keeping off and clearing away of idols. To point them out, however, is of great use, for the doctrine of Idols is to the Interpretation of Nature what the doctrine of the refutation of Sophisms is to common Logic."[1] The idols of the mind, according to Bacon, are the obstacles to the true science of nature. Bacon classifies them as the idols of the tribe, the idols of the cave, the idols of the marketplace and the idols of the theater. Each of these domains stands for a different source of error. Iconoclasm, in Bacon's sense, is clearing the mind from idols that stand between it and true knowledge of nature. The idols of the tribe are distortions in understanding due to the nature of the human tribe in general, such as mistakes that arise from the incompetency of the senses. The idols of the cave are mistakes that arise from the peculiar constitution of each individual, like the individual's investment in a particular study or theory. Using Plato's allegory of the cave, we might say that the images on the walls of Bacon's cave are not the collective experience of humans before being exposed to the light of philosophy. The idols of the cave according to Bacon differ from individual to individual, they are the individual's private prejudices and biases. The idols of the marketplace are errors that result from the discrepancy between language and reality. Those mistakes originate in language, which is the shared medium of exchange; hence Bacon's reference to the marketplace. The idols of the theater are those received into the mind from the "play books of philosophical systems." Philosophical artificial systems are called the idols of the theater because they are stagelike representations of the world, representing not the real world but their authors' own creations.

Bacon's theory of idolatry is therefore a theory of mistakes (of various kinds) that have to be overcome for the sake of science.

Bacon's discourse is analogous to that of Maimonides, who articulated the opposition between the true God and false idols: Bacon equates idols with false notions that are imprinted on the human mind. Like the idols of the religious enlightenment, they are idols of the mind, but the traditional opposition to false idols (the true God) is replaced by the true science (the Baconian method of induction).

The second example of replacement is Marx's rhetoric: "Money is the Jealous God of Israel before whom no other god may exist. Money degrades all the gods of mankind and converts them into commodities. Money is the general, self-sufficient value of everything. Hence it has robbed the whole world, the human world as well as nature, of its proper worth. Money is the alienated essence of man's labor and life and this alien essence dominates him as he worships it."[2] Man's humanity, which in Marx's view is his ability to create freely and spontaneously, is alienated in the capitalistic production process by the fact that the products no longer belong to their producers and instead dominate them. Moreover, the products of human labor become objectified in money. Their price in the market economy is the sole origin of their value, and, like God, money is the only self-sufficient value. It is the first cause of value.

From the traditions of polemics against idolatry, Marx borrows two elements: the fetish, which is the commodity, and money, the alien god that is worshiped. The commodity is a fetish because its market value is mistakenly perceived as its substance. The market value is a substitute for the use value of the product, which is the only inherent value that a product truly has. Within the fetishistic view of commodity, money becomes the alien god that confers that value.

The more man works the more he accumulates money, and the more he externalizes his essence to the alien god of money. Following Feuerbach's critique of religion, Marx says: "The more the worker exerts himself, the more powerful becomes the alien objective world which he fashions against himself, the poorer he and his inner world become, the less there is that belongs to him. It is the same in religion."[3] Marx's rhetoric of idolatry as a critique of capitalism is connected to his concept of alienation. Alienation occurs as man's creative powers are divorced from the products of his creation and as these products acquire domination over him in the capitalistic economic system. What stands in opposition to the deification of money is not the true right God but mankind's own essence. Because of the distribution of labor in capitalistic society, man, who should be giving supreme expression to his humanity in the process of production, loses it in this very process. This growing subservience impoverishes his worth as a person. Iconoclasm in Marx's case will be the act in which man regains his own alienated essence from the idols that robbed him of it: the alien gods are alienated men. The worship of the golden calf is the diminution of the human essence and its subservience to a foreign entity that gains control over man's life. What stood traditionally in opposition to the golden calf, the God who took Israel out of Egypt, is replaced here by men's creative essence. Unlike Bacon's, Marx's translation of the problem of idolatry is not connected to the epistemological sphere. It is connected rather to the religious terminology of right worship and wrong worship, and the right worship of God is replaced by the unalienated production of man.

In one of his notebooks Wittgenstein articulates his philosophical project in iconoclastic terms: "All that philosophy can do is to destroy idols. And that means not making any new ones—say out of the 'absence of idols.'"[4] Wittgenstein's philosophical iconoclasm is not intended to clear the way to the true system. Rather, the category of idolatry, which is extended to include all its possible opposites, stands against the very idea of a system. From this perspective Bacon's iconoclasm is misleading. While rejecting the four kinds of idols Bacon is replacing old idols with a new one. The metaphor of idolatry that Wittgenstein uses in describing his stand against foundationalism points to the possibility of the extension of idolatry to its opposites, which includes the new idol that was erected by Bacon.

Wittgenstein's metaphorical extension has some similarity to the Maimonidean view of negative theology. According to Maimonides, any linguistic positive description of God will constitute a belief in a false god. Since Maimonides considers language inherently limited, the predication of meaningful attributes to God will portray the world and God under the same categories and will necessarily make God into a thing of the world. The strict Maimonidean demands for total linguistic restraint exclude any possibility of articulation of what stands in opposition to the false god. At the moment such a formulation will be suggested it will mean replacing one false god with another. Maimonides, through his approach to the limits of language, extended the category of idolatry to any positive description of God.

Wittgenstein meant in his use of the metaphor to refer to epistemological idols, but extensions are possible in other spheres as well and are connected to the extension of the idea of worship. This kind of modern discourse is not replacing what stood opposite the idol but extending the category of idolatry well beyond the traditional territories. In the preceding chapter we pointed out that within the traditional discourse of idolatry there is an interesting extension of what worship is. The prophets condemned Israel's protective treaties with the superpowers of the ancient world as a form of idolatry. God's exclusivity was broadened from the only one who should be ritually worshiped to the only one who should be considered ultimate protector. Ritual worship is therefore just one of the forms of the man-God relationship, which if directed to others constitutes idolatry. The Bible itself extends the category to include attitudes that express political subjugation to those other than God. A further, typical extension of the notion of worship and the idea of deification is the position that considers granting ultimate value to someone or something which is not worthy of a form of false worship.

Granting ultimate value does not necessarily mean attributing a set of metaphysical divine attributes; the act of granting ultimate value involves a life of full devotion and ultimate commitment to something or to someone. Absolute value can be conferred upon many things—institutions such as the state, persons, goals, ideologies, and even a football team. In this extension of worship, religious attitude is perceived not as part of a metaphysics or as an expression of customary rituals but as a form of absolute devotion, an attitude that makes something into a godlike being. What makes something into an absolute is that it is both overriding and demanding. It claims to stand superior to any competing claim, and unlike merely an overriding rule it is also something that provides a program and a cause, thereby demanding dedication and devotion. The falseness of idolatry is that the object of this devotion is not worthy of it. Idolatry in this extension means leading a false life, a life dedicated to an unworthy cause. The opposition between idolatry and proper worship is not between the false and the true god but between the unworthy and the worthy god.

It is not easy to draw the exact line between attributing value and conferring absolute value, between not being indifferent and leading a life of total devotion, but when that line is crossed an idol is erected and an idolatrous life is being led. Revolutionaries who believed in their cause and participated in a revolution that demanded their full loyalty have sometimes had the painful experience of realizing later that their lives were dedicated to the wrong cause. Tragically, the unworthiness of the cause is sometimes independent of their own efforts, as when the Marxist revolution was taken over by Stalin. It is of no surprise that such experiences are documented in a book titled *The God That Failed*. The power of this title derives from its capacity to evoke, by using the metaphor of God, the absolute promise and the total investment that were involved in the Russian Revolution. Idolatry can thus be formulated in a kind of general rule: "any nonabsolute value that is made absolute and demands to be the center of dedicated life is idolatry." This formulation, although extending the sphere of idolatry, leaves room for some values that are absolute. There are some worthy gods who oppose the unworthy ones. Stronger formulations can be extended to include any value: "any human value should not be made absolute." (There is a temptation to think of this rule as if logically true, by replacing "human" with "finite" and "absolute" with "infinite," thus formulating a rule that is analytically true: "any finite value should not be made infinite." This formulation is misleading because the "finite" and "infinite" in the sentence do not refer to the same thing; human is finite in the sense of mortal or limited, and the infinite is in many ways metaphorical, expressing the importance of the value.) The internal logic of this general formulation "nothing human can be made absolute," as the core of the understanding of idolatry, threatens to include all complements of idolatry as idolatry, even the worthy God. If the knowledge of the worthy God is ultimately channeled through humans, then it cannot itself be made absolute. Siding the idol with an absolute that is superhuman will be self-refuting. What will stand in opposition to idolatry will not be any sense of absolute but the freedom from absolutes and the denial of ultimates; extension reaches its extreme limit.[5]

\* \* \*

Hume in his essay on the natural history of religion analyzes the sources of both polytheism and monotheism in human nature and in history. According to Hume, monotheism is rationally based upon the unity of nature. Nature, as seen by Hume, reflects a comprehensive unity of design. Nature's parts complement each other, and the same laws govern all natural phenomena. For Hume the most plausible outcome of the unity of nature is to assume one rational agent that stands behind that grand design of nature. Polytheism, by contrast, reflects the diversity of human events. It grows out of people's response to the fluctuations of life. Human fate does not mirror one controlling hand, it reflects tensions, conflicting claims, and a multiplicity of purposes. If life is viewed as guided by personal divine beings, the conclusion will be that at least a few gods influence human life, causing defeat and victory, wealth and poverty, illness and health. According to Hume, polytheism is created out of people's inability to detach the view of nature from the fate of man and out of a tendency to project human dispositions to the world.[6]

After validating monotheism as a better perspective on nature, Hume sets himself to value other aspects of monotheism and polytheism and he points to the relative merits of polytheism. According to Hume, unlike monotheism, polytheism is inherently pluralistic and less dogmatic. Polytheism approves of many versions and customs. Polytheists are politically far more tolerant than monotheists, who attempt to impose their unity of faith on everyone.[7] It is not our aim to evaluate the arguments of nonpagans against pagans and to issue judgment on the matter. In examining Hume's argument, therefore, we focus not on its validity or nonvalidity regarding the history, weaknesses, and merits of polytheism, but on the peculiar way Hume is inverting the values of the traditional dichotomy of pagan and nonpagan. His inversion is typical of some of the modern discourse on paganism.

Hume was not the first one to reverse the traditional evaluation. Machiavelli considered the civic virtues of pagans superior to Christian virtues,[8] and Rousseau deemed paganism preferable as a civil religion.[9] Augustine analyzed the Roman character as composed of two desires, the desire for glory and the desire for freedom. The pagan Roman citizen longed for earthly glory; he aspired to victory and raised military bravery to the status of a supreme virtue. The Christian is indifferent to such victories; he interprets everything that occurs to him as an expression of supreme providence, so it makes no difference to him if he wins or loses. What is the difference, asks Augustine, between the winners and the losers, except for the empty glory of victory?[10] Rousseau agrees with Augustine's characterization of the two types of citizens—those of the earthly city and those of the city of God, but being interested in the flourishing of the earthly city, Rousseau reverses the evaluation and considers the pagan citizen superior. It is true that the Christian soldier does not fear death, but he does not aspire to victory either. What is important in battle is the wish to return victorious rather than equanimity in the face of death.

Machiavelli, Rousseau, and Hume all show some tendency to reverse the traditional evaluation, but the greatest inverter of all was Nietzsche. The struggle against God as a struggle for man's self-realization became a central theme in Nietzsche's criticism of religion. This element has special importance for our discussion because in Nietzsche's thought it involves a call for the return to paganism. Paganism, according to Nietzsche, possesses the possibility of self-affirmation, thus constituting its superiority over the holy God of monotheism. Nietzsche interpreted the triumph of Christianity as the victory of self-denial over the life-affirming pagans, the victory of the slave morality and resentment over the morality of the nobles. The morality of the noble pagans, who identified power with happiness, beauty, justice, and love of the gods, was reversed with the rise of Christianity. The Christians, by declaring the poor as the virtuous and humility, suffering, and meekness as ideals, compensated for their incapacity to achieve the heroic life of their noble rivals. Unable to fight the nobles on their own terms through the use of force, the Christians achieved their revenge by a reversal of values, transforming the strong into the bad and the weak into the good. Thus developed a slave morality that was a total denial of life, an answer of "no" to the healthy person's will for power. The slaves, who could not free themselves of the conqueror's yoke, caused the strong to internalize the slaves' values; in the process the strong lost the source of their strength.

The nobleman who once achieved vitality through the use of power against his environment, achieves it now by his war against his own will to power. This is how bad conscience and remorse are created. The suffering that man brings upon himself, the self-mortification and self-torture involved in the feeling of sinfulness, are typical expressions of self-negation. In Nietzsche's view, within every saint there is a noble who has turned his power against himself. This is also the reason for Nietzsche's ambivalent attitude toward the saint. The saint is indeed a living model of slave morality who also contains the power of the nobility, a power that has been distorted by being turned inward.

One of the important tools of slave morality and bad conscience is the holy nonpagan God:

> This man of the bad conscience has seized upon the presupposition of religion so as to drive his self-torture to its most gruesome pitch of severity and rigor. Guilt before God: this thought becomes an instrument of torture to him. He apprehends in God the ultimate antithesis of his ineluctable animal instincts; he reinterprets these animal instincts themselves as a form of guilt before God (as hostility rebellion, insurrection against the "Lord," the "father," the primal ancestor and origin of the world); he stretches himself upon the contradiction of "God" and "Devil"; he ejects from himself all his denial of himself, of his naturalness, and actuality, in the form of an affirmation, as something existent, corporeal, real, as God, as the holiness of God . . . In this psychic cruelty there resides a madness of the will which is absolutely unexampled . . . his will to erect an ideal—that of the "holy God"—and in the face of it to feel the palpable certainty of his own absolute unworthiness.[11]

The monotheistic ideal of the holy God, the transcendent and uninstinctual God, is constructed by man as the cruelest expression of life-negation. The holy God represents as superior everything which man is not; it represents as ideal an embodied reality that is a denial of man's will to power. The monotheistic denial is expressed in one of Nietzsche's boldest formulations in *Twilight of the Idols:* "The saint in whom God takes pleasure is the ideal castrate . . . Life is at an end where the kingdom of God begins."[12] The movement from paganism is described by Nietzsche in *The Anti-Christ:* "God degenerated to the contradiction of life instead of being its transfiguration and eternal Yes! . . . In God nothingness deified, the will to nothingness sanctified."[13] Unlike the holy God of the monotheists, the pagan gods affirm life. The pagan gods portrayed as instinctual and heroic represent the will to power as an ideal, as something to cherish and affirm; they are instruments for man's liberation rather than his self-suppression. Nietzsche articulates the opposition between the nonpagan God and the pagan gods as one between the uninstinctual, transcendent, emasculated, life-denying God and the heroic, instinctual, life-affirming gods. The superiority of paganism according to Nietzsche derives from its alliance with man's own self-deification, by portraying the gods as fully human and asserting their will to power. For Nietzsche man's recognition of his limitations and his profound feeling of finiteness, which stem from the idea of a transcendental God, are nothing but cruel self-negation, the victory of envy, on the part of those who by their very nature are incapable of self-affirmation and want to chain the whole world with their own shackles. Nietzsche agrees with the analysis of the connection between denial of God and self-worship, but he reverses the evaluation of this connection. Of the modern uses of paganism that we discussed—replacement extension and inversion—inversion is the most daring. For those who do not want to accept its criticism of monotheism, it might yet serve the role of clarifying—from the perspective of the critics—some aspects of what it is that monotheism stands for.

Idolatry is a powerful category that aspires to establish a firm boundary between God and the strange gods. But since these two notions—God and the strange gods—are interlocked, defining what are the strange gods is no less complicated than defining God himself. Thus, the boundary between the nonidolatrous and the idolatrous is drawn in different locations. The category of the strange, or the wrong god, unleashed by the monotheists, proved itself to be powerful and complex. Besides marking the outside, it turned inward and served as a category of criticism within the non-pagan community. It is this complexity that gave an astonishing fluidity to "idolatry," a category that is supposed to be the firmest and strictest of all.

*Notes*

*Index*

# Notes

## Introduction

1. The term "monotheism," meaning the belief in the existence of only one God, is not an accurate term to describe religions that reject paganism. As we shall see there are trends that do not deny polytheism and yet do prohibit the worship of other gods and obligate the worship of only one God. Therefore, we generally prefer to use the term "nonpagan religions" for the religions that prohibit idolatry.

2. See Babylonian Talmud, Tractate *Yoma* 69b; Tractate *Avodah Zarah* 17a–b.

3. The term *zarah* refers to a strange form of worship in several places in the Bible: Leviticus 10:11, Exodus 30:9, Numbers 3:4 and 26:61. In a few verses the term *zar* refers to a strange god and not a strange worship: Psalms 44:14 and 81:10, Isaiah 43:12.

4. Leviticus 18:4. See also the rabbinic interpretation of this verse: *Sifrah* 13:5.

5. This rabbinic interpretation of Deuteronomy 7:4 appears in Babylonian Talmud, Tractate *Avodah Zarah* 20a.

## *1. Idolatry and Betrayal*

1. Anthropomorphic images of God are not at all foreign to the Bible, which does not present an abstract concept of God. Some authors have pointed out that different layers in the Bible exhibit different degrees of anthropomorphism. While anthropomorphism in the source J is extreme and daring, in the priestly source it is more moderate. See G. von Rad, *Genesis: A Commentary*, trans. J. H. Marks (Philadelphia: Westminster Press, 1972), pp. 25–29. On anthropomorphism in the deuteronomistic school, see M. Weinfeld, *Deuteronomy and the Deuteronomistic School* (Oxford: Clarendon Press, 1972), pp. 191–209. On the priestly tendency to abstraction, see I. Knohl, "The Conception of God and Worship in the Priestly

Source and in the Holiness School" (Ph.D. diss., Hebrew University, 1988), pp. 119–122, and his reference to Weinfeld's approach in n. 136.

2. An additional example of the analogy between idolatry and other sins is *Tosefta, Tractate Bava Kamma* 9: "If someone tears clothing or breaks utensils in his anger, he should be considered like an idolater"; cf. Babylonian Talmud, Tractate *Shabbat* 105b. See also Babylonian Talmud, Tractate *Sanhedrin* 92b: "One who changes his speech is like an idolater." In these examples the word "like" requires clarification. Does it mean "as bad as"— that the sin being compared to idolatry has the same degree of severity as idolatry itself? Or does it mean that there is some more essential similarity between the two sins? The explanation of the Babylonian Talmud in Tractate *Shabbat* to the *Tosefta* in Tractate *Bava Kamma* is an example of an attempt to interpret the similarity implied by the word "like" as a deep similarity. In the view of the Babylonian Talmud, the similarity between the person who tears clothing in his anger and the idolater is that both are enslaved to their evil desires. As R. Avin puts it in Tractate *Shabbat:* "What is the meaning of the verse, 'You shall have no foreign god among (literally, within) you, you shall not bow to an alien god'? What is the foreign god within the body of a person? This is the evil desire." This interesting interpretation is built upon the alternative wording "within you" rather than "among you," as is clearly meant in the context of the verse. As an expression belonging to the inner realm, it transforms the relation between the representing and the represented things into a broader and deeper relation than the other interpretation of "like," meaning "as bad as."

3. On the marital metaphor, see G. Cohen, "The Song of Songs," in *Samuel Friedland Lectures, 1960–1966* (New York: Jewish Theological Seminary, 1966), pp. 1–21.

4. All biblical quotations are from *Tanakh: The Holy Scriptures* (Philadelphia and New York: Jewish Publication Society, 1988).

5. For a description of the development of the image of whoredom from the Pentateuch to the prophets Hosea, Jeremiah, and Ezekiel, see M. Greenberg, *The Anchor Bible, Ezekiel 1–20* (New York: Doubleday, 1983), pp. 297–299.

6. Ibid., pp. 274–275.

7. Ibid., p. 301.

8. Ibid., p. 277.

9. The return of the alienated son is expressed in several places in the Bible, such as the verse "Turn back, O rebellious children, I will heal your afflictions!" (Jeremiah 3:22).

10. Cf. Babylonian Talmud, Tractate *Yuma* 86b: "R. Jochanan said, 'Great is repentance, for it puts aside a negative commandment of the Torah, as it is written, "If a man divorces his wife, and she leaves him and

marries another man, can he ever go back to her? Would not such a land be defiled? Now you have whored with many lovers: can you return to Me?— says the Lord." ' "

11. The following is written in *Sifrei on Numbers,* sec. 115: "Why is the Exodus from Egypt mentioned with the performance of many commandments? This may be compared to the case of a king whose friend's son was taken captive. When the king redeemed him, he did not redeem him as a free man but as a servant, so that if he did not obey the king's commands, the king could say, 'You are my servant.' When they returned to the king's domain and the king said to the redeemed captive, 'Put on my sandals and carry my things to the bathhouse,' the friend's son tried to avoid him, whereupon the king took out the bill of sale and said, 'You are my servant.' Similarly, when God redeemed the children of his beloved Abraham from captivity he did not redeem them as sons but as servants, so that if he would give them a commandment and they would not accept it he could say to them, 'You are my servants.' "

The Exodus from Egypt is a foundational event and the source of Israel's obligations to God, which constitutes an essential difference between it and other miracles. It is interesting that this midrash describes the Exodus as an event in which God bought the Israelites from Egypt according to the accepted methods of purchase. He redeemed them and he has a bill of sale for the transaction; moreover, he redeemed them as servants rather than free people. Although the word for "redeem" can be used both in the sense of "save" and in the sense of "buy," the mention of the bill of sale turns the act of saving into an act of purchase, proving that the "redemption" mentioned at the beginning of the section is a purchase accompanied by a bill of sale.

In contrast to this view of the Exodus as the source of Israel's obligation to God, there is another reading in the *Mekhilta* on the verse "I the Lord am your God" (Exodus 20:2): "Why were the Ten Commandments not written at the beginning of the Torah? This may be compared to someone who entered a state and said, 'I will be your king.' The people answered, 'What good have you done for us that you should become our king?' What did he do? He built them a fortified wall, he conveyed water to their dwellings, and he fought wars for them. Then when he said again, 'I will be your king,' they answered, 'Yes, yes.' Thus God took Israel out of Egypt, parted the Red Sea for them, gave them manna to eat, brought up water for them from a well, sent them quail to eat, and fought a war for them against Amalek. Then, when he said to them, 'I will be your king,' they answered, 'Yes, yes.' " The Exodus is conceived here not as an act of purchase but as a benefit. It does not directly obligate the Israelites to be God's servants, but it is the reason why they accept God's kingship voluntarily. According to this view, the Exodus is not a unique event but one of a series of benefits that God performed for Israel.

12. In the Bible gentiles are forbidden to worship idols only in the land of Israel, which is the territory of the God of Israel. The gentiles who were exiled to Samaria were punished because they did not act according to "the rules of the God of the land" (see II Kings 17:24–41). Aside from this, they are permitted to worship idols and are not punished for it. One of the extreme formulations of this view appears in Deuteronomy, where there is a claim that God himself allotted the worship of the host of heaven to the nations (4:19). The universal vision of the prophets is a vision for the end of days and not a present prohibition of idol worship for the gentiles. The prohibition of idolatry for the gentiles as well as part of the "seven commandments of the gentiles" are innovations by the Talmudic sages, which free the prohibition on idolatry from its dependence on the unique historical connection between Israel and God. Concerning this prohibition, see *Tosefta,* Tractate *Avodah Zarah* chap. 8, 4; Genesis Rabbah 16:16; Babylonian Talmud, Tractate *Sanhedrin* 56a.

13. Such views are widespread among scholars. See, for example, M. Smith, "Common Theology of the Ancient Near East," *Journal of Biblical Literature,* 71 (1952): 135–147, n. 16. A more extensive discussion of this question may be found in the first part of Chapter 8, below.

14. Concerning the question of reliance upon foreign powers and idolatry, see Chapter 8.

15. The conception of idolatry as an evil desire within people, similar to their sexual desire, may be found in the Babylonian Talmud, Tractate *Yuma* 69b and Tractate *Sanhedrin* 64a.

16. The connection between the prohibition of idolatry and God's jealousy appears in several places in the Bible; see above, nn. 3, 4.

17. The JPS edition translates *kana* in this verse as "impassioned," but the metaphor being developed here requires the traditional translation of "jealous" [trans.]. Goitein understands the tetragrammaton itself as meaning "jealous"; see S. Goitein, *Iyunnim ba-Mikra* (Tel Aviv: Yavneh Press, 1957), pp. 318–331.

18. Similar quotations may be found in *Mekhilta of R. Ishmael,* sec. 65, and in *Mekhilta of R. Shimon ben Yohai* on the portion Jethro 20:5. In the latter source the second story appears differently: General Agrippa asked Rabban Gamaliel, "Is he jealous of anyone not of the same type, as it is written, 'It has been clearly demonstrated to you that the Lord alone is God' (Deuteronomy 4:35)?" Rabban Gamaliel answered, "He is not jealous of someone superior or of someone like himself but only of someone inferior, as he says, 'For my people have done a twofold wrong: They have forsaken me, the Fount of living waters'—and even if they had only forsaken me, the

Fount of living waters, they would be unfortunate, how much the more so that they 'have hewed them out cisterns, broken cisterns, which cannot even hold water' (Jeremiah 2:13)." The question here is based on the fact that the end of the verse quoted from Deuteronomy asserts, "There is none beside Him," yet he is jealous of idols, which implies that they exist.

19. In the Bible there are very few images of God as a woman. The verse in Isaiah, "Now I will scream like a woman in labor, I will pant and I will gasp" (42:14), which compares God to a woman undergoing childbirth, is rare in biblical literature, and the images appearing just before and after this image in Isaiah speak of God in the masculine gender. In rabbinic writings the word *shekhina* (used as a name of God) is the name of a female rather than a male: The verbs used in connection with this term are of feminine gender. This name, which is very frequent in rabbinic literature, constitutes a departure from biblical usage and a willingness to portray God as a woman. Urbach claims that the use of *shekhinah* is characteristic of those places where there is a close presence of God; see E. E. Urbach, *The Sages: Their Concepts and Beliefs,* trans. I. Abrahams (Cambridge, Mass.: Harvard University Press, 1987), pp. 37–65. According to this view it is perhaps intimacy that gives God a feminine attribute. In the kabbalistic literature the term *shekhina* is no longer conceived as one of God's names, but rather as the feminine aspect of the divinity. Concerning the development of this name, see G. Scholem, *On the Mystical Shape of the Godhead: Basic Concepts in the Kabbalah,* trans. J. Neugroschel (New York: Schocken, 1991), pp. 140–196.

20. The JPS translation notes: "Admah and Zeboiim were destroyed with neighboring Sodom and Gomorrah; cf. Genesis 10:19, 14:2,8."

21. Concerning the distinction between the two types of loyalty and authority and the process of depersonalization of obligation, see M. Weber, *Economy and Society,* ed. G. Roth and C. Wittich (Berkeley: University of California Press, 1978), pp. 214, 226–227, 256–266. Concerning the complex relationship between the personal and the nonpersonal aspects of obligation in the feudal period, see G. Poggy, *The Development of the Modern State* (Stanford: Stanford University Press, 1978), pp. 16–36. For the many distinctions relating to the changing attitudes to disloyalty, see J. Shklar, *Ordinary Vices* (Cambridge, Mass.: The Belknap Press of Harvard University Press, 1984), pp. 138–192.

22. The use of the verb *yd'*, to know, for intimate relationships is found in Genesis 4:1: "Now the man knew his wife Eve"; the JPS translation notes that the Hebrew verb *yada* is often used in a sexual sense.

23. See n. 11 above.

24. A feeling of discomfort with the attribute of jealousy may be found in the *Mekhilta*'s interpretation of the verse "For I the Lord your God am a jealous God" (Exodus 20:5): "I rule over jealousy and jealousy does not rule

over Me, just as I rule over sleep and sleep does not rule over Me, as it is written, 'See, the guardian of Israel neither slumbers nor sleeps!' (Psalm 121:4)." Another interpretation offered there for the verse is: "I punish them for idolatry but I am merciful and gracious in other matters." In the first interpretation God is not a jealous God but is a ruler over jealousy, and in the second interpretation jealousy is not one of God's characteristics but only a tool he uses to punish the idolaters; otherwise God is merciful and gracious.

25. For a discussion of the various uses of the term "jealousy" in the Bible and a distinction between "jealous for" and "jealous of," see Y. Levinstadt, *Encyclopedia Mikrahit*, VII, 196–198. For an extremely interesting account of the deeply anthropomorphic complexities of God's jealousy in the Bible, see Y. Muffs, "Bein Din Lerahamim: Tefilatam shel Neviim," in *Torah Nidreshet* (Tel Aviv: Am Oved, 1984), pp. 74–79. For a discussion of the relationship between jealousy, dependency, rivalry, and self-doubt, see L. Tov-Ruach, "Jealousy, Attention, and Loss," in A. O. Rorty, ed., *Explaining Emotions* (Berkeley: University of California Press, 1980), pp. 465–488.

26. For the distinction between the two meanings of "honor," see P. Berger, "Obsolescence of the Concept of Honour," in M. Sandel, ed., *Liberalism and Its Critics* (Oxford: Blackwell, 1984).

27. See *Mekhilta of R. Ishmael* va-Yehi sec. 8, and Babylonian Talmud, Tractate *Yuma* 69b. The definition of bravery as "restraint" creates a new possibility for theodicy since the flourishing of idolaters is not a sign of God's weakness but of his power of restraint. Concerning the relation between this conception of restraint and the conception of God's providence, see D. Hartman, *A Living Covenant* (New York: Free Press, 1985), chaps. 1, 2, 11.

28. Y. Kaufmann, *Toldot ha-Emunah ha-Israelit,* vol. 1 (Tel Aviv: Bialik Institute, 1937), pp. 221–254.

## 2. Idolatry and Representation

1. Concerning the connection between the two verses, see B. Childs, *The Book of Exodus* (Philadelphia: Westminster Press, 1974), pp. 406–409.

2. Did the giving of the Torah on Mount Sinai involve only the sense of hearing? In Exodus we find the verse, "The Lord came down upon Mount Sinai" (19:20), while in Deuteronomy the following is written: "From the heavens He let you hear His voice to discipline you; on earth He let you see His great fire; and from amidst that fire you heard His words" (4:36). Concerning the tension between vision and hearing during the giving of the Torah on Mount Sinai, see A. J. Heschel, *Torah min ha-Shamaim be-Aspaclaria shel ha-Dorot* (New York: Shonstin, 1962), pt. 1, pp. 262–294; pt. 2, pp. 58–67.

3. C. S. Peirce, "The Icon, Index, and Symbol," in *Collected Papers,*

vol. 8, ed. Charles Hartshorne and Paul Weiss (Cambridge, Mass.: Harvard University Press, 1931–1958).

4. Nelson Goodman, *The Languages of Art* (Indianapolis: Bobbs-Merrill, 1976), pp. 3–43.

5. See Isaiah 40:18–20, 44:9–20; Jeremiah 10:1–5; Habakkuk 2:18–19.

6. The biblical reduction of paganism to mere fetishism can be understood as an intentional misrepresentation for the sake of polemics. Y. Kaufmann explains that the Bible never confronts pagan myths or other conceptions of the pagan gods aside from the fetishistic elements, not as a result of intentional ridicule of paganism but as a sign that the pagan religions were not truly understood. According to Kaufmann the "monotheistic revolution" in Israel was successful to the extent that the Bible recognized only marginal pagan practices and nothing more. See Y. Kaufmann, *The Religion of Israel: From Its Beginnings to the Babylonian Exile,* trans. Moshe Greenberg (Chicago: University of Chicago Press, 1960), pp. 7–20, 133–147. For an extensive discussion of Kaufmann's views, see Chapter 3 below. For an unfetishistic rabbinic view of Roman icons, see *Midrash Exodus Rabbah* 15:17, and S. Liberman, *Hellenism in Jewish Palestine* (New York: Jewish Theological Seminary, 1962), p. 126.

7. For information on the iconoclastic debate, see *Icon and Logos: Sources in Eighth-Century Iconoclasm,* trans. and introd. D. J. Sahas (Toronto: University of Toronto Press, 1986). Concerning the claim that there is no divinity in the icon, see ibid., pp. 64, 65, 76, 84–86. For an example of the counterclaim, see pp. 68, 77. Concerning iconoclasm in the sixteenth century, see C. M. N. Eire, *War against the Idols* (Cambridge: Cambridge University Press, 1986). For additional references on the attribution of powers to symbols in the worship of saints, see Eire, p. 15, n. 32; on the iconoclastic debate in the seventh and eighth centuries, see p. 19, n. 50. One of the most interesting cases of the attribution of the power of the represented thing to the representing thing is Eire's example on p. 17. The Jews were accused of stealing the missal wafer in order to continue torturing Jesus. Toward the end of the Middle Ages churches were named after the blood that dripped from the wafer when the Jews tortured it, because the wafer was the symbol of God's body.

8. For descriptions of the function of images, see E. Bowen, *Holy Images: An Inquiry into Idolatry and Image-Worship in Ancient Paganism and Christianity* (London: G. Allen and Unwin, 1940); H. Frankfort, *Kingship and the Gods* (Chicago: University of Chicago Press, 1984), pp. 303–305; D. Freedberg, *The Power of Images* (Chicago: University of Chicago Press, 1984), chaps. 2, 14; E. Kitz'inger, "The Cult of Images in the Age before Iconoclasm," *Dumbarton Oaks Papers* 8 (1954): 85–150; and M. Camille, *The Gothic Idol* (Cambridge: Cambridge University Press, 1989), chaps. 1, 5.

9. I Samuel 5:1–7:1. It is interesting to examine the Philistines' reactions to the ark when it was brought by Israel to the war against them. The Philistines first identify the ark with Israel's God: "When they learned that the Ark of the Lord had come into the camp, the Philistines were frightened; for they said, 'God has come to the camp' (I Samuel 4:6). Israel on the other hand regarded the ark as a representation of God because it is God's footstool and throne, and God is called Lord of Hosts Enthroned on the Cherubim." On this difference see J. Milgrom, *The JPS Torah Commentary: Numbers* (Philadelphia and New York: Jewish Publication Society, 1990), pp. 373–375.

10. On the myth of the Dumuzi and the Mesopotamian conception of symbolism, see T. Jacobsen, *Treasures of Darkness* (New Haven: Yale University Press, 1976), chaps. 1, 2.

11. See n. 7 above.

12. For an extensive discussion of the origin and the development of the concept of the fetish, see W. Pietz, "The Problem of the Fetish I, II, and III," in *Res* 9 (1985), *Res* 13 (1987), and *Res* 16 (1988).

13. There is a similar description in Maimonides, *The Guide of the Perplexed,* trans. S. Pines (Chicago: University of Chicago Press, 1963), 1:36.

14. The attribution of powers to sacred objects that represent God is widespread within the nonpagan religions themselves. In certain kabbalistic traditions the prohibition against erasing even a single letter in the Torah scroll is interpreted as a prohibition against erasing God himself. The extreme caution involved in the laws for writing a Torah scroll thus derives from the fact that the obligation to write the scroll is connected with the act of multiplying the presence of God in the world through the Torah scrolls. For conceptions of such immanent representations of the divinity in Kabbalah see M. Idel, *Kabbalah: New Perspectives* (New Haven: Yale University Press, 1988), pp. 188–189. One of the manuscripts Idel cites says that someone who writes a Torah scroll is making God. In contrast to such views we can cite the attitude of Maimonides toward those who turn the mezuzah into a good-luck charm by adding holy names on its parchment: "It is not enough for these fools that they have voided the fulfillment of the commandment [adding the names makes the parchment unfit as a mezuzah], but they have also taken a great commandment which is the unification of the name of God and His worship, and used it as if it were a good-luck charm for their own benefit" (Maimonides, *Code of Jewish Law,* Laws of Mezuzah, 5:4).

15. Two arguments may be found in the iconoclastic literature of the sixteenth century. One is that the worship of statues is a substitute for the worship of God, while the other is that the statues are not capable of representing the deity properly because the infinite and the spiritual cannot be given material representation. The material representation of God would

lead to the conception that he is a material being. This claim is repeated many times by Calvin and others; see Eire, *War against the Idols,* p. 201.

16. See Chap. 1, n. 1, above.

17. See S. Lieberman, "Mishnat Shir ha-Shirim," a Hebrew appendix to G. Scholem, *Jewish Gnosticism, Merkabah Mysticism, and Talmudic Tradition* (New York: Jewish Theological Seminary, 1965). For a discussion of the *Shi'ur Komah* literature, see Scholem, *On the Mystical Shape of the Godhead: Basic Concepts in the Kabbalah,* pp. 15–55. On notions of the image of God, see Idel, *Kabbalah,* pp. 119–136 and n. 14. Traditions of seeing God directly exist therefore in the Bible, early Jewish mystical literature, and the midrash. In one of the earliest midrashim, the *Torat Kohanim,* sec. 1, ch. 2, we find: "R. Dosa said: God said, 'No man may see Me and live—they cannot see Me when they are alive but they can do so after their death.'" Also see *Sifrei on Numbers,* sec. 103.

18. The Sassian monarch sat on a throne with a veiled face or behind a curtain. He was therefore inaccessible and unseen. On this practice, see G. Windengren, "The Sacral Kingship in Iran," in *The Sacral Kingship* (Leiden: E. J. Brill, 1959), p. 247.

19. R. Abraham ben David differs with Maimonides' opinion in the *Code of Jewish Law,* Laws of Repentance, 3:7: "Three types of people are called heretics: one who says that there is no deity and the world has no ruler, one who says there is a ruler but there are two or more, one who says that there is one sovereign but he is a body and has an image." R. Abraham ben David comments as follows: "Even though this is a principle of our faith, one who believes that He is a body due to his understanding of the language of the biblical verses and the Midrash according to their literal meaning is not worthy of being called a heretic." There are other versions of this criticism that are expressed much more sharply; e.g., "Many who are better than he [Maimonides] believe in the corporeality of God." For a detailed analysis of the controversy see I. Twersky, *Rabad of Posquieres* (Cambridge, Mass.: Harvard University Press, 1962), pp. 282–286.

On the controversy that evolved around the Maimonidean denial of anthropomorphism and the opposition that supported anthropomorphic views, see B. Septimus, *Hispano-Jewish Culture in Transition* (Cambridge, Mass.: Harvard University Press, 1982), pp. 75–103.

20. On the nature of the cherubim and the ark as God's throne and therefore as his representations, see M. Haran, "The Ark and the Cherubim: Their Symbolic Significance in Biblical Ritual," *Israel Exploration Journal,* 9 (1959): 39–48, 89–94.

21. Views that the northern golden calves functioned like the ark in Jerusalem are discussed in M. Aberbach and L. Smolar, "Aaron Jerobam and the Golden Calves," *Journal of Biblical Literature,* 86 (1900): 135 and n. 34.

22. The prohibition against making metonymic representations may be found in *Mekhilta,* commentary on the verse: "You shall not make for yourselves any gods of silver or any gods of gold" (Exodus 20:20). Concerning the extension of this prohibition to pictures and sculptures of human form or the constellations even in nonritualistic context, see the Babylonian Talmud, Tractate *Rosh Hashanah* 24a–b; Tractate *Avodah Zarah* 43a–b. The scope of the prohibition against painting and sculpturing was debated by medieval commentators of the Talmud; see *Ramban* Tractate *Avodah Zarah* 43b "Hah de-Akshinan."

Images from Hellenistic mythology dating from the second century A.D. have been found in mosaics in synagogues and in tablets affixed to coffins in the Galilee. These discoveries raise deep questions about the strictness of the practical observance of the prohibition against the making of sculptures and images in Jewish society of the Hellenistic period. E. R. Goodenough, in his book *Jewish Symbols in the Graeco-Roman Period* (New York: Pantheon Books, 1953–1956), IV, 2–44, claims that the existence of these images in synagogues in a context of ritual worship implies that the rabbis did not determine the lifestyle of the communities and that their leadership had become undermined at that time. Opposing opinions are expressed by E. Urbach, "The Rabbinic Laws of Idolatry in the Second and Third Centuries in the Light of Archeological and Historical Facts," *Israel Exploration Journal* (1959–60), no. 3, 149ff., no. 4, 229ff. Urbach claims that these pictures did not have any symbolic ritual significance but served only for esthetic purposes, and furthermore that this usage derived from a change in attitude toward the prohibition on the making of sculptures and pictures during the second and third centuries, a change which took place within the world of the sages. For a further discussion of Jewish attitudes to visual art see *No Graven Images: Studies in Art and the Hebrew Bible,* ed. J. Gutmann (New York: Ktav Publishing House, 1971).

23. It is Onkelos's policy to replace representations of God with things he created in order to avoid corporealization. Maimonides discusses this many times in *The Guide of the Perplexed;* see, e.g., 1:21, 27, 28.

24. Concerning this debate, see M. Luther, "The Easter Sermon," *Werke* (Weimar, 1883ff.), vol. 38, p. 66. On Luther's preference for representations that would be understood as allegorical, see J. Korner, *The Moment of Self-Portraiture in German Renaissance Art* (Chicago: University of Chicago Press, 1992), chap. 15.

25. See n. 4, above.

26. In the opening paragraphs of *Philosophical Investigations,* Wittgenstein attacks the concept of meaning as a tag that refers to an internal picture.

27. I. Heinemann, in his book *Darchei ha-Haggadah* (Jerusalem: Magnes, 1954), p. 12 and n. 106, attempts to bridge the controversy by claiming that

everyone interprets doubled expressions as saying two different things, and there is no one who believes that the Torah speaks in the language of people. However, it seems that this is not the case and that there is an essential difference between the schools of R. Akiva and R. Ishmael on the issue.

28. The extension of the expression to the theological realm already appears in the literature of the post-talmudic sages. See *Teshuvot ha-Geonim,* ed. J. Musafia, response of R. Hai Gaon, 98, Jerusalem 1967, and B. Lewin, *Ozar ha-Geonim, Berakhot,* 1:131, and *Hagigah,* p. 30.

29. See H. A. Wolfson, *Studies in the History of Philosophy and Religion,* ed. I. Twersky and G. Williams, vol. 2 (Cambridge, Mass.: Harvard University Press, 1977), chaps. 6, 7.

30. *Guide of the Perplexed,* 1:59. For a moderate view of the theory of negative attributes as a criticism of language, see Wolfson, *Studies in the History of Philosophy and Religion,* II, chap. 5; J. Gutman, *Dat u-Mada* (Jerusalem, 1955), pp. 103–118. For a more skeptical view about the possibility of any metaphysical knowledge of God which is connected to the theory of negative attributes, see S. Pines, "The Limitations of Human Knowledge according to al-Farfabi ibn Bajja and Maimonides," in I. Twersky, ed., *Studies in Medieval Jewish History and Literature* (Cambridge, Mass.: Harvard University Press, 1979), pp. 89–110. For an important discussion of this issue, see J. Stern in *Iyyun* 38 (1989): 137–166. On Maimonides' epistemology see A. Altman, "Maimonides on the Intellect and the Scope of Metaphysics," in *Von der Mittelalterlichen zur modern Aufklarung* (Tubingen: J. C. B. Mohr, 1987), pp. 60–129.

### 3. Idolatry and Myth

1. Kaufmann, *The Religion of Israel: From Its Beginnings to the Babylonian Exile,* pp. 60–63; H. Frankfort, *Ancient Egyptian Religion* (New York: Harper and Row, 1961); H. and H. A. Frankfort, eds., *Before Philosophy* (New York: Penguin Books, 1951); H. Frankfort, *The Problem of Similarity in Ancient Near East Religions* (Oxford: Clarendon Press, 1951); F. Rosenzweig, "Das Neue Denken," in *Kleinere Schriften* (Berlin: Schocken, 1937). See also F. Rosenzweig, *The Star of Redemption,* trans. W. W. Hall (Notre Dame: University of Notre Dame Press, 1985), book 1, pp. 64–80; M. Buber, *Reden ueber das Judentum* (Berlin: Köln, J. Henger, 1932), pp. 125–142; E. Renan, *Histoire Générale et Système Comparé des Langue Simitiques* (Paris: Imprimerie impériale, 1858), p. 7. Renan claims that "the Semitic peoples never had a mythology," identifying the Semitic peoples with the monotheistic viewpoint and the absence of mythology. The reason he gives is that the monotonous desert landscapes led the dwellers in these

deserts to develop a concept of an abstract divinity and prevented them from acquiring the imagination needed for creating myths.

2. "Myth" and "mythology" should be distinguished. "Mythology" includes all stories about the gods, whereas "myths" are those stories connected with the revivification rituals discussed below. We consider "mythology" distinct from "saga" in that the central heroes in myth are the gods (even though they are not the only heroes), whereas in sagas the central heroes are mortals who perform acts similar to those of the gods. An ancient claim (from the third century B.C.) asserts that myths about the gods derive from stories about ancient kings who were deified. This claim is called Euhemerism, after the first person who made the claim. Whatever the source of myth, our distinction is a structural one—according to the dominant type of hero in the story. One might also make a "class" distinction: myths and sagas are aristocratic stories in which not just anyone can serve as a hero, as is the case in folk tales. The aristocracy of myth is like the aristocracy of tragedy according to Aristotle. Myth, like tragedy, is about the elite.

3. J. Fontenrose, *The Ritual Theory of Myth* (Berkeley: University of California Press, 1971); S. H. Hooke, ed., *Myth and Ritual* (London: Oxford University Press, 1933); S. H. Hooke, ed., *Myth, Ritual, and Kingship* (Oxford: Clarendon Press, 1958); T. H. Gaster, *Ritual Myth and Drama in the Ancient Near East* (New York: Harper and Row, 1950); C. Kluckhohn, "Myth and Rituals: A General Theory," *Harvard Theological Review* (1942): 45–79.

4. M. Eliade, *The Myth of the Eternal Return,* trans. W. R. Trask (Princeton: Princeton University Press, 1971); Y. Garber-Talmon, "The Concept of Time in Primitive Myths" (in Hebrew), *Iyyun* 2 (1951): 201–214. The mythic time we discussed is in the past, but there is also a future mythic time related to eschatological myths such as the myth of Gog and Magog. Myth may be distinguished from vision by the difference between stories about the past, "In the beginning there was," which is mythic time, and tales about the future, "It will be at the end of days," which is the time of the vision.

5. For criticism of Kaufmann's view, see B. Uffenheimer, "Myth and Reality in Ancient Israel," in S. N. Eisenstadt, ed., *Axial Age Civilizations* (Albany: State University of New York Press, 1986), from which it appears that the direct source of Kaufmann's view on the issue of absolute will as the line of distinction between the pagan and the monotheistic is Herman Cohen. But even if Cohen was the intermediary between Kant and Kaufmann, Kant is undoubtedly the source of the claim.

6. Kant's idea of the holy will is important for giving God's absolute will an ethical rather than a Gnostic character. In Leibniz's terminology, God acts as "sub specie boni." Kaufmann himself does not use the Kantian

expression "holy will," but his words can be interpreted that way. In contrast, we claim that the biblical God has, in Kantian terminology, a "good will" but not a holy will. The biblical God gets angry, has regrets—in short, he has tendencies that need to be overcome, and with his good will he overcomes them. The possessor of a holy will does not have any tendencies that need to be overcome.

7. In Hebrew most words are based on two-, three-, or four-consonant roots, and all sorts of prefixes, infixes, and suffixes may be added to form new words that are related in meaning. The very fact that the same consonants in the same order are used in several words is generally taken as an indication that these words have something important in common. In this case there is a difference of opinion as to whether the root has two or three consonants, the main ones being "r" and "tz," with "h" as a possible third, although it does not appear in most of the words based on the root.

8. An obvious motif for the relation between paganism and myth is the relation between nature and paganism that is given expression by myth. The idea is that myth expresses the reverence the pagans felt for nature by transforming the objects of their reverence—the forces of nature—into gods. Paganism in this view is a religion of nature, in which nature is given divine attributes. All this differs from the monotheistic religions, which are centered around a God who is not a part of nature and whose major manifestations are not solely or primarily in nature but in history and society. This view admits that there are manifestations of the embodiment of the deity in nature in the monotheistic religions as well but insists that the direction is from the deity to nature, and not from nature to the deity, as it is in paganism.

It may be argued equally convincingly that the pagans did not perceive nature as a deity but saw the deity as dwelling or embodied in nature. According to this view the causal order must be reversed: it is not the case that nature is deified because it is so impressive; rather, because nature is so impressive it is considered worthy of being an embodiment of the deity.

Another approach to the relation between the deity and nature as reflected in myth is expressed in the idea that nature as a whole is a divine living entity rather than the arena of the deity's activities. The divine drama consists of the changes that occur in nature, which are perceived as changes in the deity itself. In this view nature is not the artistic creation of a divine artisan—a heavenly "smith"—but a living entity.

A more promising connection between nature and the deity as mediated by myth and ritual may be found in the idea that paganism expresses an "organic" conception of reality—involving man, nature, and the deity—whose model is sexual reproduction. In the pagan worldview sexual reproduction is an accepted method of connection between the gods—this is the source of the importance of female deities and of the existence of goddesses as well as gods. The accepted method of connection between the gods and the world is also sexual reproduction—for example, through plant seeds, which are seen as the seed of the gods. The connection between the gods and human beings may also be sexual. The relation between sex and paganism according to this view is thus not a matter of sexual permissiveness—as opposed to the sexual zealotry of the monotheistic religions—but an internal relation that touches the ideological essence of paganism. Myth in this view is an epical expression of an organic reality whose model is sexual reproduction. This view of idolatrous sexual intercourse was transformed by the monotheistic religions into verbal intercourse. Between God and the world there is an abyss that God bridges by "verbal" rather than "sexual" intercourse.

Even if the source of the mythic story is the personification of nature, the meaning of the myth is not that of a story about nature. Myths speak about gods and goddesses even if they originally referred to mountains and rivers. The claim that myth is the personification of nature is a hypothesis about origins rather than a claim about meaning.

9. The monsters that God fought did not undergo the same transformation that had been undergone by the cherubim, for example, which became ritual symbols. Figures of the cherubim decorated the walls of the temple in Jerusalem, and engraved images of them dwelt in the holy of holies within the temple. The cherubim were perceived as servants, like those God had appointed to guard the way to the tree of life in the Garden of Eden (M. Haran, *Temples and Temple Service in Ancient Israel,* Oxford: Clarendon Press, 1977, p. 254).

10. H. Jonas, *Gnosis und Spaetantiker Geist,* 2 vols. (Goettingen, 1934); H. Jonas, *The Gnostic Religion* (Boston: Beacon Press, 1963). We do not mean to claim that the discovery of the Gnostic writings in Naj-Hammadi, which Jonas did not know about at the time he wrote his works, do not contain new and exciting revelations (see, e.g., W. H. Wuellner, ed., "Jewish Gnostic Naj Hammadi Texts," in *Protocol of the Third Colloquy of the Center of Hermeneutical Studies,* University of California at Berkeley, 1975). Our claim is only that Jonas succeeded in reconstructing the essential contours of Gnosticism from the Christian polemic writings.

11. Concerning the technique of concealment, see A. Zinoviev, *The Yawning Heights,* trans. G. Clough (New York: Random House, 1979); J. Elster, *Sour Grapes* (Cambridge: Cambridge University Press, 1983), chap. 2, sec. 8. There are, of course, many varied techniques of censorship. One of them is an external negation that uses concealment but that is really a form of internal negation because the negated view is quite well known. The idea is to say what one wishes to say as though it were obvious,

without polemics and in an authoritative tone, even when the issue is actually highly debatable. Thus it is possible to imagine a trenchant controversy about creation and preexistence where the narrator begins by saying, "In the beginning of God's creation," as if it were obvious. Related to this technique is that of not acknowledging one's opponent as a worthy rival. Thus, for example, the Bible transforms terrifying monsters like the leviathan into God's pets (Psalm 104:26). On this issue, see Uffenheimer, "Myth and Reality in Ancient Israel."

12. N. Avigad, "Excavations at Beth She'arim," *Israel Exploration Journal* 7 (1957): 252ff.; E. R. Goodenough, *Jewish Symbols in the Greco-Roman Period,* 12 vols. (New York: Pantheon Books, 1953–1965); E. R. Goodenough, "Symbolism, Jewish," in *Encyclopaedia Judaica,* vol. 15 (New York: Macmillan, 1971), pp. 569–570.

13. P. Tillich, *Gesamte Werke* (Stuttgart: Evangelisches Verlagswerk, 1959–1975), V, 187ff.

14. See the apocalypse of Enoch (Ethiopic, Slavonic, and Hebrew) in J. H. Charlesworth, ed., *The Old Testament Pseudepigrapha: Apocalyptic Literature and Testaments* (New York: Doubleday, 1983), as well as the prefaces of the translators: E. Isaac, "Ethiopian Apocalypse of Enoch"; F. I. Anderson, "Slavonic Apocalypse of Enoch"; and P. Alexander, "Hebrew Apocalypse of Enoch." The midrashic view of Enoch is ambivalent, in that he is seen both as a righteous man and a sinner (*Bereshit Rabba* 10:25), perhaps in order to neutralize the Christian myth.

It is interesting to note the distinction between a "mythic gap" in a text and a "midrashic gap." Whenever there is a mythic gap in a text, there is also a midrashic gap, but not conversely. The difference between mythic and midrashic gaps is that mythic gaps are filled by creatures with an independent will, whereas midrashic gaps are filled by God's servants. The distinction between the two types of gaps is not a distinction between what is inside or outside the midrash. The midrash itself sometimes contains gaps that are filled in mythically.

In the Slavonic Apocalypse of Enoch there are so many angels with so many different tasks that Anderson is justified in claiming that there does not seem to be anything left for God to do (p. 97). This is an example of a bureaucracy in which a staff without an independent will takes control of all the tasks, turning the master with the will into a nominal authority without a function.

15. On this and related issues, see A. Margalit, "Animism Animated," *S'vara* 1 (1990): 41–49. The idea that myth is a "sickness of language" is not new. Max Muller, in his study of myth (*Chips from a German Workshop,* New York: Scribner, 1869), was perhaps the first to use the expression though not the idea.

16. E. Cassirer, *The Philosophy of Symbolic Forms,* vol. 2, *Mythical Thought,* trans. R. Mannheim (New Haven: Yale University Press, 1955–1957).

17. The concept of the third race may be found in P. Veyne, *Did the Greeks Believe in Their Myths?* trans. P. Wissing (Chicago: University of Chicago Press, 1988), pp. 208–210. According to W. K. C. Guthrie, *A History of Greek Philosophy,* 2 vols. (Cambridge: Cambridge University Press, 1962–1965), divinity and immortality were synonymous to the ancient Greeks. But while some of the Greek authors considered as hubris the ambition of human beings to be gods and to ignore their mortality, other Greek thinkers, including Aristotle, thought that man's goal was to be immortal (*Nichomachean Ethics* 1177b). What constitutes, in the last analysis, insolence toward the divinity? According to one view, the essence of hubris is harming the gods' interests—thus stealing fire from the gods for human use is insolence. It is also insolent to relate to the gods as if they were members of the same social class. Equivalence in attitude constitutes insolence, but the assumption that the gods and humans belong to the same social framework does not in itself constitute insolence. In Homer the gods approach humans because of the human element within them, while in some of the monotheistic religions, especially in Christianity, we approach God because of the divine element within us.

18. Karl Kerenyi's claim that Gnostic myth is only halfway to mythology, "nur halbwegs Mythologie," is justified, since Gnostic myth contains, to a considerable extent, a conscious attempt to dress up a theological doctrine in narrative clothing for the purposes of religious instruction. See G. A. G. Stroumsa, *Another Seed: Studies in Gnostic Mythology* (Leiden: Brill, 1984).

19. Wittgenstein, in his penetrating criticism of Frazer's theory (*Remarks on Frazer's Golden Bough,* trans. A. C. Miles, Atlantic Highlands, N.J.: Humanities Press, 1979), attacks the offers of causal explanations of the significance of myth, in the sense of its implications for people's lives. Causal explanations here refer to explanations in terms of the source of the story. The explication of myth must focus on what is "impressive" about it, that is, what it contains that can influence the lives of those for whom the myth is a living story. The question of the source of myth has very little relevance for the issue of what is impressive about myth.

20. J. Huizinga describes the worldview of the Middle Ages in a chapter called "The Decline of Symbolism," in his book *The Waning of the Middle Ages,* trans. F. Hopman (New York: St. Martin's Press, 1985). He writes: "The symbolic mentality was an obstacle to the development of causal thought, as causal and genetic relations must needs look insignificant by the side of symbolic connections. Thus the sacred symbolism of the two

luminaries and the two swords for a long time barred the road to historic and juridical criticism of papal authority. For the symbolizing of Papacy and Empire as the Sun and the Moon, or as the two swords brought by the Disciples, was to the medieval mind a far more striking comparison; it revealed the mystic foundation of the two powers" (pp. 204–205).

21. The entire enterprise of biblical criticism may actually be described as an attempt to deal with the Bible's many versions of one story, where the paradigm is the story of the creation (the first version is from Genesis 1:1 to 2:3; the second version, from 2:4 to 2:22). In the first version God created Adam and Eve as a couple, whereas in the second he created Adam first and Eve afterward; in the first version human beings are the last creation, in the second the plants and animals are created after Adam (although before Eve); in the first version the world was created by God's word, in the second it was the work of his hands; and so on. Claude Lévi-Strauss, in his book *Anthropologie Structurale* (Paris: Plon, 1958), defines a myth as the set of all the versions of the myth (p. 240). He opposes the attempt to rank myths according to their "degree of authenticity." The biblical story of creation, according to this approach, would be the set of the two versions presented in Genesis, as suggested by Leach, for example, following Lévi-Strauss (see E. R. Leach, "Genesis as Myth," in J. Middleton, ed., *Myth and Cosmos: Readings in Mythology and Symbolism,* New York: Natural History Press, 1967).

22. W. R. G. Horton, "African Traditional Thought and Western Science," *Africa* 37 (1967): 155–187; J. Skorupski, *Symbol and Theory* (Cambridge: Cambridge University Press, 1976), part 3. The idea is that there is no contradiction between myth and logos; rather, myth is the logos of closed societies. In contrast, Hans Blumenberg believes that the fact that myth continues to exist even in societies which promote science (logos) attests that myth and logos are two different things. According to Blumenberg himself the purpose of myth is to allay existential anxiety by transforming diffuse anxiety into focused fear. See H. Blumenberg, *Work on Myth,* trans. R. M. Wallace (Cambridge, Mass.: MIT Press, 1985).

H. W. Bartsch, in his book *Kerygma and Myth: A Theological Debate,* trans. R. H. Fuller (London: SPCK, 1953), presents an approach that is the polar opposite of Horton's. In his view myth is precisely the expression of the unobserved in terms of the observed. This means that myth presents the unobserved divinity by means of observable figures. It thus seems as if we are presented with a choice: is myth a "religious" story in which the unobserved is spoken about in terms of the observed (that is, as story about the divinity), as Bartsch claims? Or is it about the observed, the world, in terms of the unobserved—the divinity as a "theoretical being"? For societies in which myth plays an active role, the claim is that myth is both religion and science, both literature and drama—and a thousand and one other things. The functional complexity of myth is like that of life in general. We are concerned here with its religious function, as a story about the divinity, and for this purpose Bartsch's "observation" is more important than Horton's.

23. G. S. Kirk, *Myth: Its Meaning and Functions in Ancient and Other Cultures* (Cambridge: Cambridge University Press, 1970), chaps. 1, 2; M. Douglas, "The Meaning of Myth," in E. Leach, ed., *The Structural Study of Myth and Totemism* (London: Tavistock Publications, 1967). There is a clear sense in which fairy tales of the sort collected by the brothers Grimm are serious, whether because of their deep sexual content according to psychoanalytic theory, as proposed by Bruno Bettleheim in his book *The Uses of Enchantment* (New York: Knopf, 1976), or because of the historical reality of famine and hunger, which is the source as well as the theme of these stories according to Robert Darnton. Hunger and sex are certainly serious matters, but these are not topics that the typical hearer of these stories identifies as their themes. The identification of the deeply serious content of fairy tales requires investigation on the part of the observer, whereas the seriousness we are speaking about here is appreciated by the typical hearer. In general fairy tales are more optimistic than myth, if only because of their happy endings.

24. On pagan myths in Christianity, see E. Wind, *Pagan Mysteries in the Renaissance* (Harmondsworth: Penguin, 1967), especially his discussion of the domestication of pagan myths in the Renaissance.

25. W. V. O. Quine, *Word and Object* (Cambridge, Mass.: MIT Press, 1960), chap. 2.

26. See L. Ginzberg, "Allegorical Interpretation" in the *Jewish Encyclopedia* (New York: Funk and Wagnalls, 1906–07), vol. 1.

27. Origen, *Contra Celsum,* trans. H. Chadwick (Cambridge: Cambridge University Press, 1980); R. P. C. Hanson, *Allegory and Event: A Study of the Sources and Significance of Origen's Interpretation of Scripture* (London: SCM, 1959), p. 245.

28. E. McCracken, *Arnobius of Sicca: The Case against the Pagans, Ancient Christian Writers,* 2 vols. (Westminster, Md.: Newman Press, 1949).

29. D. Rokeach, *Jews, Pagans, and Christians in Conflict* (Leiden: Brill, 1982), chap. 2. An interesting example of this is the case of Solomon Ibn Gabirol. His allegorical interpretations of Genesis, which attempt to reveal the esoteric significance of the book as being about spiritual uplifting toward the divinity, could be adopted by any neo-Platonist. Thus his book, which was originally written in Arabic and appeared in Latin in the twelfth century, was not identified as the work of a Jewish philosopher, and for many years the author of the book was unknown. See J. Schlanger, *La Philosophie de Salomon Ibn-Gabirol* (Leyden, 1968).

30. A. Erman, *The Literature of the Ancient Egyptians,* trans. A. M. Blackman (London: Methuen, 1924), p. 243; entry "Song of Songs," *Encyclopedia Biblica,* vol. 7 (Jerusalem, 1976).

31. F. W. J. Schelling, "Einleitung in die Philosophie der Mythologie," in *Saemtliche Werke,* pt. 22, vol. 2 (Stuttgart, 1856).

32. G. Scholem, *On the Kabbalah and Its Symbolism,* trans. R. Mannheim (New York: Schocken, 1969), chap. 3.

33. In the *Tractatus Logico-Philosophicus* the world is the totality of facts. This totality does not include as one of its facts the factuality of the world itself, that is, the world being the way it is. We are supposed to see this from the totality; it is not an additional fact. The totality of facts is what we might call fate, since this is the world that it is our fate to live in. The meaning of this world for us is also not another fact among the facts that constitute the world. Wittgenstein calls this meaning God. God cannot be described, because a description requires a way of mapping the constituents of the description onto the thing being described. This cannot be done with the totality of all facts because then we would have another fact that was not included in the totality. But if it is impossible to say anything about God in the sense of asserting a factual proposition about him, it is possible to show the meaning of the world. This step of showing without saying is what Wittgenstein calls the mystic. (See also E. Zemach, "Wittgenstein's Philosophy of the Mystical," in I. M. Copi and R. W. Beard, eds., *Essays on Wittgenstein's Tractatus* (London: Routledge, 1966).

The idea of the distinction between showing and saying is expressed nicely by Plato in the "Meno," where Socrates teaches ("reminds") the boy geometry. He uses the example of a hypotenuse of a triangle whose length is an irrational number, the square root of 8. An irrational number, in Plato's view as well that of the ancient Greeks in general, is a number that cannot be expressed as a number even though it can be seen, as we can see the hypotenuse of an isosceles triangle each of whose sides has a length of 2 units. From this example Plato goes on to deal with the virtues, or ethics, whose statements and features can be seen but not asserted.

34. Is myth more similar to painting or to music? On one hand, Horace's famous remark, "Poetry is like painting," directs us to painting. On the other hand, there is Lévi-Strauss's well-known remark that myth is like music. Underlying these vague remarks are different views of language and, more important, different religious intuitions about religious representation. Analogous to the three arenas in which religious dramas take place—nature, history, and the soul—there are three means of expression of the religious experience. The typical means of expression for nature is painting and sculpture, for history speech, and for the soul, music. Pagan myth, being connected with nature, is like painting; myth, as a projection

upon nature of the drama of the soul, is like music. This is all very vague but not meaningless. Thus we find Luther, for example, extolling music as a medium for sublime religious expression, while he considers sculpture and painting forms of idolatry that distort the religious experience.

In our own day there is a controversy that may shed some light on our question as well—the controversy between two trends in poetry, the symbolists and the imagists. Imagist poetry, according to Ezra Pound, is "the sort of poetry which seems as if sculpture or painting were just forced or forcing itself into words." He calls symbolist poetry "the sort of poetry which seems to be music just forcing itself into articulate speech." The idea here, in our view, is that music has a formal syntax and a personal and interpersonal system of associations. If myth is like music then what is conveyed by it in relation to the cyclicity of nature is more similar to Vivaldi's *Four Seasons* than to Lucas Cranach's transition from the "Golden Age" to the "Silver Age." It appears that to the monotheists the pagan sort of religious expression seems like representational (plastic) art, while their own sort seems expressive (musical).

35. See N. Goodman, *Of Mind and Other Matters* (Cambridge, Mass.: Harvard University Press, 1984); N. Goodman and C. Z. Elgin, *Reconceptions in Philosophy and Other Arts and Sciences* (London: Routledge, 1988). For an explication of ritual in terms of Goodman's theory of symbols, see I. Scheffler, *Inquiries: Philosophical Studies of Language, Science, and Learning* (Indianapolis: Hackett, 1986), part 1, chaps. 6, 7.

36. We do not follow the path of connecting typology directly with myth. This path should nevertheless be mentioned here, since the reason we do not follow it clarifies our use of the concept of myth. The path we are referring to is that of Jung. Jung actually asked what the psychological conditions are for the generation of myth, or, more precisely, what the conditions are for the generation of "mythopoetic" thought. He claimed that we have a natural tendency to create archetypes which are common to all humanity and which express people's deep wishes. Although the number of universal archetypes is small and limited, like the number of linguistic phonemes, each culture does not necessarily make use of all of them. Just as the phoneme pool is universal and each language takes the phonemes it uses solely from this pool, so each culture takes its archetypes from a fixed pool. Moreover, just as there is a phonetic relationship between languages because the phonetic pool is small and universal, so there is a resemblance between the appearance of the archetypes in various cultures. Typology from the psychological viewpoint is the collection of tendencies we have to tell stories about the archetypes. Myths, according to Jung, are stories about the archetypes that give our lives meaning, rather than collective illusions, as Freud believed.

According to Jung, modern people are alienated from myth because they have converted their natural tendency to myth into acquired habits of scientific activity. Thus people have cut themselves off from stories that give meaning to their lives. Idolatry, according to this view, is not embodied in myth but, rather, is distanced from myth. The alienation implicit in the "alien worship" that constitutes idolatry is people's alienation from what might give meaning to their lives. Religion, according to Jung, is a concentrated and systematic expression of our ability to create myths, which is also our ability to live meaningful lives. These last ideas of Jung's do, of course, touch upon the core of our argument, but the psychological concept of archetype as typology, which is Jung's main concern and through which the association with myth is created, is not our own concern in typology.

37. Concerning Augustine's doctrine of symbols, see B. D. Jackson, "The Theory of Signs in St. Augustine's De Doctrina Christina," in R. A. Markus, ed., *Augustine: A Collection of Critical Essays* (New York: Anchor Books, 1972), pp. 92–147; R. A. Markus, "St. Augustine On Signs," in Markus, ed., *Augustine*, pp. 61–92.

38. E. Durkheim, *The Elementary Forms of Religious Life,* trans. W. J. Swain (London: Allen and Unwin, 1976). The distinction between magic and religion acquired a polemical tone ("What I have is religion, what you have is magic"). Our interest in this distinction is explanatory rather than polemical. Durkheim's distinction is old but not outdated. This does not mean that the phenomena are in complete accordance with the distinction. The conceptual distinction is sharp, but its application is blurred. The reason for this is that there are societies which do not have a sufficiently developed cultural division of labor to allow the distinction to be applied, just as the distinctions between magic and science and between magic and art cannot be applied to them even though there is room for a conceptual distinction in each of these pairs. There are, of course, other characteristics of the distinction between magic and religion. The relationship between the magician and the person who seeks his help is that of a professional and a client rather than that of a spiritual leader and a follower. Furthermore, the magician has the freedom to decide when to hold the ritual, whereas the religious practitioner is dependent on a rigid calendar. For our purposes, however, Durkheim's distinction is the decisive one.

## 4. Idolatry as Error

1. Maimonides contrasts what people say with what they believe. Belief is not what one says but "the matter imagined in the mind." Internalization therefore refers to what the person really believes and not what he asserts. See *Guide of the Perplexed,* 1:50.

2. Our interest in the causes of people's idolatrous errors relates to those who commit the errors rather than those who cause others to commit these errors. But some of the anti-idolatrous polemics, such as Josephus Flavius's *Against Apion* (33, 34) are directed at the "instigators" of the errors, the poets. The criticism of the poets in the anti-idolatrous polemical literature is not new. It is drawn from the intrapagan criticism of folk religion as relying upon poets who distort the image of the gods. The most refined and perhaps the most influential of these critics is Plato. Plato contrasts the poet with the legislator and the philosopher. (Josephus contrasts the rational lawgiver Moses with the idolatrous poets as irrational architects of society.) The Muse-inspired poet, the "divine lunatic," is perceived by Plato as irrational in contrast with the legislator and the philosopher. Nevertheless, he considers poetry one of the active forces in society, along with money, honor, and political power. Two of the three specific errors that Plato ascribes to the poets have to do with the distorted conceptions of the gods that they disseminate. The picture that arises from poetry is that the divinity is not absolutely good and that his providence is like an arbitrary lottery rather than a hand directed toward the good. This error concerning the gods—that they err from a lack of understanding—should not be accepted from Homer or any other poet (*The Republic* 379). The picture of deities that can change and assume material form is also unacceptable. The gods are not the magicians described by the poets (383). Portraying the gods as undergoing transformations implies that they are not absolutely good, because the absolutely good does not undergo transformations: something which undergoes a transformation either is changing from a deficient state to a better one or, if it was already in a perfect state, is changing to a deficient one.

3. L. Strauss, *Philosophy and Law,* trans. F. Baumann (Philadelphia: Jewish Publication Society, 1987).

4. One of the characteristics of the general Enlightenment that has settled into our cultural consciousness is its secular, or at least deistic, nature. Therefore the collocation "religious Enlightenment" is liable to sound oxymoronic, like the phrase "the sound of silence." But in our opinion it is a successful collocation with explanatory power, and it is preferable to the term "religious rationalism," which was embraced by the thinkers who expressed the views we include under the heading of religious Enlightenment (Ibn-Rushad, Maimonides, Thomas Aquinas). The justification for the use of the label "religious rationalism" is based on the contrast between reason and revelation as the source of our knowledge about divine matters, where rationalism is perceived as the view that reason is the source of authority even for our knowledge of divine matters (natural theology). The shift from religious rationalism to religious Enlightenment changes the

role of the intellect in religious understanding. The intellect is a tool for the critique of religious errors and illusions, especially those that we call idolatrous illusions, and not so much a source for the grasping of positive truths about the deity. The intellect serves to control the power of the imagination, which is the source of religious illusion. The power of the imagination is nevertheless a vital power in religious communication with the masses. The religious Enlightenment does not stand in opposition to the church as the secular Enlightenment does, but this difference should not obscure the basic similarity between the two types of Enlightenment. We claim, moreover, that the secular Enlightenment is an extension of themes that were already present in the religious Enlightenment.

5. On the distinction between "hot" (motivational) cognition and "cold" (structural) cognition, see R. Nisbett and L. Ross, *Human Inference: Strategies and Shortcomings of Social Judgment* (Englewood Cliffs, N.J.: Prentice-Hall, 1980), pp. 12–13, 228–231. Concerning the implications of this distinction, see J. Elster, *Making Sense of Marx* (Cambridge: Cambridge University Press, 1985), chap. 8; A. Margalit, "The Past of an Illusion," in E. Ullmann-Margalit, ed., *The Kaleidoscope of Science* (Dordrecht: D. Reidel, 1986), pp. 79–95.

6. According to one version (K. Mannheim, *Ideology and Utopia,* trans. L. Wirth and E. Shils, London: K. Paul, 1936, p. 61), there is a historical connection between the concept of ideology and Bacon's concept of the idols, in addition to the connection between the concept of ideology and Locke's concept of ideas.

7. See P. Coby, *Socrates and the Sophistic Enlightenment: A Commentary on Plato's Protagoras* (Lewisburg: Bucknell University Press, 1987), on the sophists as representatives of the pagan enlightenment.

8. Pines, "The Limitations of Human Knowledge according to Al-Farabi, Ibn Bajja, and Maimonides," pp. 82–109; the appendix is especially relevant.

9. For an explication of the concept of presumption, see E. Ullmann-Margalit, "On Presumption," *Journal of Philosophy* 80 (1983): 143–163.

10. The bishop of Paris, Stephen Tempier (1277), claimed that some people hold that something may be true in accordance with philosophy but not be true in accordance with Catholic faith. See M. Pine, "Double Truth," in *Dictionary of the History of Ideas,* vol. 2 (New York: Scribner, 1973), p. 31.

11. Z. R. J. Werblowsky, "Monotheism: Original or Primitive?" (in Hebrew), *Iyyun* 9 (1958): 152–162. See also our discussion of Maimonides' views in Chapter 2.

12. According to Kant the errors of the imagination are a side effect of the faculty of the imagination that is necessary for cognition, as the perception of an object is always partial and its conceptual completion is accom-

plished by the imagination. The "cost" of the ability to complete the parts of the object that are not perceived is the ability to imagine what does not exist at all. According to Maimonides (*The Eight Chapters of Maimonides on Ethics,* trans. J. I. Gorfinkel, New York: AMS Press, 1966), the imagination permits us to imagine what is not even possible. Maimonides' example of an impossible thing may seem a bit strange to us nowadays, as it is "an iron ship sailing in the sky," but when we reflect that Wittgenstein, who was trained as an aeronautical engineer, thought that flight to the moon was impossible—and this only a few years before the first space flight—how can we fault Maimonides?

13. On Plato and error, see *The Sophist* 240; see also 217, 254–264; *Philebus* 470.

14. In the appendix to part 1 of the *Ethics,* Spinoza deals with the causes of religious prejudices, the most important one being "that God made all things for man, and man that he might worship God." The importance of this appendix for our discussion is in the connection Spinoza makes between errors whose source is the faculty of the imagination (structural cognitive errors) and motivational errors. What is the error of those who believe that God does everything for the sake of mankind? Spinoza's answer is sublimely simple: "all men are born ignorant of the causes of things, and . . . all have a desire of acquiring what is useful." Since people seek what is beneficial to them and are aware of their desires, they believe that they have free will— the most severe illusion, in Spinoza's view. They also project their illusive view onto the world, as if the world were run by forces with quasi-human desires and freedom, to the point where they reach the conclusion "that the Gods direct all things for the use of men, that men may be bound down to them and do them the highest honor." Thus people have things they didn't work for: the sun for giving light and the sea for breeding fish, teeth to chew with and eyes to see with. There must have been someone who provided all these needs for mankind and he requires recompense—honor and reverence. In this way a prejudice became a superstition: ". . . the Gods and men are all mad." This picture encounters some difficulties—storms, earthquakes, diseases—but these are immediately given an explanation: "the anger of the Gods aroused against men through some misdeed or omission in worship." Human utilitarianism, accompanied by natural ignorance, led to this subjective view of the world (what is useful for people is good, and its opposite is bad). However, the combination of natural ignorance and utilitarianism does not suffice to create illusion. What is required is a cognitive mechanism that feeds the illusion: "they firmly believe there is order in things, and are ignorant of them and their own nature." This is the function of the imagination, which is capable of imposing order from our egotistic point of view; our concepts "are nothing other than modes of imagining in

which the imagination is affected in diverse manners, and yet they are considered by the ignorant as very important attributes of things."

15. See G. S. Kirk and J. E. Raven, *The Presocratic Philosophers: A Critical History with Selection of Texts* (Cambridge: Cambridge University Press, 1971), who quote Xenophanes' assertion that Homer and the Hesiod attributed all sorts of degrading deeds to the gods, including theft, adultery and deceit (p. 169), and his observation that mortals think of the gods as beings who were born, wear clothes, speak, and act as if they were people with a body like ours (p. 170). They also quote Heraclitus's opinion on this matter (p. 244). Also see J. Barnes, *The Presocratic Philosophers,* vol. 2 (London: Routledge and Kegan Paul, 1979), pp. 154ff.

16. Freud discusses the mechanism of projection in detail in only one case, that of Dr. Schreber (see "The Case of Schreber," in *The Standard Edition of the Complete Psychological Works of Sigmund Freud,* trans. J. Strachey, London: 1958, vol. 12). Freud finds in this case reverse projection. The subject, who feels persecuted, has a homosexual wish, but he cannot live with the belief "I love him," which is the latent content of his belief. Therefore he uses a defense mechanism that transforms the sentence into "I do not love him," but this thought too is unthinkable for him because it is about a beloved object, even if the object is a forbidden one. Finally, the mechanism of projection turns the sentence into "He hates me." Projection, in Freud's view, may also be applied to an imaginary object which is given existence by illusion. Schreber's God kept being subdivided, something that is characteristic of people with persecution complexes. In this they differ from people suffering from hysteria, whose tendency is toward the unification of content.

17. Feuerbach actually has two different things to say about projection. In his book, *The Essence of Christianity,* trans. G. Eliot (New York: Harper, 1957), the projection is of constitutive characteristics of man's character onto nonhumans. In Feuerbach's opinion this is the essence of religion, where theology is the enterprise that grants absolute value to the thing onto which the human characteristics are projected, and the imagination vivifies this projection onto an alien entity by means of concrete images. In his book of lectures, *The Essence of Religion,* trans. R. Manheim (New York: Harper and Row, 1973), however, Feuerbach suggests a different form of projection, not from man onto the deity but from nature onto man through the mediation of an anthropomorphized deity. Let us concentrate on the first sort of projection and exemplify it by the sentence "God is merciful." The true subject of the sentence, as opposed to its grammatical subject, is man's nature. The next step is the reversal: I, the utterer of this sentence, am not merciful, and I am estranged from my humanity. I attribute mercy to the deity because I identify in myself, in potential, my ability to be merciful,

but I am aware that I am not actualizing this nature of mine. Therefore projection is not a crazy deification of my individual personality but a projection of man's nature at its best.

18. The modality of the scientific worldview is not consistent with that of the religious worldview, in which there is a place for objects that are not in space and time yet act upon objects that are in space and time (the deity in theistic conceptions). It is also not consistent with the modality of objects that are not in space and time but "visit" space and time in the guise of objects in space and time and influence occurrences in space and time by a sort of miraculous quasi-causality (gods and angels) and with the modality of objects in space and time that do not exist continuously but appear and disappear or that exist in time but not in space (such as spirits).

19. See A. Margalit, "Animism Animated," pp. 41–51.

20. I. Kant, *Transcendental Dialectics,* introduction to book 1; also appendix to *The Critique of Pure Reason.*

## 5. The Wrong God

1. St. Augustine, *The City of God,* book 6, chap. 9, 31.

2. G. W. F. Hegel, *Hegel's Lectures on the Philosophy of Religion,* ed. and trans. E. B. Spiers and J. Burdon-Sanderson (London: Routledge, 1974), III, sixth lecture.

3. Concerning the problem of "accommodationism" in the church, see J. Bettray, *Die Akkomodationsmethod des P. M. Ricci in China* (Rome, 1955).

4. J. J. Rousseau, *The Social Contract,* trans. M. Cranston (Baltimore: Penguin Books, 1979).

5. Concerning the Mesopotamian treaties and the presence of the gods, see Weinfeld, *Deuteronomy and the Deuteronomic School.*

6. Astral worship may be connected with the idea of providence, where each person has a sign in the sky in the form of a star or constellation. This type of providence is not a caring providence but a knowing and directing one. An interesting question is who began the identification of the mythological gods with the stars, and when. One claim is that it was actually the philosophers, led by Plato, and the astronomers who began this process, especially the identification of Apollo with the sun (see the entry "astrology" in the *Encyclopaedia Britannica,* 11th ed.). This identification is thus not the property of poets or folk religion, but an act of the philosophical elite.

7. G. Frege, "On Sense and Reference," in *Translations from the Philosophical Writings of Gottlob Frege,* ed. P. Geach and M. Black (Oxford: Blackwell, 1970), pp. 56–78.

8. See the entry "Hesperus" in the *Encyclopaedia Britannica,* 11th ed., XIII, 408: "Although as a mythological personality he is regarded as distinct from

Phosphorus . . . the two stars were early identified by the Greeks." A simple explanation for this phenomenon, if it was indeed such, suggests itself immediately. The Greeks did not find out soon enough about the identity of the stars Hesperus and Phosphorus. This was a relatively late discovery—at any rate later than the time of the formation of separate rituals for the two gods. After the astronomic discovery was made that the evening star and the morning star are identical, the two rituals did not manage to be merged, because rituals are much more conservative than astronomic discoveries, and astronomic identity is not immediately translated into ritual identity. Therefore one cannot infer from the differences between the rituals that the foci of worship were different as well. However, although the suggested explanation may explain why rituals are likely to lag behind discoveries, it does not explain why the rituals were not merged after some time had passed. The phenomenon of the merging of rituals was fairly common, yet it does not seem to have occurred in the case of Hesperus and Phosphorus.

Another possible explanation is the following. The Greeks worshiped the planet Venus in one way when it was seen in the west at twilight and in a different way when it was seen in the east at dawn. Therefore, since two different locations of the planet are in question, the identification must be understood as holding between the god and the location of the planet rather than between the god and the planet itself. We find such a phenomenon in the case of the early Egyptians. For them the worship of the sun was associated with different names of the god, where the names denoted the different situations of the sun: the sun when it was rising, the sun at zenith, and the sun when it was setting. It is not easy to judge whether these are the names of different gods or the names of the same god (Aten) in different situations. Obviously our knowledge of the facts in each of the cases we have mentioned is far from being certain, but we are basically concerned with conceptual explication rather than with facts. The examples we have given point out the difficulty involved in the hasty identification of the god with its heavenly body. It is very possible that what is involved here is not after all astral worship but the worship of gods whose relation to the heavenly bodies is a complex one.

9. U. Simon, *Heaven in the Christian Tradition* (1958); see also M. Stern, *Greek and Latin Authors in Jews and Judaism,* vol. 2 (Jerusalem: 1980), p. 103, n. 96; Urbach, *The Sages: Their Concepts and Beliefs,* chap. 4. Simon claims that because of the prevalent use of expressions like "the fear of Heaven" (a euphemism for "the fear of God") among the Jews, Roman writers (such as Juvenal) ascribed worship of Heaven to the Jews. What is interesting is that Simon himself does not hesitate to say that among many nations heaven itself was the supreme deity and the object of worship. It is doubtful that the evidence upon which belief in heaven as a god is ascribed to many

nations is any more solid than that upon which the Roman ascription of this belief to the Jews was based.

10. The distinction between the free soul and the soul tied to the body is a functional one. The free soul provides the stamp of individuality, while the connected soul provides life and consciousness. See J. Bremmer, *The Early Greek Concept of the Soul* (Princeton: Princeton University Press, 1983).

11. G. E. Moore, "'Real' and 'Imaginary' in G. E. Moore," in *Lectures on Philosophy,* ed. C. Lewy (London: Allen and Unwin, 1966), pp. 20–43.

12. The god of the sun as a winged disk appears both among the Egyptians and among the American Indians, almost certainly without any cultural connection.

13. We are adopting A. Tversky's concept of similarity, according to which similarity is a weighted function of common and distinctive features. See "Features of Similarity," *Psychological Review* 84 (1977): 327–352.

14. N. Goodman, "On Likeness of Meaning," in *Problems and Projects* (Indianapolis: Bobbs-Merrill, 1972), pp. 221–231; A. Margalit, "Illustrations and Reconstructions" (in Hebrew), *Iyyun* (1987): 101–109.

15. In giving an account of the identity of the objects of idolatry there is a danger of falling into the most outstanding idolatrous fallacy: the error of substituting the agent or the representation for the original. The explication of intentional identity in terms of linguistic theories seems prima facie an error of substitution. For there is no doubt that someone who reveres Apollo, loves Aphrodite, or fears Poseidon does not revere, love, or fear linguistic entities. A worshiper of Aphrodite's golden curls will not be satisfied with the colorless substitute of an Aphrodite-hair-description.

Our claim is that a thought about an existent entity is different from a thought about a nonexistent entity. The difference is not something occurring in the mind or brain of the thinker. The content of a thought is not something determined solely within our minds; it is also determined partly by the situation in the world (as in Hilary Putnam's motto, "Meaning is not in the head"). When Bush is thinking about Gorbachev there is a real object of his thought and the relation "is thinking about" exists between Bush and Gorbachev. But if Bush is thinking about Aphrodite there is no real object of his thought and so there is no relation between Bush and Aphrodite. In such a case the complement of Bush's thought, namely "Aphrodite," is a placeholder for an Aphrodite-description. Such descriptions characterize the method of thought rather than the object of thought, since there is no such object. Aphrodite-descriptions thus have the force of adverbs. We may say, "Bush is thinking Aphrodite-ly," just as we say "Bush is thinking slowly." "To think Aphrodite-ly" is a way of thinking characterized by the fact that this is the way the thinker tries to identify the object of his thought. Bush's method of identification is constitutive of the identity of the thought for the observer. If the methods of identification of Aphrodite-thinkers are the same as those of Venus-thinkers, and there is also a historical connection between these methods of identification, then we say that an Aphrodite-thought is the same as a Venus-thought, and in short we say that Aphrodite is Venus. A Venus-worshiper is not worshiping a description, but descriptions of Venus permit the identification of his thought. The identity of the thought about Venus is constituted by the conditions of identification of Venus and not by the identity of Venus, as there is no such thing. Conditions of identification do not guarantee that there is something to identify, but it is enough that they serve as a means for the identification of thoughts.

Some thoughts are dependent on actual identity. Let's say you are in a museum and you hear the voice of a museum guide in the next hall saying, "See, this statue is broken," but you are unable to see into that hall. If you don't know the identity of the statue the guide is pointing to you will not be able to identify the thought. If, however, the guide announces, "There are broken statues in the museum," then you do not need to know the actual identities of the statues in order to identify the thought. Does monotheistic belief require the actual identity of God? A mystic approach to religion may be interpreted as a demand for actual identity in order to understand religious thought, but this is not an accepted view. Even someone whose belief depends on revelation does not require that the revelation should occur to him. Therefore revelation is not a requirement for actual identity in order to locate the thought about the deity. Concerning the role of actual identity in the location of thoughts, see S. Blackburn, *Spreading the Word* (Oxford: Clarendon Press, 1984), chap. 9. Concerning the issues discussed in this note, see A. N. Prior, *Objects of Thought,* ed. P. T. Geach and A. J. P. Kenny (Oxford, 1971), pp. 111–130.

16. P. T. Geach, "On Worshipping the Wrong God," in *God and the Soul* (New York: Schocken Books, 1969). Concerning intentional identity in general, see P. T. Geach, "Intentional Identity," in *Logic Matters* (Berkeley and Los Angeles: University of California Press, 1972), pp. 146–153.

17. Maimonides' theory of categories, like Aristotle's, is not a linguistic theory. It is an ontological theory which has traces in language that are expressed in determining which collocations have no meaning. See H. A. Wolfson, *The Philosophy of the Church Fathers* (Cambridge, Mass.: Harvard University Press, 1964), pp. 195–230.

18. *Guide of the Perplexed* 1:60. Another example, of a ship, is in the same chapter.

19. Our analysis is based on an important shift in Maimonides' argument. In *Guide of the Perplexed,* 1:50–60, he stresses the "negative" part of

the theory of negative attributes but then turns, in the next three chapters, to the names of God.

20. Another test of the distinction between description and noun is a pronunciation test, which works only in some languages, of which English is one. When a two-word phrase consists of an adjective and a noun, then the words are pronounced like two separate words, and so the stress is on the noun. When the phrase is a name, however, it is pronounced as one word, and if each word has only one syllable then the stress is on the first syllable, which in this case is the adjective. For example, the stress in "black bird" (as a description) is on "bird"; the stress in "blackbird" (the noun) is on "black." The same is true of the example used in the text. The stress in "the white house" (any old house that happens to be white) is on "house"; the stress in "the White House" is on "White."

21. The closest viewpoint among Christian thinkers to the interpretation of Maimonides we are suggesting here is that of Dionysus the Areopagite, especially in his book *The Divine Names*.

22. Our interpretation of Maimonides' theory of names has undoubtedly been influenced by Kripke's theory of the way names function in language (S. Kripke, *Naming and Necessity*, Cambridge, Mass.: Harvard University Press, 1980). It is our guess that Kripke himself was influenced by the picture in the mishnaic tractate *The Ethics of the Fathers* of the way the Torah was transmitted from person to person through the chain of tradition from the time of the constitutive event of the giving of the Torah on Mount Sinai.

23. Concerning Aphrodite see P. Friedrich, *The Meaning of Aphrodite* (Chicago and London: University of Chicago Press, 1978).

24. R. Rorty, "Is There a Problem about Fictional Discourse?" in *Consequences of Pragmatism* (Minneapolis: University of Minnesota Press, 1982), pp. 110–139.

25. K. L. Walton, "Fearing Fictions," *Journal of Philosophy* (1978): 5–27. See also G. Evans, *The Varieties of Reference* (Oxford: Clarendon Press, 1982), chap. 10.

## 6. The Ethics of Belief

1. W. James, "The Will to Believe," in *The Will to Believe and Other Essays in Popular Philosophy* (Cambridge, Mass.: Harvard University Press, 1979), pp. 1–31.

2. E. Ullmann-Margalit, "Opting: The Case of 'Big' Decisions," in Wissenschaftskolleg zu Berlin, *Jahrbuch 1984/85,* pp. 441–454.

3. Concerning the concept of teleology, see J. Lear, *Aristotle: The Desire to Understand* (Cambridge: Cambridge University Press, 1988).

4. B. Williams, "Deciding to Believe," in Kiefer and Munitz, eds., *Language, Belief, and Metaphysics* (1973), pp. 136–151. Williams casts doubt upon the possibility of adopting a belief voluntarily, even through the use of an indirect approach, since the condition for the adoption of a belief voluntarily is forgetting that the reason for its adoption is one's will rather than some other justification. Williams means that it is impossible to adopt a belief purely voluntarily. But if the will to believe is accompanied by justifications for the change in belief, then it is certainly possible to adopt a belief even if the first cause of its adoption is the will to believe its truth.

5. A. Margalit and Y. Gutgeld, "Pensées on Pascal's Wager" (in Hebrew), *Iyyun* (1986): 101–110. B. Pascal, *Pensées,* trans. A. J. Krailsheimer (Harmondsworth: Penguin Books, 1966). Also see J. Elster, *Ulysses and the Sirens* (Cambridge: Cambridge University Press, 1979), ch. 11, esp. pp. 47–54.

6. The first commandment, "I the Lord am your God" (Exodus 20:2), is interpreted by Maimonides as a positive commandment *(The Book of the Commandments)*. It is not clear whether this is a commandment to believe in the existence of God or to know of his existence. It is also unclear whether Maimonides thought that it is possible to command belief or whether he thought the commandment is to declare one's belief. Maimonides himself declared his total faith in principles such as the resurrection of the dead and the coming of the Messiah, which he did not believe (or at least did not believe literally). He considered it important to make these declarations as a sign of belonging to the religious community.

Be that as it may, the question is whether Maimonides considered it a requirement to believe or to know. The distinction here relates to the seriousness of the requirement. Thus there is nothing absurd in a teacher's demand that her class know the proof of the Pythagorean Theorem by next week, but it would be ridiculous for her to demand that they believe the Pythagorean Theorem by next week. Knowing can be interpreted as acquiring a procedure, such as a proof, that is within the control of a person who is capable of understanding it. Indeed, Isaac Abarbanel interpreted Maimonides' requirement as a requirement to adopt a procedure. In their Aristotelian context, knowledge and belief both constitute making a judgment about the truth of a proposition, with the difference being that knowledge is making a judgment on the basis of proof. Proof in the Aristotelian sense means categorical proof—that is, not only a valid deductive proof in which the truth of the premises necessitates the truth of the conclusion, but also one in which the truth of the premises is self-evident. The premises acquire their self-evidence either by relying on observations that cannot be denied or by being based on principles that are clear to the intellect. Therefore a person who has adopted the proof and understands it is not only logically but also psychologically compelled to believe the truth of its conclusion. If he denies the conclusion, this means that he did not understand the proof. Not everyone is capable of understanding proofs, but everyone is capable of voluntarily accepting the authority of the person presenting the proof.

All this can be ascribed to Maimonides in a fairly unforced reading. However, Maimonides' standpoint concerning proof is far from being clear, especially since the issue under discussion is the proof of God's existence, which relies upon the premise that the world was created ex nihilo, and this premise is not self-evident in Maimonides' opinion. Therefore the proof of God's existence is hypothetical rather than categorical, not to mention the problem that according to the theory of negative attributes it is not even valid because it suffers from duality of meaning in all its premises.

There is also another difficulty—although this is not a difficulty for Maimonides—which is related to the religious evaluation of belief grounded in proof. Thomas Aquinas, who was hospitable to proofs, deliberated about this issue. He considered belief based on proof to be an intellectual achievement but not a religious or moral achievement. Others were even sharper in their views. Ambrose, for example, claimed that God did not come to redeem his people by means of dialectics. Proofs have an educational or polemical role but do not have a role in belief. For Maimonides as well proofs have a political and educational role but not a cognitive one. The only proofs that have a cognitive role are negative ones of the sort that prevent us from adopting erroneous and therefore alien beliefs.

There are other ways to interpret the first commandment. In fact, there are many good reasons not to consider the verse "I the Lord am your God" as a commandment at all, since commandments presuppose the existence of a commander, and therefore the one who gives the command cannot command belief in his existence. The role of this sentence is therefore a preamble to the commandments and not a requirement of belief.

7. In these chapters on idolatry as error, we have been assuming that belief is propositional belief—that a believer is a person with a disposition to affirm or deny propositions—even for the ethics of belief. It is, however, an open question whether religious belief is propositional belief. Martin Buber, for example, argued forcefully against the tendency to transform religious belief of the biblical sort from "belief in" to "belief that," i.e., propositional belief. He ascribed the change in attitude toward belief to Paul, who was influenced, in Buber's opinion, by the tendencies of the Hellenistic philosophers. One may establish a church on "belief that" but not an intimate relationship of secure trust in God, as is demanded by

biblical belief. If the core concept of truth is really "belief in," then there is no gap between idolatry as extreme disloyalty—"whoredom"—and idolatry as an error of belief, as the error in belief would then be an error in a personal relationship rather than an error with respect to propositions. (Relying on a false friend is different from believing a false proposition.)

It is our opinion that "belief in" cannot be based on "belief that." This is not only because it would entail the loss of noncognitive elements (such as a warm attitude) in the transition from the sentence "Abraham believes in God" to the sentence "Abraham believes that God exists." Another reason is that propositional complements to "belief that" can provide reasons and causes of "belief in," but sentences involving "belief in" and sentences involving "belief that" are not equivalent in meaning.

"Belief in" may have different complements—belief in security borders, in antibiotics, or in Volvos, as well as belief in an idea, such as belief in socialism. Even if the belief in an idea may be broken down into a sequence of propositions that constitute the idea, a believer in the idea is not necessarily someone who is capable of affirming or denying these propositions. Let's say Rita believes in socialism and so does her friend Rosa. Rosa's belief can be translated into a sequence of statements that Rosa would affirm or volunteer. (She believes that the means of production should be owned by society and that all the products of labor should be distributed equally as the fruit of collective social labor, and so on.) Rita's belief is different—it is simpler but more complicated to describe. Rita has a warm attitude toward socialism. She likes the word "socialism" very much, and this attitude includes the entire semantic field connected with that word—phrases such as "equality," "the right to strike," "the solidarity of the workers," and so on. These are "good" words for her. She doesn't know exactly what they mean, but she gets up early in the morning to prepare sandwiches for the strikers and she curses the scabs roundly. She doesn't know what they are striking for, but strikers are automatically in the right. When asked about it, she refers the questioner to Rosa: "Ask her, she knows how to 'speak well.'" Rita is devoted to an idea with her entire simple soul. She believes in socialism even if she is nearly incapable of saying anything about it except that it is good and right. Even if this description is somewhat of a caricature, the world is full of believers of this sort—both religious and nonreligious. Propositions are not generally relevant for the evaluation of their beliefs, and the question of error in their case is not a cognitive question.

8. The influence of Frankfurt's concept of second-order desires on our view will be obvious to anyone who reads H. G. Frankfurt *The Importance of What We Care About* (Cambridge: Cambridge University Press, 1988), pp. 11–46.

### 7. From Idolatrous Belief to Idolatrous Practice

1. *The Works of Emperor Julian,* trans. W. C. Wright (Cambridge, Mass.: Harvard University Press, 1962), 115 E, p. 345.

2. For example of such an approach, see M. Smith, "Common Theology of the Ancient Near East," n. 16. According to this approach the denial of the existence of other gods starts as late as the second Isaiah.

3. See Kaufmann, *The Religion of Israel: From Its Beginnings to the Babylonian Exile,* pp. 127–133. Kaufmann makes two claims: first there is no polytheism or monolatry within the biblical religion, and second the Israelites did not practice polytheism in any serious manner. In addition to the challenge to the first claim by the monolatrous view of biblical religion, some scholars claim that the Israelites practiced polytheism as late as the fall of Judah in 587–586. According to this view the biblical religion was monolatrous, and the Israelites did not practice even monolatry as the Bible condemns them again and again. For views that claim the widespread practice of polytheism, see A. B. Davidson, *The Theology of the Old Testament* (Edinburgh: T. and T. Clark, 1911), p. 60; M. Smith, *Palestinian Parties and Politics that Shaped the Old Testament* (New York: Columbia University Press, 1971), p. 57. Jeffrey Tigay examined the controversy in light of Hebrew inscriptions from the period and arrived at conclusions similar to Kaufmann's; see J. H. Tigay, *You Shall Have No Other Gods* (Atlanta: Scholars Press, 1986), pp. 37–41.

4. On the angel Metatron who sits on the throne and is mistakenly perceived by the mystic as an independent sovereign power, see Babylonian Talmud, Tractate *Hagigah* 15a, and Tractate *Sanhedrin* 38b. In the Babylonian Talmud Tractate *Yuma* 77b there is a fascinating story about the angel Gabriel, who receives from God an order to destroy Israel. Gabriel acting like a clever bureaucrat delays the performance of the order and saves Israel.

5. Origen quotes Celsus's argument against the Christians: ". . . and whatever there may be in the universe whether the work of God or of angels or of other daemons or heroes, do not all these things keep law given by the greatest God? And has there not been appointed over each particular thing a being who has been thought worthy to be allotted power? Would not a man, therefore, who worships God rightly worship the being who has obtained authority from him?" (Origen, *Contra Celsum,* trans. H. Chadwick, Cambridge: Cambridge University Press, 1953, VII, 70).

6. E. R. Dodds, *Pagan and Christian in an Age of Anxiety* (New York: Norton, 1970), pp. 37–68. On the difference between the pagan elite and the masses, see R. Macmullen, *Paganism in the Roman Empire* (New Haven: Yale University Press, 1981), pp. 67–94.

7. Origen never denies the existence of the pagan gods but he claims

that they are demons. Paradoxically this argument limits God's power and control over the universe, because it denies the pagan assumption that every power in the universe is authorized by God and therefore worthy of worship. See *Contra Celsum,* VII, 68, 69. The view that the pagan gods are demons and that basically idolatry is demonolatry is also expressed by Tertullian and Augustine. See Tertullian, *De Idololatria,* trans. J. H. Wasznik and J. C. M. Van Winden (Leiden: E. J. Brill, 1987), 10, 5.

8. The prohibitions regarding Christians' participation in pagan public games are discussed in Tertullian, *De Spectaculis,* trans. T. R. Clover (Cambridge, Mass.: Harvard University Press, 1977). Regarding the prohibitions on participation in military service, public office, and homage to the emperor, see Tertullian, *De Idololatria,* 17, 2–19; 15, 1–10. For a general discussion on Tertullian's position, see T. D. Barnes, *Tertullian* (Oxford: Clarendon Press, 1985), pp. 85–115.

9. On Halevi's attack on philosophical relativism, see L. Strauss, *Persecution and the Art of Writing* (Chicago: University of Chicago Press, 1952), chap. 4.

10. Halevi himself maintains also the concept of idolatry that is performed by worshiping an alien god, and not only idolatry which involves alien worship to God. On Halevi's distinction between two kinds of idolatry, see *Kuzari,* 4:13.

11. The magic of talismans and images that Nachmanides describes is associated with the Middle Ages and the Hermetic tradition. On this subject see L. Thorndike, *A History of Magic and Experimental Science* (New York: Columbia University Press, 1923–1958), II, 214ff. On the later development of astral magic, which is connected to the use of images, see D. P. Walker, *Spiritual and Demonic Magic from Ficino to Campanella* (Notre Dame: University of Notre Dame Press, 1975), pp. 1–24. For the power of stars and their identification with pagan gods see J. Seznec, *The Survival of the Pagan Gods* (Princeton: Princeton University Press, 1953), pp. 37–83. Rashba, a generation after Nachmanides, gives his approval to talismanic medicine and tries to distinguish it from idolatry. See *Teshubot ha Rashba,* ed. H. Dimitrovsky (Jerusalem: Mossad ha Rav Kook, 1990), p. 303.

12. Nachmanides describes the sin of cutting the plants in other places in his commentary. See *Nachmanides,* Genesis 3:22, Exodus 30:1.

13. This metaphor was mentioned by a disciple of Nachmanides, R. Shem Tov ibn Gaon in *Keter Shem Tov* in Maor Va Shemesh fol. 25a. For an earlier formulation, see R. Isaac the Blind, *Commentary on Sefer Yezirah,* p. 6.

14. The Kabbalah in Scholem's analysis, is a mythic reinterpretation of basic concepts of Judaism that began to emerge in the twelfth century. Scholem's views on the mythic qualities of the Kabbalah are expressed in

G. Scholem, *Major Trends in Jewish Mysticism* (New York: Schocken, 1961), pp. 18–39, and *On the Kabbalah and Its Symbolism,* chap. 3. Moshe Idel argued for a different approach to the history of the Kabbalah which is of great importance to the understanding of the role of mythical components in rabbinic Judaism. According to Idel, the Kabbalah is a continuation of traditional and early mythical elements within Jewish sources rather than a mythical revolution that occurred in later stages; see Idel, *Kabbalah New Perspectives,* pp. 156–172.

15. A detailed analysis of the theurgical function of the commandments appears in Idel, *Kabbalah New Perspectives,* chap. 8.

16. The different views of the *sefirot* as the essence of the divinity or as instruments or vessels of God, are thoroughly discussed in I. Tishbi, *The Wisdom of the Zohar,* trans. D. Goldstein (Oxford: Oxford University Press, 1989), I, 95–117, 131–161, and Idel, *Kabbalah New Perspectives,* pp. 137–146.

17. According to Abulafia, the Kabbalists who believe in the doctrine of *sefirot* are worse than the Christians. Whereas the latter believe in the Trinity, the kabbalists believe in a system of ten distinct divine forces. On the different orientation of the ecstatic kabbalists and their rejection of the theosophy of the *sefirot,* see Idel, *Kabbalah New Perspectives,* pp. ix–xviii; M. Idel, *The Mystical Experience in Abraham Abulafia,* trans. Jonathan Chipman (Albany: State University of New York Press, 1988), pp. 7–10.

18. The Hebrew text of R. Meir ben Simon was published by G. Scholem in *Sefer Bialik* (Tel Aviv, 1934), p. 149. For an extensive discussion of the criticism, see G. Scholem, *The Origins of the Kabbalah,* trans. from the German A. Arkush (Princeton: Princeton University Press, 1990), pp. 393–414.

19. On the Bahir's position concerning prayer to the *sefirot,* see Scholem, *The Origins of the Kabbalah,* pp. 194–197.

20. *Ma'amar Sod ha-Yihud* of Abraham ben Eliezer ha-Levi, MS Jerusalem 4 537 fol. 146a.

21. Isaac Ben Sheshet, one of the important rabbinic authorities of the fourteenth century, was asked about praying to the *sefirot.* In his answer he condemns such a prayer as idolatrous and recommends a direct prayer to God himself. The only form of kabbalistic prayer that he is willing to approve of, albeit hesitantly, is the prayer to God to manifest himself in the relevant *sefirah.* See *Shelot u-Teshubot Issac Ben Sheshet,* (ha-Rybash) (Jerusalem, 1968), 157.

22. Babylonian Talmud, Tractate *Sanhedrin* 64a.

23. Ibid., 74a.

24. Ibid., 61b.

25. Examples of situations in which intention is necessary to describe the action itself are mentioned in the Babylonian Talmud, *Sanhedrin* 62b.

26. See *Tosafot, Sanhedrin* 61b, "Raba."

27. See *Ramban, Shabbat* 72b, "Ela."

28. *Yad Ramah, Sanhedrin* 64a, "Piskah."

29. *Rashi, Sanhedrin* 60b, "ve-Lahashov."

30. *Yad Ramah, Sanhedrin* 60b, "Mahi."

31. See Chapter 1 above.

32. Mishnah, Tractate *Avodah Zarah* 1:1–3.

33. Babylonian Talmud, Tractate *Shabbat* 105b.

34. The first chapter of Tractate *Avodah Zarah* in the Mishnah deals with a broad set of rules that regulate the contact between Jews and pagans. Y. Baer claims that these prohibitions in the Mishnah influenced the prohibitions that were formulated by the Church Fathers concerning dealings with pagans. See Y. Baer, "Israel, the Christian Church, and the Roman Empire," in *Scripta Hierosololymitana*, vol. 7 (Jerusalem: Magnes Press, 1961), pp. 79–145.

35. J. Katz, *Exclusiveness and Tolerance: Studies in Jewish-Gentile Relations in Medieval and Modern Times* (Westport, Conn.: Greenwood Press, 1980), chap. 3.

36. The opinion of R. Tam is mentioned in the *Tosafot*, Tractate *Avodah Zarah* 2a, "Asur."

37. Babylonian Talmud, Tractate *Hulin* 13b.

38. R. Gershom's opinion is printed in: S. Idelberg, *Teshuvot Rabeinu Gershom Meor Hagolah* (New York: 1957), 21, pp. 75–77.

39. J. Katz, "Sovlanut Datit be-Shitato shel Rabbi Menachem Hameiri ba-Halakhah ube-Philosophia," *Zion* (1953): 15–30.

40. Menahem Ha-Meiri, *Beit Habehirah, Tractate Avodah Zarah*, ed. A. Sofer (Jerusalem: 1944), p. 48. See also pp. 3, 28, 33, 46, 53.

41. J. Katz explains Ha-Meiri's tolerant approach as a result of the influence of Maimonidean rationalism on him. We suggest that in the case of Maimonides, rationalism or the insistence on correct metaphysics as a goal of the police, is a cause for the intolerance that Maimonides exhibits in dealing with idolaters and heretics. Maimonides himself never attempts to moderate the intolerance of the tradition in these matters, and sometimes he even exceeds it. (See for example *Mishneh Torah*, Laws of Idolatry, 5:6, 10:6.) Ha-Meiri reaches religious tolerance because in this case he has freed himself from Maimonides by defining idolatry as unconnected to beliefs.

42. For Maimonides' statements concerning Christianity, see Rambam, *Perush ha-Mishnah*, Tractate *Avodah Zarah* 1:1, and *Mishneh Torah*, Laws of Idolatry, 9:7. (The ruling in the *Mishneh Torah* was omitted from later editions.) In the seventeenth and eighteenth centuries there was an important change in the attitude of rabbinic authorities to Christianity. Great

rabbinic authorities, among them R. Yakob Emdin and R. Yehezkel Landau, reevaluate Christianity as a nonpagan religion. On this change, see Katz, *Exclusiveness and Tolerance,* chap. 13, and J. Katz, "Shlosha Ma'amarim Apologetim be-Gilguleihem," *Zion* 23–24 (1958–59): 181–186.

## 8. Idolatry and Political Authority

1. Among scholars who analyzed the covenant in this way, see Weinfeld, *Deuteronomy and the Deuteronomic School,* pp. 59–157. Weinfeld's comprehensive discussion of Deuteronomy as a contract modeled on a covenant between a king and a vassal emphasizes the political aspect of God's demand that Israel should be loyal to him; see pp. 81–91. On the use of the title "king" in reference to God, see p. 84, n. 4. On other covenants see D. R. Hillers, *Covenant: History of a Biblical Idea* (Baltimore: Johns Hopkins University Press, 1967), pp. 46–71.

2. The source of the expression "a woman cannot be partially married" is the Babylonian Talmud, Tractate *Kiddushin* 7b.

3. In the period of the judges there was no organized standing army nor was there systematic tax collection by a central body. The judge of the people did not inherit his role; instead, the Bible tells us, the spirit of the Lord came to rest upon him. Shemariyahu Talmon claims that already in the Book of Judges there is noticeable criticism of this form of government because of the anarchy it creates. This criticism appears through the story of the concubine in Giv'a and the story of the children of Dan, which conclude the Book of Judges with the verse: "In those days there was no king in Israel; every man did that which was right in his own eyes" (Judges 21, 25). This despite the anticentralist stance expressed in Gideon's declaration and his refusal to accept the monarchy. Thus in the book itself there is a tension between the two positions. See S. Talmon, *King, Cult, and Calendar in Ancient Israel* (Jerusalem: Magnes Press, 1986), pp. 38–52.

According to Mendenhall the essence of the monotheistic revolution is in the proclamation of God as king. The founding event of Israel as a community is in the act of covenant in which groups and individuals not belonging to one ethnic group accepted the kingdom of God and rejected the rule of the great powers. The return to the monarchy in the days of David and Solomon is in his opinion the return to the pagan days that preceded the covenant. See G. E. Mendenhall, *The Tenth Generation* (Baltimore: Johns Hopkins University Press, 1973), pp. 1–31.

4. The ambiguity with regard to the monarchy continues among the exegetes, who disagree about whether the comment on the appointment of a king in the book of Deuteronomy is a commandment to appoint a king or only a statement that such an appointment is permissible. The exegetical problem is tied to the verse in Deuteronomy that says, "And thou shalt say,

I will set a king over me" (17:14), thereby stipulating the appointment of the king on Israel's request. On this dispute, see the Babylonian Talmud, Tractate *Sanhedrin* 20b, *Sifrei Devarim,* sec. 156. For the attitude of medieval Jewish thinkers to the monarchy, see L. Strauss, "On Abravanel Philosophical Tendency and Political Teaching," in J. B. Trend and H. Loewe, eds., *Issac Abravanel, Six Lectures* (Cambridge: Cambridge University Press, 1937), pp. 95–129.

5. Frankfort, *Kingship and the Gods,* pp. 259–312, and Conclusion.

6. The prohibition against the multiplication of horses is interpreted by the rabbis in the *Sifrei Devarim* not as a prohibition against the growth of the military power but as a prohibition against the king's private ownership of the horses, implying a prohibition against an extravagant lifestyle in the king's court. In this way the midrash moderates conspicuously the meaning of the reduction of the military forces. In the words of the *Sifrei,* sec. 158: "'But he shall not multiply horses to himself,' perhaps it means that he should not multiply horses for his chariots and cavalry, the verse says 'to himself,' he should not multiply for himself, but he may for his chariots and cavalry." The possibility rejected by the *Sifrei* is that which is most apparent in a straightforward reading of the verses, which is that the reliance on God demands a reduction in military forces. Of David it is told in II Samuel 8:4: "And David took from him one thousand seven hundred horsemen, and twenty thousand footmen; and David lamed all the chariot horses, but reserved of them enough for a hundred chariots." King Solomon is condemned in the Bible for multiplying chariots for a standing army; see I Kings 10:26–29.

7. What is unique in the Israeli monarchy and its dependence upon the kingdom of God can be seen in the description of the coronation of Yoash as king of Judea. Yehoyada made a covenant described in the following manner. "And Yehoyada made a covenant between the Lord and the king and the people that they should be the Lord's people between the king also and the people" (II Kings 11:17). At the time of the coronation of the king a covenant is also made between the Lord and the people. This is an example of a double covenant that the Lord used to make with the vassal. He would have the people swear to be loyal to him and then have them swear to be loyal to the vassal. See Weinfeld, *Deuteronomy and the Deuteronomic School,* pp. 77–84.

8. The expression "na'ase lanu shem" has been interpreted in a number of ways. Some interpretations do not see this expression in a ritualistic context. A different midrash claims that the tower was built out of the fear of that generation of the possibility of an additional flood (*Bereshit Raba,* 11:1). *Ibn Ezra* follows a similar line: "So that you should see the city from afar, for those who walk outside as tenders of sheep. Also that their name should remain after them for as long as the tower remains, and that is the meaning of the verse, 'let us make for us a name.'"

9. One of the interesting discussions in the context of the status of the covenants Israel makes with neighboring powers is based on the verses in Ezekiel 17:11–22. These verses describe the rebellion of Zidqiyyahu, the king of Judea, against the Babylonians after he had established a covenant with them. Zidqiyyahu appealed to Egypt against the Babylonians, and Ezekiel describes the punishment of Judea in connection with the violation of the treaty. One of the possibilities for understanding this section is that the trespass of the oath which the king of Judea swore to the king of Babylon is the transgression of the covenant of God because God is perceived as the guarantor of the covenant and its performance. See M. Tsevat, *Journal of Biblical Literature* 78 (1959): 201–204. A similar position is taken by the author of Chronicles, who counts among the sins of Zidqiyyahu his rebellion against the king of Babylon (II Chronicles 36:13). This view is found unacceptable by Moshe Greenberg, who sees Ezekiel's prophecy mainly as an analogy to what will happen to the king of Judea as a result of breaking God's covenant: Greenberg, *Ezekiel, The Anchor Bible* (New York: Doubleday, 1983), pp. 318–324.

10. On Alexander's demand and the worship of the Persian kings, see L. R. Taylor, *The Divinity of the Roman Emperor* (Philadelphia: Porcupine Press, 1975), pp. 1–13, Appendix 1.

11. On the interesting issue of deification as a political tool, see Taylor, *The Divinity of the Roman Emperor,* pp. 232–238, and A. Momigliano, "How Roman Emperors Became Gods," in *On Pagans, Jews, and Christians* (Middletown, Conn.: Wesleyan University Press, 1989), pp. 92–107. For a presentation of this topic in the context of the general problem of the status of beliefs, see P. Veyne, *Did the Greeks Believe in Their Myths?* trans. P. Wissing (Chicago: University of Chicago Press, 1988), p. 89.

12. On the centrality of creation for Nachmanides, see Exodus 3:13, 6:2, and esp. 13:16 and 20:2.

13. The question of creation or eternal existence of the world in the writings of Maimonides is very complex. Although Maimonides sides with the opinion that the world is created he proves the existence of God from the eternity of motion. See *Mishneh Torah,* Yesodei ha-Torah 1:7, and *Guide of the Perplexed,* 1:71.

14. See Y. Leibowitz, *Yahadut Am Yehudi u-Medinat Israel* (Jerusalem: Am Oved, 1975), pp. 13–36.

15. See *Chidushei ha-Ran,* Tractate *Shabbat* 72b, "ela me-ahava ve-yir'a," as well as *Chidushei ha-Ritva* there.

16. Maimonides follows the interpretation of R. Hananel found in Tractate *Shabbat* 72b.

17. The claim of Hameiri against Maimonides is also found in *Chidushei ha-Ran* (see n. 16).

18. Josephus Flavius, *Antiquities of the Jews,* part 3, 18:6.

19. The refusal to pay the tax is described by Josephus in *Wars of the Jews,* 2:88a: "And in his day one man from the Galilee by the name of Judah incited another of his people to rebel against the Romans, saying that it would be a disgrace if they would bend their shoulders to suffer and pay the tax to the Romans, so that in addition to the kingdom of heaven they also would bear the yoke of flesh and blood."

20. Ibid., 17:5.

21. A disagreement between the Zealots and the Pharisees on a matter related to the question we are dealing with is quoted in the mishnah in Tractate *Yadayim,* 4:8. We of course do not claim that there was no disagreement among the rabbis concerning the attitude toward Roman rule and the degree to which it should be opposed. On this disagreement see, for example, Babylonian Talmud, Tractate *Shabbat* 23b, and Tractate *Avodah Zarah* 18a.

22. See E. R. Dodds, *Pagan and Christian in an Age of Anxiety* (New York: Norton, 1970), pp. 102–138 (including n. 1).

## Conclusion

1. Bacon, *The Essays* (Harmondsworth: Penguin Books, 1985), p. 277.

2. *Writings of the Young Marx on Philosophy and Society,* trans. L. D. Easton and K. H. Cuddat (New York: Doubleday, 1967), pp. 245–246.

3. Ibid., pp. 289–290.

4. L. Wittgenstein, *The Big Typescript,* Manuscript 213 and 413.

5. For a modern theological articulation of idolatry as granting absolute value to the state, see E. Fackenheim, *Encounters Between Judaism and Modern Philosophy* (New York: Basic Books, 1973), pp. 188–198.

6. D. Hume, *The Natural History of Religion* (Stanford: Stanford University Press, 1957), pp. 26–32.

7. Ibid., pp. 48–51.

8. See N. Machiavelli, *The Discourses,* trans. L. J. Walker (Harmondsworth: Penguin Books, 1983), II, 277–280.

9. See J. J. Rousseau, *The Social Contract,* trans. M. Cranston (Harmondsworth: Penguin Books, 1982), book 4, chap. 8, pp. 176–187.

10. St. Augustine, *The City of God,* trans. H. Bettenson (Harmondsworth: Penguin Books, 1984), book 5, chaps. 12–26, pp. 197–224.

11. F. Nietzsche, *On the Genealogy of Morals,* trans. W. Kaufman and R. J. Hollingdale (New York: Vintage Books, 1967), p. 22.

12. F. Nietzsche, *Twilight of Idols,* trans. R. J. Hollingdale (Harmondsworth: Penguin Books, 1990), p. 55.

13. F. Nietzsche, *The Anti-Christ,* trans. R. J. Hollingdale (Harmondsworth: Penguin Books, 1990), p. 138.

# Index